# Best Hikes Near
## SEATTLE

# Best Hikes Near
## SEATTLE

PETER STEKEL

GUILFORD, CONNECTICUT
HELENA, MONTANA

AN IMPRINT OF THE GLOBE PEQUOT PRESS

To my parents, May and Ed Stekel

To buy books in quantity for corporate use
or incentives, call **(800) 962–0973**
or e-mail **premiums@GlobePequot.com.**

# FALCONGUIDES®

Falcon and FalconGuides are registered trademarks and Outfit Your Mind is a trademark of Morris Book Publishing, LLC.
All interior photos by Peter Stekel (http://home.comcast.net/~peterstekel)
Compass on p iii © Shutterstock

Text design by Sheryl P. Kober
Maps created by Tim Kissel © Morris Book Publishing, LLC

Library of Congress Cataloging-in-Publication Data
Stekel, Peter.
 Best hikes near Seattle / Peter Stekel.
   p. cm.
 Includes bibliographical references.
 ISBN 978-0-7627-4725-2
 1. Hiking--Washington (State)--Seattle Metropolitan Area--Guidebooks. 2. Seattle Metropolitan Area (Wash.)--Guidebooks. I. Title.
 GV199.42.W22S427 2009
 796.5109797'772--dc22
                              2008031454
Printed in China
10 9 8 7 6 5 4 3 2 1

# Contents

## Overview

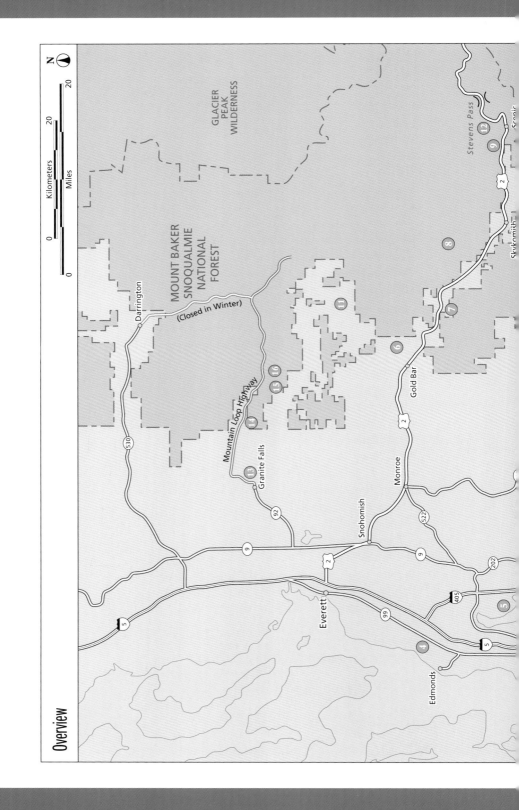

MOUNT BAKER
SNOQUALMIE
NATIONAL
FOREST

GLACIER
PEAK
WILDERNESS

Darrington

(Closed in Winter)

Mountain Loop Highway

Granite Falls

530

Stevens Pass

Scenic

Skykomish

Gold Bar

Monroe

Snohomish

Everett

Edmonds

N

Kilometers    0         20         20

Miles         0         20         20

5

9

92

2

2

99

522

405

9

202

5

4

5

13

14

15

16

11

6

7

8

9

12

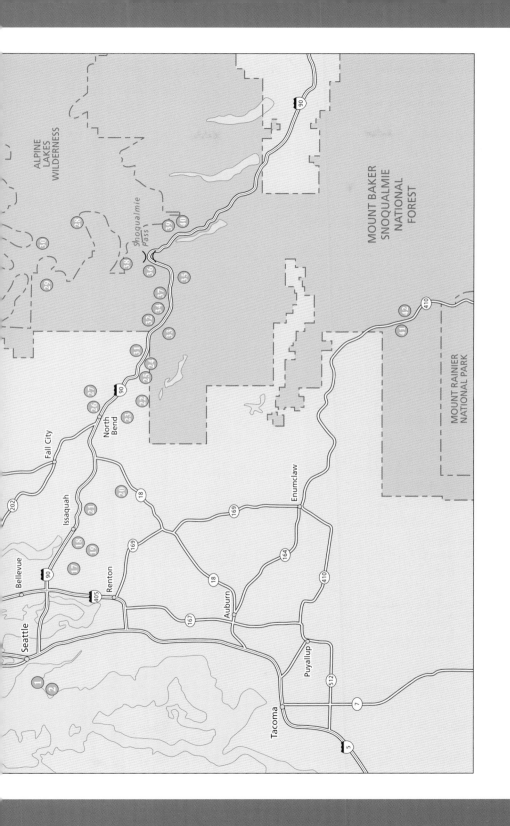

Leopard lily

# Acknowledgments

"In wildness is the preservation of the world."
—Henry David Thoreau

I walked every one of these trails. No doubt about it. Dawn Meekhof and/or Michele Hinatsu walked nearly every one of these trails with me. My thanks to both these friends for helping make the miles pass with good company, good humor, and good conversation. Jennie Goldberg, Laurel Hansen, Victor Kress, Boo Turner, Neil Gitkind, and Karen George also accompanied me on some of the trails for this book.

The best part about hiking is hiking with a companion. Thanks also to all my hiking partners over the years, especially Rich Stowell, Gregg Fauth, Tommy James, Alice Goldberg, Bill Tweed, Scott Atkinson, Susan Buis, Jim and Bronwyn Buntine plus replicates, Ken Corathers, Steven Jacobs, Margaret Hill Stowell, Bob Specht, Ronnee Helzner, Garrett Munger, Les Chow, Peggy Moore, Sylvia Hultain, Nate Stephenson, and everybody at Camp Wolverton BSA and Post 90, Pacific Palisades, along with scientists and naturalists at Sequoia and Kings Canyon National Parks. You have made thousands of trail miles fun, exciting, and educational. Many thanks to all the Cooperistians whose presence brings humor and laughter where ere they are encountered.

Thanks to David B. Williams for tossing this gem my way.

Every writer stands on the backs of giants. Therefore, I want to acknowledge those writers of previous guidebooks. They came first and did most of the hard work: Ron Adkison, Joan Burton, Bob Dreisbach, Harvey Manning, Mike McQuaide, Marge and Ted Mueller, Jeff Smoot, Bob and Ira Spring, Bryce Stevens, Karen Sykes, Andrew Weber, and John Zilly. I hope I haven't forgotten anyone.

Also, thank you to Garmin and Magellan, manufacturers of handheld GPS units, for giving me such a good deal.

Without the people who pushed Congress to create the Wild Sky and Alpine Lakes Wilderness Areas, many of the trails in this book would not be very attractive for hiking. Thank you for your time, effort, and vision.

Many immeasurable thanks to Gordon Lightfoot and Mason Williams. Also, thanks to The Band: Robbie Robertson, Garth Hudson, Richard Manuel, Levon Helm, and Rick Danko. Life without music isn't life.

This book would never have happened without the love and support of Jennie Goldberg. *Sigh.*

# Introduction

In spite of many things—homes and highways, factories and farms, an expanding population—the Pacific Northwest retains the same allure that first pulled people here from all over the world during the 19th century: The impression of limitless space from the shores of Puget Sound and on into deep green forests and beyond; a feeling that anything is possible here—fame, success, wealth, a life of accomplishment and purpose.

> Seattle is a beautiful city in a gorgeous setting, with opportunities available in every direction to hike, bike, climb, ski, kayak, and canoe.

To all this, add the attraction of vast outdoor recreational opportunities available to people of all skill levels or experience. Places to hike, bike, climb, ski, kayak, and canoe can be found in every direction. Because of their proximity, the Cascade Mountains, Alpine Lakes Wilderness, and the new Wild Sky Wilderness (dedicated May 31, 2008) can feel like one extended backyard playground. From the greater Seattle area it's possible to find yourself on a hiking trail within 60 minutes of leaving the city. Welcome to the heavenly Pacific Northwest! When all superlatives are exhausted, it's nice to realize that, even for a city, Seattle is a beautiful place situated within a gorgeous setting.

With all the possible outdoor sports to divert a person's attention, hiking remains the easiest and least expensive. Of course, it's possible to spend hundreds of dollars on boots, another few hundred dollars on the latest, greatest rain jacket, clothing, and day pack, but you can get by just fine with less. Really. No special equipment is necessary and, as long as the weather and terrain are not extreme, a simple backpack, sturdy shoes with ankle support, comfortable pants or shorts, and some extra warm clothing are all you need to get started. This makes hiking a fantastic way for people to jump into outdoor recreation. Today, as in the past, hiking is an egalitarian activity—which is why it continues to have such broad support and interest among all ages and backgrounds of people.

## Weather

Seattle is a great place to live. Our climate is perfect. With mild winter temperatures, cool summers, and summer drought, it's possible to play outside nearly every day of the year. Sure, it rains here once in a while, but 36 inches a year isn't that much! Nobody ever talks about how much it rains annually in Mobile, Alabama (60 inches), Miami, Florida (49 inches), or Houston, Texas (44 inches). Even Boston (40 inches) and New York City (39 inches) get more rain than Seattle. Of course there's the Hoh Rain Forest in Olympic National Park (145 inches) but, let's face it, that's why it's called a rain forest!

Downtown Seattle skyline from Alki Beach Trail

Though our climate may be perfect, the same can't be said for our weather. Our average number of rainy days (158), cloudy days (226), and days of sun (58) is what people really care about when they moan and groan about how much it rains in Seattle. October to March is the wet season in the Northwest; 67 percent of our rain falls between those months. July and August are the driest; November to February, the wettest. Seasonal Affective Disorder (SAD) is a big worry for people who require more sunlight than the sun is able to provide during the short days of winter. Some people even take Vitamin D supplements.

Because of topography, where all this rain and cloud measuring is done becomes very important. Precipitation and sky cover increase from west to east. And with elevation, all that rain turns to snow. So places like North Bend (along Interstate 90) with 60 inches and Monroe (along U.S. Highway 2) with 47 inches of precipitation are wetter and cloudier than Seattle. It behooves hikers to pay attention to what is going on in these two towns, since they are central to many hikes in this book. Referring to the Washington State Department of Transportation Web site for road conditions is a good way to check on the weather. To get started, point your browser to www.wsdot.wa.gov/traffic/seattle.

The latest weather conditions and forecasts are available at www.wrh.noaa .gov/sew and www.accuweather.com. NOAA weather radio is also available for conditions and forecasts. Radios that pick up only the NOAA broadcast can be purchased at any consumer electronics store.

Hikers need to also be aware of this thing called the "Puget Sound Convergence Zone." Weather coming in from the Pacific Ocean is split by the Olympic Mountains. Some flows south, through Chehalis Gap, where the Chehalis River runs into the ocean. Some more of it flows north, through the Strait of Juan de Fuca. The Cascades create an eastward barrier, redirecting the two weather flows through Puget Sound. When the two opposing currents collide (from Everett to Tacoma) the air rises, cools, and produces locally heavy rain or snow.

Clearly, climate is what you want, and weather is what you get. Ah, for those mild winters and cool, dry summers! And that's why everybody keeps talking about our "liquid sunshine" and "sun breaks." As we all can joke, it only rains twice a year in Seattle: August to April and May to July. And the significance of daylight saving time can't be missed —it gives us an extra hour of rain. Optimistic hikers can always be recognized by the sun visor on their rain hat. We don't live in the Pacific Northwest—we live in the Pacific Northwet.

Everybody talks about the weather, but nobody does anything about it. Still, skiers don't let little things like snowstorms get in the way of having a good time, and hikers don't see any reason to stay at home when it's raining. The hiking season in Seattle never ends. It's that topographical thing again—there is always some place to go that will be warmer or drier than somewhere else, even in winter. Sure the sweltering months of July and August (average high temperature of 75 degrees Fahrenheit), with an occasional heat wave, drive the less serious hikers out of their homes and into the hills. But the real fun is had when the "bad" weather arrives.

Embrace the rain, because it's always going to be a factor when hiking in the Pacific Northwest. There are advantages. Popular places see fewer people on rainy days—though plenty of folk aren't hesitant about going then. Rainy days present great opportunities for leaving stuffy houses. A wet autumn hike means not having to share any huckleberries on the trail—except with the usual tooth-and-claw forest dwellers. All the fall colors are yours and yours alone to enjoy. And at the end of the day, no matter how wet you are you can always go home and take a hot shower and drink a hot toddy. The Boy Scout adage of "Be Prepared" is a wise admonishment for wet weather. Bring along the best rain gear you can afford, and carry additional warm (and dry) clothes along with plenty of food and energy snacks. Wrap them all up in a plastic garbage bag, shove it into your pack, and be on your way!

## Trail Etiquette

In any kind of weather it's considered rude to pass fellow hikers without some friendly greeting. We're all on this blue orb together, so let's make the best of it and acknowledge one another's presence with a "Hello." Maybe even stop to chat. If the person you encounter is plugged into his or her music machine and can't hear you, eye contact and a nod of the head go a long way in lieu of verbal greeting.

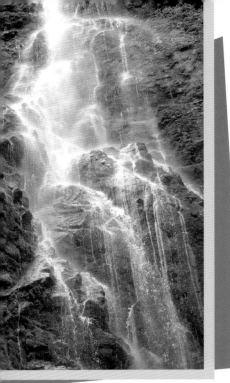
Skookum Falls in the White River Valley

When proceeding down the trail, it's considered polite to yield to the poor souls huffing and puffing up. Sometimes hikers laboring against gravity will graciously (even gratefully) take the initiative and stop, permitting speedy downhillers to zoom by. This brief respite also allows an opportunity for breath catching, pack strap adjusting, weary bone resting, and snack ingesting. Particularly at these times, a cheery greeting or smile is always appreciated from passing hikers.

Trails are designed and built to high standards, and cutting switchbacks is not only impolite but expensive. Erosion is encouraged when many feet follow the initial insult. All this hastens the demise of that section of trail, which will then require somebody to return with rakes and shovels and other implements of construction to repair what has been so inconsiderately wrought.

If you must hike plugged in to music, keep the volume down. You may not care much for your eardrums, but there are others on the trail who appreciate either conversing with their friends or being alone within the silence of their thoughts.

We all need rest from time to time. Try to find a place off the trail. If this isn't possible and you must sit on the trail, keep your feet, legs, and backpacks from dangling in the path where they might encumber other hikers or cause them to trip, stumble, and fall.

When catching up to other hikers, whether you are going up or down the hill, if they do not hear the tramp-tramp-tramp of your feet, a slight clearing of the throat or an "Excuse me" is usually enough to get them to step aside and allow you to pass.

## Dogs

The USDA Forest Service requires that all dogs on trails be kept on a 6-foot leash at all times. A tight lease will not present a trip-wire to other hikers. A leashed dog will eliminate the need to pull fighting dogs apart and also is a kindness extended to your fellow travelers who are walking without a pet. There is a pretty stiff fine if you are caught failing to follow the leash rule. During the summer it is common to find rangers patrolling the popular trails as well as checking cars for Northwest Forest Passes.

## Going to the Bathroom in the Woods

After you leave the parking lot, the likelihood of finding a toilet gets farther and farther away. So what happens if you're halfway up the trail and hear the call of nature?

Some believe in digging a hole. Others disagree, believing that critters come by and dig it up, and claim that it's better to scatter some forest duff over the pile. No matter what your philosophy, an important question is, what happens to the toilet paper?

How often have you looked behind a boulder or large tree and found a sodden wad of toilet paper poking out from beneath a rock? Somebody evidently had some business back there before walking off contented. Now here you are a few hours or a day or a week later, and the paper is still there.

There is a better way. Put the used TP in a plastic bag inside a lunch sack, and take it home with you. At home flush the TP down the toilet to the side sewer, to the trunk line to the main line to the sewage treatment plant at West Point in Magnolia. Let METRO take over from there.

Something else to keep in mind: Locate your toilet at least 100 feet from lakes, rivers, and streams. Try to stay that far away from trails, too. And remember what your mother taught you: Afterwards, wash your hands.

The Forest Service asks that you be kind to your pet. Familiarize yourself with trail situations that can be hazardous for a dog. Update all vaccinations, and provide flea and tick control. If you and your dog should become separated, make sure your pet has identification. Dogs, like people, need to build up their endurance before attempting a long hike. People wear shoes; dogs obviously don't. Trails contain sharp rocks that can tear a dog's feet. When you stop to eat or drink, share your bounty with Fido. Dog lovers should check out *Best Hikes with Dogs in Western Washington* by Dan Nelson (Mountaineers Books).

Be kind to other hikers. Keep Fido or Fifi under control—and pick up after your pet.

Cleaning up after your dog

### What to Bring

It's popular to list the "Ten Essentials" of what hikers must carry in their pack. Of course one person's essential is another's not so essential.

Bird-watchers won't leave home without binoculars and a bird book. You can't botanize without a field guide for flora. Can't angle without a pole and lures (does anyone use bait anymore?). Can't take photographs without a camera (bring extra batteries and memory cards for digital cameras).

As far as what survival gear to carry, a day hiker may need less than a backpacker. Shorter, simpler trails might require a shorter list of essentials. A walk to Weeks Falls requires significantly less of everything than a hike to Twin Falls, which in turn demands less than an overnight backpacking trip to Snoqualmie Lake, which needs less than a multiday trip and . . . you get the point. Even the "hardcore" survival list of essentials is debatable.

For instance, a compass and topographic map are always listed as essential. At their worst, many people can find north using a compass but have no idea what declination is (and how to correct for it) or how to place themselves onto a map. Making the leap from three dimensions (the real world) to two dimensions (a topo map) takes knowledge, training, and experience. And if you don't know where you are, a map and compass aren't going to help. For them to work, you need to have a starting point—a datum.

The uninitiated might think that hauling around a GPS eliminates the need for map and compass skills, since it will provide a datum—your location—at all times.

Surprise Lake in the Alpine Lakes Wilderness

Ignoring the technological weaknesses of GPS (interference, issues with accuracy, need for batteries, must be kept out of water), it's important to note that having a datum doesn't mean you know how to get from where you are to where you want to be. That still takes, at least, a map. A GPS can provide the map as well as way-points, a route, or a track, but the user still must know how to read it.

The most essential of essentials is intangible. It's what you heard from your mother your whole life: "Use your head!" Many problems in the outdoors can be obviated by paying attention, being prepared for weather, being familiar with the route, and knowing the time needed to complete it in plenty of daylight. Staying found is better than trying to find your way home when lost.

With all of this in mind, here is an extensive list of essentials. Select the ones that are best for a particular experience or situation. Leave behind the ones you feel are extraneous.

Carry a liter of water (more on hot days), and don't forget to drink it. If your urine is not clear, frequent, and copious, you're not drinking enough. Bring food. Energy bars are good for snacks, but bring real food too. Remember, hiking up McClellan Butte is not part of a diet plan.

Some sort of navigating device (see above) is preferable to hiking blind. *Best Hikes Near Seattle* contains trail descriptions and an area map along with GPS way-points. Consider this navigation guide as the barest of the barest and not the only guide.

A first-aid kit is nice to have but introduces its own set of essentials. People prone to blisters will want lots of Band-Aids, moleskin and/or molefoam, and anti-septic. Hikers who regularly take medication should carry that with them, plus an extra dose or two in case they are late in getting home. Asthmatics will want to have inhalers with them. Allergic to bees and wasps? Don't forget your EpiPen and antihistamines, although EpiPens should be considered a last resort. Consult your physician or allergist about a regimen of desensitizing shots.

Other first-aid kit items might include gauze pads (many purposes and func-tions), waterproof tape, scissors (for cutting gauze pads, tape, or bandages), Band-Aids (many sizes and shapes), antibacterial ointment (check expiration date), pencil and paper (for recording health data in case of serious injuries), fire starter, and oral thermometer. This list is by no means exhaustive. Add or delete items according to what personal experience has taught you.

Though many hikes in this book are in deep forest, and it seems the sun never shines in the Pacific Northwest, sunglasses and sunscreen are excellent items to carry. So is a cap (with a bill), a hat (to keep your head warm), gloves (ditto), wool or pile sweater (ditto), rain jacket (doubles as a windbreaker), pocketknife, small flashlight (check the batteries), extra dry socks, a clean shirt for the drive home, toilet paper and extra plastic bags for waste, and a whistle.

Put it all into a backpack, and off you go!

As for what to wear when hiking, it's up to you. Some prefer shorts to long pants (shorts wearers should carry wind pants in case the temperature drops) and T-shirts to long-sleeved sport shirts (to protect sun-sensitive bodies). Sports bras give support and comfort for women. Single or double walking sticks help with steep or uneven stretches and serve to steady you on snow, talus, or stream crossings.

As for nonessentials, cell phones top the list. Few things are more annoying to the rest of us than hearing someone deep in a telephone conversation while hiking. Besides, unless you're hiking at Tiger, Cougar, and Rattlesnake Mountains or around Mount Si and North Bend, cell phones aren't going to work anyway. Go ahead and carry one if you feel you need to, but turn it off and save the battery just in case you really do need it for the drive home.

Another nonessential, as far as I'm concerned, is an MP3 player. If your need for being plugged in to your own private soundtrack is that important, there isn't much need to be outdoors. Hiking is more than just exercise—it involves using all your senses. Don't close off your ears.

Keep in mind that bear hunting starts in early August. Deer season opens mid-October across much of the state, and elk season opens at the end of the month. If you hear shooting, stop. Raise your voice to let hunters know you're near. While moving through the landscape, wear bright clothing. Talk while you walk to alert hunters of your presence.

## More on Maps

Every responsible hiker carries topographic maps whether they understand how to read the contour lines or not. For Tiger, Cougar, Rattlesnake Mountains and Mount Si, the large-detail Green Trails maps can't be beat. For other areas, U.S. Geological Survey (USGS) 7.5-minute quadrangle maps are great for topographic detail. Regular Green Trails maps work well for geographic and cultural details; their major weakness is being larger scale than USGS maps. Whichever you use, and a case can be made for carrying both, they are superior to sketch maps such as the ones appearing in this book. This guide's maps are intended solely to give hikers an overview of the area covered in the text.

The Alpine Lakes Protection Society (ALPS) publishes a shaded-relief topographic map that covers most of the hikes in this book. Its larger scale means it isn't as detailed as a USGS or Green Trails map, but it does have the distinct advantage of covering a huge amount of territory. For that reason alone, it's a map well worth carrying.

## The "Art" of Mileage

Without pushing a wheel equipped with an odometer, computing trail mileage is an art, not a science—and a tricky art at that. There is what you see on trail signs, what you see written on maps, what you read in guidebooks, what your GPS unit says, and what your own internal odometer tells you is the distance between points. Sometimes the numbers jibe. More often, they don't. Occasionally the numbers can be disturbingly different.

It's best to take all published mileages with a grain of salt, or at least a pinch. Plan hikes by consulting maps and by relying on past experience of what you can (and can't) do for a given type of terrain. Five miles of flat will expend less time and effort and be kinder to your body than an equal distance that also gains 4,000 vertical feet!

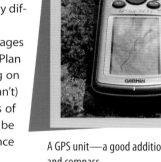

A GPS unit—a good addition to your map and compass

Mileages in this book are based on GPS readings taken during each hike using a Garmin GPSmap 76CSx and WGS 84 map data. In some cases this information varied extremely from trail markers and the bulk of other published sources. In those instances, the GPS data was tossed out in favor of majority rule.

Most of the base maps for *Best Hikes Near Seattle* were generated by the Garmin GPSmap 76CSx and downloaded to a Dell 8250 PC with 1.5 GB of RAM, running Windows XP and Garmin base map software. They were then provided in hard copy to a graphic artist who drew the final maps, including roads and place names determined to be essential in helping the reader make decisions or identify important landmarks.

## Getting More Information on Where to Hike

You'll find that the trails in *Best Hikes Near Seattle* are either within 60 miles or sixty minutes of Seattle. With the Internet, it's hard to find any hike in the Seattle area that isn't mentioned at least once on a Web site somewhere. So why publish a book when everything is available online?

Getting a group of hikes together in a compendium that facilitates decision-making is the best reason for a hiking guide. Searching the Web by hike name and sorting through thousands of hits is a tedious and sometimes unrewarding process. The Internet works best if you already know the name or location of a hike.

For people new to an area and with no geographical knowledge, nothing beats a book—and you can take it along with you.

Is another hiking book for the Seattle area really needed? Aren't there already dozens of hiking guides for the region? Have the trails changed that much since the last book was published? Have the access points moved? The answers are yes, yes, some, and no—at least, not a lot of them.

It's true. There are lots of hiking guides. You may already own several of them. I sure do! Hiking guides are highly individualized, and each reader finds something different to explore or discover based on each author's approach. Some writers prefer a historical approach; others feel the need to attack motorized recreation and resource extraction, while many prefer to focus on plants and animals.

Most trails haven't changed much since the last crop of books were published. The biggest changes have occurred in access roads and trailheads. Roads have been paved, and vault toilets have been built. If you encounter other recent changes, please e-mail them to editorial@globepequot.com.

## Flora and Fauna

All but a few of the trails in *Best Hikes Near Seattle* stay below the mountain vegetation zones of Pacific silver fir and mountain hemlock and remain in the lowland Douglas fir and western hemlock forest. For the former, climb the high mountains and ridgetops to where trees refuse to grow. The latter zone is most familiar to hikers in the Seattle area, since it's the vegetation that surrounds where they live and work. Left to the land's own devices, from the shores of Puget Sound to a few hundred feet below Snoqualmie or Stevens Pass, the dominant trees would be Douglas fir, western hemlock and western red cedar. Common shrubs in all zones include huckleberry, blackberry, Himalayan berry, blueberry, devil's club, stinging nettle, mahonia, sword fern, and salal. The most common tree associated with our conifer forests is the red alder.

Looking for abundant pond wildlife

Old-growth forest is not a type of vegetation but refers to the maturity level of a stand of trees. For instance, lowland forests begin assuming old-growth characteristics after 175 to 250 years of growth and reach their prime between 350 and 750 years. Younger stands of trees lack the traits indicative of old-growth forests: large size, trees occurring in a mix of different ages and sizes, greater spacing between individuals, much woody debris on the ground and in the creeks, many snags (standing dead trees), and a shrub layer that thrives on filtered sunlight.

Birds like the goshawk, northern spotted owl, and pileated woodpecker are more common in old-growth forests. So are northern flying squirrels, martens, and red tree voles.

Other animals that hikers are likely to see or hear in the Seattle area include the American black bear, mule deer, elk, American robin, winter wren, raven, deerfly, frog, and mosquito.

Blueberries—Yum!

## Little Bird, Big Mouth: The Winter Wren

When breeding season is done, most birds either fly the coop to sunnier climes or hunker down locally to quietly await the following spring. Not the winter wren (*Troglodytes troglodytes,* or "ignorant, old-fashioned cave dweller"). Though rarely seen, this secretive little bird energetically sings year-round. It sounds like a squeaking monster gone haywire from too much coffee—producing a continuous stream of melodious notes and trills that lasts five to ten seconds.

The winter wren is the only wren found outside the New World, occurring also in Europe, Asia, and North Africa. Males are polygynous (they have more than one mate) and often build "dummy" nests to draw away predators. Preferred nesting sites include natural cavities like old woodpecker holes, a rocky crevice, under tree stumps, and within the roots of an upturned tree. They prefer dense coniferous forests. Persons lucky enough to see this 3- to 5-inch-tall bird will spot it teetering and bobbing, flitting about in low tangles of vegetation and around logs where it is searching for a meal of insects. The winter wren is reddish brown with pink legs. The bill is short and thin.

But mostly hikers *hear* winter wrens. They bring a spot of musical joy into our winter hikes that belies the English translation of its Latin name.

RECREATION
PASS
REQUIRED

Please display
valid pass
when parked
at this site.

36 CFR 261.17

A Northwest Forest Pass or a costly citation—your choice

## Wilderness Restrictions and Regulations

Fires are prohibited above 4,000 feet on the west side of the Cascades and above 5,000 feet on the east side in the Mount Baker–Snoqualmie National Forest. Other forest areas may have fire restrictions due to high use and/or no fuel. Check for specific regulations pertaining to the area you plan to visit. Fires are highly restricted in city or county parks to supplied barbecue grates in picnic areas. No fires are allowed on any Department of Natural Resources land noted in this book.

Hikers entering the Alpine Lakes Wilderness are asked to self-register at trailheads and dangle a permit from their packs. Dogs must be kept on a short leash—though many hikers are inclined to allow Rover to rove. Regulations for the new Wild Sky Wilderness were still being decided at press time.

Camping with pack and saddle animals is allowed only at designated sites in the national forest and is prohibited in many other areas. Pack and saddle animals are not allowed within 200 feet of lakes except to get a drink or pass on a trail. Forage is poor throughout the region.

The most controversial restriction is the Northwest Forest Pass required by the Federal Lands Recreation Enhancement Act (FLREA). An outgrowth of the older Fee-Demo program, FLREA requires user fees from people who want to park their cars and recreate on federal land. For all the Mount Baker–Snoqualmie National Forest hikes described in this book, you will need a Northwest Forest Pass or risk an expensive citation.

In 1958, following the post–World War II popularity of spending time in the outdoors, the Outdoor Recreation Resource Review Commission proposed that recreation could be managed like any other industry. Prior to this, public lands visitors weren't viewed as representing an important, commercial market. Also, recreation on public lands wasn't seen as having exploitable commodity value. Later, during the Reagan administration, government began to see the outdoors not as a place where citizens ventured for the quiet contemplation of nature but as a profit center for private enterprise catering to a consumer base. This philosophy culminated in the 1996 Recreation Fee–Demonstration Program.

During the Clinton administration there was a move away from logging, mining, and grazing on public lands and a move toward selling recreation instead. The trend since then has been to commercialize, motorize, and package fee-based experiences on America's public lands. For the working poor—whose weekly entertainment budget is stretched thin enough—these user fees can be profound. Once upon a time, our public lands were supported by our tax dollars and were free for all to use. This is becoming less and less the case.

Privatization has its proponents and they all make a good case for it. Free market capitalists think there should be no public lands at all since they compete with private land owners who could be providing the same services. Libertarians say public lands should be self-funded via user fees and from profits created by selling natural resources. The recreation industry expects privatization to benefit the products and services they manufacture, distribute, or provide.

Some suspect this move toward privatization has been encouraged by creative budgeting. Between 1994 and 1996, the Forest Service saw a slashing of its recreation budget. The agency was finally forced to admit it had no money for recreation, and Congress agreed to implement temporary fees. Since then the Forest Service budget has increased but hasn't kept pace with inflation, deferred maintenance, and regional expenses. This leads many to believe that the fees are likely to remain in place, despite the requirement that Congress reimplement FLREA in the coming years.

Understandably finding itself in a perpetual funding crunch, the Forest Service has been forced to make recreation decisions based on what provides much-needed revenue. Hence, more emphasis has been placed on activities like RV camping since those activities require more amenities and generate more money. Lost in the shuffle are those activities like hiking that cannot be managed to enhance revenue. As a result, many trails are not being maintained except by volunteers. If no volunteers exist, trails fall into disarray, disuse, and then disappear.

Fee-Demo and FLREA have never grossed more than $50 million in a year. On top of this, the Government Accountability Office (GAO) estimates that fee collection and enforcement of FLREA consumes 50 percent of the funds it generates. It is also worth noting that several years ago a fee-based push in Washington state parks, following budget cuts, was not successful. Neither have been various attempts to commercialize some state and county parks with public-private partnerships. When private interests are allowed to control public land and turn it into a private, money-making operation, the inevitable result is that people who can't afford to pay are excluded from resources that are supposed to belong to all of us.

Perhaps the answer to this quandary can be found in the original study done by the Outdoor Recreation Resource Review Commission in the 1950s. They suggested it was appropriate to charge a fee for some services on public lands (e.g., admission to national parks, use of campgrounds), while other uses should be free (access to national forests, hiking, primitive car camping, etc.). That seems like a more reasonable balance.

## Effects of the November 7, 2006, Storm

Roads, bridges, campgrounds, and trails on public lands throughout the Cascade Mountains were severely damaged in 2003–2004 winter storms. On November 7, 2006, it happened again. Though progress continues to be made in repairing access roads and trails throughout the Cascades, there is still an immense amount of work to be done.

The Index-Galena Road (Forest Road 63) experienced huge amounts of damage at eight separate locations. At this time only one location still needs repair, and it's a whopper. The North Fork Skykomish River moved its southern bank and swallowed up a long swath of roadbed. Estimates of anywhere from five to ten years before a new road can be constructed have been projected. Lack of will on the part of local government and land use agencies is not the reason for this. There are complex engineering, environmental and funding issues, as well as permitting processes to consider. Revenue from the Northwest Forest Pass is simply not up to the task. Public-private partnerships can't come up with enough money either. It requires congressional funding. Yet in this era of budget cutbacks, can the government justify the expense of replacing a road that serves such a small community of homeowners and recreationists, especially since the North Fork can be accessed from Beckler River Road?

North Fork Road—wiped out by a November 2006 storm

Mount Baker–Snoqualmie National Forest is a big place. There are 1.7 million acres with thirty-three campgrounds, 2,600 miles of roads, and 1,500 miles of trails. When 2006 came around, the Darrington Ranger District was still trying to recover from $2.7 million worth of damage following the 2003–2004 floods. As of 2008, two winter storms' worth of damage remains largely unfunded and unaddressed. By some reports, $70 million might be needed to repair storm damage throughout the Cascades. Add this to many more millions of dollars needed to address back-logged maintenance resulting from years of congressional budget neglect.

Many popular and well-known areas in the forest were unavailable during the 2007 field season when *Best Hikes Near Seattle* was being researched and written. Trails and bridges that were washed away had yet to be repaired or replaced. Forest roads were gone. Some trails, not so badly damaged as others, were accessible but still in poor shape. Joel Connelly, reporting for the *Seattle Post-Intelligence* in April 2007, wrote that the 2007 trail maintenance budget for the entire Mount Baker–Snoqualmie National Forest was $15,000—3 percent of the money needed to repair bridges on the Big Four Ice Caves Trail. Volunteer labor organized by Washington Trails Association and others have done commendable work in opening up some areas, but there is simply too much for volunteers to do.

In late 2007 the Mountain Loop Highway between Granite Falls and Darrington was finally opened. It had been closed north of Barlow Pass since autumn 2003, when floodwaters damaged bridges and cut the highway and over forty side roads. Repairs cost $10 million, and snow soon required the yearly closing of the road.

Some would argue that a hiking guide is not the proper place to lobby citizens of the United States. On the other hand, what's the alternative? If hikers, anglers, paddlers, equestrians, hunters, picnickers, birdwatchers, boaters, botanizers and everyone else who uses our public lands don't tell our elected representatives that we expect those public lands to be fully funded and cared for, who else is going to do it? As some politicians like to say when discussing taxes, it's our money. It's time to remind those politicians that we want it spent wisely. There are over 5.4 million annual visitors to Mount Baker–Snoqualmie National Forest. Make your voice heard.

# How to Use This Book

Each region begins with an introduction that provides a general overview for the hike chapters featured within that region. To aid in quick decision-making, each hike begins with a summary. Next come the hike "specs," including where the hike starts; hike distance and type of hike; approximate hiking time; difficulty rating; trail surface; best hiking season; other trail users; status on dogs; what agency manages the land; town nearest the trailhead; information about fuel and other services available in the area, along with availability (and type) of a toilet at the trailhead; whether a Northwest Forest Pass is necessary; useful maps; whom to contact for updated trail information; and any special hazards you might encounter on the trail.

"Finding the trailhead" gives you directions from downtown Seattle to where the hike begins. Also provided are the *DeLorme Washington Atlas and Gazetteer* coordinates of the trailhead.

"The Hike" presents this author's impressions of the trail. It isn't possible to cover everything you will see, and who would want that anyway? Taking a hike is not just about exercise or getting outside. It's also about exploring a place and learning about it on your own. The hike description is meant as a guide.

"Miles and Directions" includes specific mileages and GPS coordinates to identify turns, trail junctions, and points of interest. "Options" suggests hike extensions or interesting detours. Where it appears, "Hike Information" lists other data such as historical facts, miscellaneous local information resources, recommendations of a few places to eat, and anything else that didn't fit elsewhere in the trail description.

Appendixes at the end of this guide list clubs and organizations that advocate for trails and suggest books to read for more information about where you have been, or are going to be, hiking.

# Map Legend

## Transportation

- [80] Freeway/Interstate Highway
- [101] U.S. Highway
- [1] State Highway
- [1431] Other Road
- = = = = Unpaved Road
- ⊢—⊢—⊢ Railroad

## Trails

- ▬ ▬ ▬ Selected Route
- - - - - - Trail or Fire Road
- → Direction of Travel

## Water Features

- Body of Water
- River or Creek
- Waterfalls

## Symbols

- (20) Trailhead
- ≍ Bridge

## Symbols (continued)

- ■ Building/Point of Interest
- ▲ Campground
- ▮ Gate
- Lighthouse
- ▲ Mountain/Peak
- P Parking
- ≍ Pass
- ⛟ Picnic Area
- 🚻 Restroom
- Scenic View
- ○ Towns and Cities
- ⊢——⊣ Tunnel
- N ↕ True North (Magnetic North is approximately 15.5° East

## Land Management

- Local & State Parks
- National Forest & Wilderness Areas
- Natural Area
- Watersheds

**Trail Finder**

| Hike No. | Hike Name | Hikes for Children | Hikes for Backpackers | Training Hikes | Wildflower Hikes | Weekday Hikes (to avoid crowds) | Historical Hikes | View Hikes |
|---|---|---|---|---|---|---|---|---|
| 1 | Alki Beach Trail Stroll | ● | | | | | | ● |
| 2 | Alki Stair Climb | | | | | | | ● |
| 3 | Fort Lawton–Discovery Park | ● | | | | | ● | ● |
| 4 | Meadowdale County Park | ● | | | | | | ● |
| 5 | O. O. Denny Park | ● | | | | | | |
| 6 | Wallace Falls State Park | | | | | ● | | |
| 7 | Lake Serene | | | | | ● | | |
| 9 | Deception Falls | ● | | | | | | |
| 10 | Surprise Lake | | | | ● | | | |
| 11 | Boulder Lake | | | | ● | | | |
| 12 | Iron Goat Trail | | | | ● | | ● | |
| 13 | Robe Canyon Historic Park | | | | | | ● | |
| 14 | Robe Canyon | | | | | | ● | |
| 15 | Heather Lake | | | | ● | ● | | |
| 16 | Lake Twenty-two | | | | ● | ● | | |
| 17 | De Leo Wall | | | | | | | ● |
| 22 | Cedar Butte | | | | | | | ● |
| 23 | Rattlesnake Mountain | | | | | | | ● |

**Trail Finder**

| Hike No. | Hike Name | Hikes for Children | Hikes for Backpackers | Training Hikes | Wildflower Hikes | Weekday Hikes (to avoid crowds) | Historical Hikes | View Hikes |
|---|---|---|---|---|---|---|---|---|
| 24 | Weeks Falls | ● | | | | | | |
| 25 | Twin Falls | | | | | ● | | |
| 26 | Little Si | | | | | ● | | ● |
| 27 | Mount Si | | | ● | | ● | | ● |
| 28 | Myrtle Lake | | ● | | | ● | | |
| 29 | Taylor River | ● | ● | | | ● | | |
| 30 | Snoqualmie Lake–Lake Dorothy | | ● | | | ● | | |
| 31 | Dirty Harry's Peak | | | ● | | | | ● |
| 32 | Bandera Mountain | | | ● | ● | | | ● |
| 33 | McClellan Butte | | | ● | | | | ● |
| 34 | Mason Lake and Mount Defiance | | ● | | | ● | | ● |
| 35 | Annette Lake | | ● | | | ● | | |
| 36 | Melakwa Lake | | ● | | | ● | | |
| 37 | Olallie Lake | | ● | | | ● | | |
| 38 | Snow Lake | | ● | | | ● | | |
| 39 | Lake Lillian | | | | | | | ● |
| 41 | Skookum Falls | ● | | | | | | |
| 42 | Snoquera Falls | ● | | | | | | |

# Urban Walks

Trail's end at Puget Sound

Some days, it just doesn't pay to leave town. Traffic is horrendous and Interstate 5 is a barely moving parking lot. The bridges across Lake Washington may resemble barges transporting automobiles to Alaska up the Inside Passage. It could be snowing in the mountains. Or there isn't enough time to spend on getting to a trailhead.

When your legs are dying to stretch and your heart and lungs demand aerobic exercise, the Seattle area is fortunate in having many large city and county parks that take the sting out of having to remain close to home. Those listed here all have access to Puget Sound and, with only slight variations, are family-friendly. Since about four million people live along the shores of Puget Sound, don't expect to have these urban parks to yourself, although they can be amazingly empty on weekdays.

Puget Sound is an estuary—a place were salt and fresh water coalesce before the mix reaches the ocean. It's connected to the Pacific Ocean (and the Strait of Georgia to the north) by the Strait of Juan de Fuca. The Sound is actually a system of flooded glacial valleys carved by a million years of continental glaciation. At one time, a lobe of ice reached as far south as Olympia and at least as far east as Grouse Ridge (near exit 38 on Interstate 90). The beaches and bluffs around the edge of Puget Sound represent the accumulated sediments from this glaciation. About 20,000 years ago Seattle was buried by 3,400 feet of glacial ice—the height of five Space Needles.

> When your heart and lungs demand aerobic exercise, the Seattle area is fortunate to have many large parks that take the sting out of remaining close to home.

Duplex along Washington Avenue built for Army brass at Fort Lawton

*Sometimes it's impossible to be rid of Seattle—those days when Interstate 5 is a barely moving parking lot and you don't get anywhere until the news on NPR recycles a second time. Or the weather is terrible and the thought of driving to go hiking is anathema. Those days it's best to remain home reading a good book or exploring Seattle's urban walks.*

*The Alki Beach Trail draws people year-round and is one of the most popular walks anywhere in Seattle. Summer crowds are definitely a hindrance, but Alki is a great place for leg-stretching the rest of the year. Views are just as good—even better when winter snow covers the Olympics. Walk, jog, or bring your bike. Exercise the dog, or come down for a cuppa joe and some fish-and-chips.*

**Start:** Trailhead at Harbor Avenue SW and West Seattle Bridge off-ramp; alternative start at Sixty-third and Alki Avenues SW

**Distance:** 7.0 miles out and back; 3.5 miles one-way with return on METRO #37 bus (check schedule at http://transit.metrokc.gov)

**Approximate hiking time:** 3 to 4 hours

**Difficulty:** Easy

**Trail surface:** Sidewalk

**Seasons:** Year-round

**Other trail users:** Bikes, horses (police in summer months), runners, skateboarders, in-line skaters, baby strollers

**Canine compatibility:** Leashed dogs permitted on trail but no dogs allowed on beach

**Land status:** City of Seattle Department of Parks and Recreation; Port of Seattle; METRO/King County; Seattle City Light

**Nearest town:** Seattle

**Services:** Restaurants, bars, coffee— lots of coffee; no toilet at trailhead; flush toilets at Jack Block Park (with outdoor cold showers—seasonally operative), Seacrest Park, on Alki Avenue at 57th (with outdoor cold shower), and Alki at 63rd

**Northwest Forest Pass:** No

**Maps:** USGS Duwamish Head

**Trail contacts:** Seattle Department of Parks and Recreation, 100 Dexter Avenue N, Seattle, WA 98109; (206) 684-4075; www.seattle.gov/parks. Seattle City Light, 700 Fifth Avenue, Suite 3200, P.O. Box 34023, Seattle, WA 98124-4023; (206) 684-3000; www.seattle.gov/light. Port of Seattle, P.O. Box 1209, Seattle, WA 98111, (206) 728-3000; www.portseattle.org. King County Parks and Recreation Division, 201 South Jackson Street, Suite 700, Seattle, WA 98104; (206) 296-8687; www.metrokc.gov/parks/parks

**Special hazards:** Bikes, in-line skaters, dogs, cars, inattentive people; no water at trailhead

**Finding the trailhead:**

From I-5 north or south take exit 163 and drive west on the West Seattle Bridge (older maps might refer to it as the West Seattle Freeway). Or from Highway 99 south, exit to the West Seattle Bridge (aka the "High Bridge" versus the "Low Bridge" that spans Duwamish Waterway and swings open for ship traffic). Take the Harbor Avenue exit, turning right at the traffic signal at the end of the ramp. Drive 0.2 mile, pass the Active Space building, and park shortly beyond GT Towing. Finding a parking space any farther than this during spring and summer, especially on hot, sunny days, is problematic. Taking the bus is always a good idea. The #37 runs only during the commuter rush. The #56 takes an alternate route, over Admiral Way, to the beach (get off at 63rd and Alki). The Elliot Bay Water Taxi from downtown is always an option during the season it runs (contact METRO/King County for times of operation). Begin your walk at the farthest point from Alki Beach, where you're more likely to find a parking space. More parking is available under the West Seattle Bridge in the Park and Ride lot. *Delorme: Washington Atlas and Gazetteer:* Page 79 C-5.

## THE HIKE

Walk north beside Southwest Harbor Avenue under a lovely, wide tree-lined asphalt multiuse trail. Pass Jack Block Park on the right. Pass in succession Seacrest and Don Armeni Parks. Both afford fantastic views of Elliot Bay and the downtown Seattle skyline. Views only get better as you round Duwamish Head to Luna (aka Anchor) Park. A stairway provides access to a small sandy beach. From 1907 to 1913 Luna Park was the site of a large amusement park. The stairs are closed seasonally to provide sanctuary to marine mammals.

From here the multiuse trail splits. Walkers should take the water side of the trail, leaving the wider part for bikes and other self-propelled wheeled vehicles. This portion of the trail was formerly a railroad trestle. A seawall was constructed to protect the tracks, and the area between Puget Sound and the cliffs to the left (south) was filled in, eventually becoming Alki Avenue. The condos are more recent and began arriving on the scene during the 1980s when they replaced single-family homes.

The trail remains atop the bulkhead until the beach is reached at 57th Avenue SW. Notice the embedded plaques, which illustrate the history of Seattle with words and pictures. Designed by an artistic team led by Donald Fels, the project was funded with money from

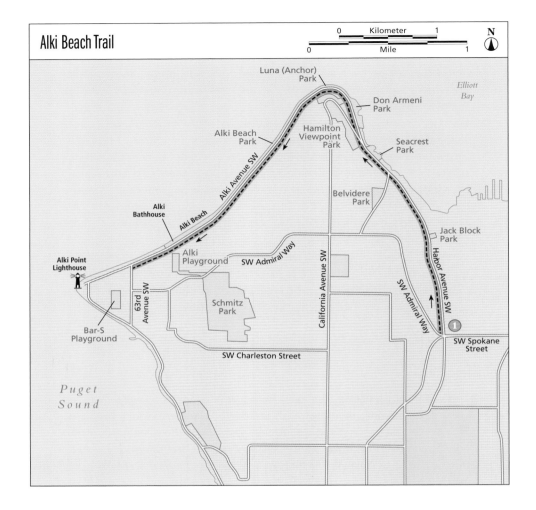

Seattle's 1% for the Arts program during the 1990s reconstruction of the Alki Beach Trail.

Beginning at 57th Avenue SW is Alki's small business district of restaurants, some of which convert themselves into bars after 10:00 p.m. The beach begins here, as well as the crowds. In summer stop and enjoy the volleyball games, or simply take a load off your feet and savor some people watching.

When ready, get back on the path and keep walking until you reach the end of the trail. Numerous places afford access to the water. The colorful building on the right is the Alki Bathhouse. Rebuilt and opened in 2005, the bathhouse serves as a meeting room and neighborhood art studio. Classes are taught throughout the year.

Beside the bathhouse is a small replica of the Statue of Liberty, originally a gift in 1952 from Reginald H. Parsons and the Seattle Council of the Boy Scouts of America. In 2007 the statue was recast and, in September 2008, installed on the same site. (Community involvement and fundraising has been crucial in this project.) Just before the end of the trail, at Alki Avenue and 63rd Avenue SW, is a concrete column commemorating the 1852 founding of Seattle by the Denny Party.

From here, one-way walkers should check the bus schedule. During the morning and late afternoon, catch a ride on the #37 bus back to your car. Or wait for the free shuttle bus that picks up and delivers passengers to the Elliot Bay Water Taxi. Round-trip walkers can turn around here and retrace their steps.

## MILES AND DIRECTIONS

**0.0**  Southwest Harbor Avenue and West Seattle Bridge trailhead: N47° 34.456' / W122° 22.240'

**0.6**  Jack Block Park: N47° 34.928' / W122° 22.417'

**1.4**  Don Armeni Park: N47° 35.551' / W122° 22.995'

**2.4**  Luna (Anchor) Park at Duwamish Head: N47° 35.702' / W122° 23.213'

**3.2**  Alki Bathhouse: N47° 34.763' / W122° 24.565'

**3.5**  Sixty-fourth Avenue SW and Southwest Alki Avenue: N47° 34.666' / W122° 24.960'. Option: One-way hikers, head for your bus.

**7.0**  Return to trailhead: N47° 34.456' / W122° 22.240'

**Options:** Railroad aficionados can extend the walk 1.0 mile east with an excursion from the Harbor Avenue trailhead to Chelan Cafe for lunch. There are numerous places along the way to observe the railyard used by the nearby steel plant and container ship facility.

## HIKE INFORMATION

Don Armeni Park has a boat launch. Luna (Anchor) Park has views of Puget Sound and downtown Seattle. Both are administered by the Seattle Department of Parks and Recreation. Don Armeni Park is home to scores of resident Canada geese. Please don't feed the birds—it only encourages them to stay, and they need to learn how to migrate.

The Elliot Bay Water Taxi runs between Seacrest Park (this will change when a permanent dock is built) and Pier 54, downtown (check www.transit.metrokc.gov for latest fares and schedules). A free shuttle bus runs from the water taxi dock to West Seattle Junction.

Jack Block Park, administered by the Port of Seattle, provides a nice detour. There is parking, flush toilets, a drinking fountain, and a picnic area. Elliot Bay,

Anchor Park

Harbor Island, Duwamish Waterway, and the container facility can be seen from numerous observation platforms and viewpoints. The sculpture over the entrance is supposed to represent the keel and ribs of a sailing ship.

Alki Point Lighthouse (3201 Alki Avenue SW) offers tours for the general public on Saturday and Sunday from June through August (1:30 to 4:00 p.m.). Tours are thirty minutes long and cover lighthouse history and operations, artifacts, and U.S. Coast Guard roles and missions. Group tours can be arranged by calling (206) 217-6203. Please respect the privacy of the people living in the two residences adjacent to the lighthouse.

Alki Kayak Tours (www.kayakalki.com; 206-953-0237), located at the Seacrest Boathouse on Southwest Harbor Avenue, rents sea kayaks. They also lead guided kayak tours of Elliot Bay and the Duwamish Waterway. People interested in exquisite Mediterranean cuisine will want to have dinner at Phoenicia (206-935-6550). It's the best!

> *"The walker's companions are the stones in his boot, the rain in his face, the unreadable map . . . but a wide open space."*
> —*Proverb*

# Alki Stair Climb and College Street Ravine

*Getting prepared for the hiking season can involve time in the gym. But time spent on a treadmill or stairclimbing machine isn't very interesting. Fortunately Seattle is blessed in having some steep hills. Though the hills stymied road building, our city fathers saw to it that pedestrians were provided with stairs. Such wisdom! And what better way to get in shape than to utilize those stairs? Adjacent to Alki Beach are two tall sets of nearly 200 stairs to climb. Combine them with a pleasant walk in a quiet neighborhood. Afterward try a delightful amble through the wild College Street Ravine. Surrounded by a dense urban neighborhood, the ravine is home to migratory birds and small mammals like foxes, coyotes, opossums, squirrels, and raccoons.*

**Start:** Alki and 53rd Avenues SW
**Distance:** 2.5-mile loop (does not include repeated stair climbs)
**Approximate hiking time:** 1.5+ hours (depending on how many times you climb the stairs before starting up College Street Ravine)
**Difficulty:** Easy
**Trail surface:** Sidewalk, forest path
**Seasons:** Year-round
**Other trail users:** Runners
**Canine compatibility:** Leashed dogs permitted
**Land status:** Seattle Department of Parks and Recreation; private property
**Nearest town:** Seattle

**Services:** Restaurants. Bars, convenience market, coffee—lots of coffee; no toilet at trailhead; flush toilets at Jack Block Park (with outdoor cold showers—seasonally operative), Seacrest Park, on Alki Avenue at 57th (with outdoor cold shower), and Alki at 63rd
**Northwest Forest Pass:** No
**Maps:** USGS Seattle
**Trail contacts:** Seattle Department of Parks and Recreation, 100 Dexter Avenue N, Seattle WA 98109; (206) 684-4075; www.seattle.gov/parks
**Special hazards:** Stinging nettle, Himalayan berry; off-leash dogs; possible automobile traffic

**Finding the trailhead:**
From Interstate 5 north or south, take exit 163 and drive west on the West Seattle Bridge (older maps might refer to it as the West Seattle Freeway). Or from Highway 99 south, exit to the West Seattle Bridge (aka the "High Bridge" versus the "Low Bridge," which spans Duwamish Waterway and swings open for ship traffic). Take the Harbor Avenue exit, turning right at the traffic signal at the end of the ramp. Follow Harbor Avenue to the north and then around Duwamish Head as it turns west and becomes Alki Avenue SW. Park your car between 53rd and 57th Avenues SW. *Delorme: Washington Atlas and Gazetteer:* Page 79 C-5.

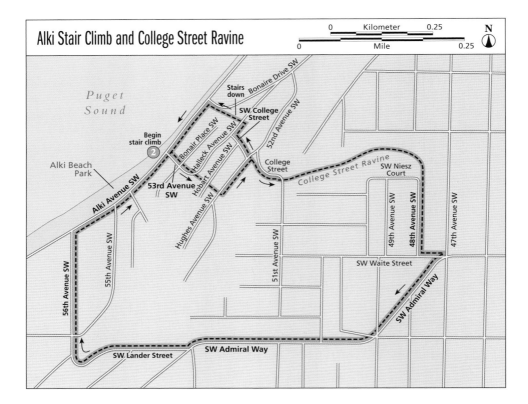

## Alki Stair Climb and College Street Ravine

**THE HIKE**

B egin at Alki and 53rd Avenues SW. Walk up the street to concrete steps—a route considered an extension of 53rd Avenue SW. The stairs are uneven in height and depth—not OSHA approved! Climb 145 stairs and cross Hobart Avenue SW to the remaining 51 stairs, which take you to Hughes Avenue SW.

Turn around, descend the stairs, and start all over again. This time, mix it up a bit. Try doing intervals. Run; then walk. Take two steps at a time, then three, then four. This is a popular place for fitness walkers, but you will have it all to yourself during the dark mornings of winter. Most dogs in the neighborhood are friendly and accustomed to people.

At the top of the stairs, try something different. Turn left (east) onto Hughes Avenue SW and walk downhill to Halleck Avenue SW. Turn right (east), enjoying the view of Puget Sound. Spot the stairway and descend 140 steps, through an overgrown forest straight out of the Enchanted Tiki Room, to Bonair and Alki Avenues SW.

Turn left and walk back 0.1 mile to 53rd, passing the bus stop for the #37 bus and free water taxi shuttle to Seacrest Park, and start all over again. Total distance for this loop is 0.9 mile.

Had enough of stairs? Then instead of dropping down to Alki Avenue at the Halleck Avenue stairs, continue uphill on Hughes. Curve onto Southwest College Street, hoof it uphill some more and turn right (southwest) on 52nd Avenue SW, then jog back onto Southwest College Street. Head directly to a Parks and Recreation sign identifying the start of the College Street Ravine as the Duwamish Head Greenbelt next door to 2302 51st Avenue SW. Please don't disturb the residents.

Community activist and former Seattle city councilmember Charlie Chong was instrumental in organizing neighbors in the late 1980s to save this green space from developments. The ravine was acquired with funding through the 1989 King County open space and trails bond. We should all be thankful to Charlie Chong, who died in 2007. The wild critters certainly must be.

Walk up the ravine, being careful of stinging nettle alongside the path. During the wet seasons the ground can be awfully moist, so be prepared or be willing to get your feet wet. Locals tend to bring boards down to the ravine to cover the most egregiously moist zones.

The Alki stairs

College Street Ravine has shade aplenty, provided by mature red alder trees. The developing understory of native plants includes sword fern, buttercup, geranium, and young western red cedar. There are many exotics such as Himalaya berry and holly. English ivy is particularly common. In the ravine's lower reaches, various spots are given over to poison hemlock (remember Socrates?), which resembles 6-foot-tall parsley. Note the red streaks, or striations, on the stem. All parts of the plant are poisonous.

Far too soon, pop out of the ravine onto 48th Avenue SW and Southwest Niesz Court, in a quiet residential neighborhood. If you've had enough, turn around and retrace your steps down College Street Ravine to the Alki Stair Climb. Otherwise follow 48th to Southwest Waite. Turn left (east), soon turning right (west) onto Admiral Way. If so inclined, there are many bus stops for the #56 to carry you back down to Alki Avenue. Otherwise saunter down to SW Lander Avenue and turn right (north). Lander becomes 56th Avenue SW and soon delivers you back to Alki Avenue. Turn right (east) to return to your car or the trailhead.

## MILES AND DIRECTIONS

**0.0**  Alki and 53rd Avenues SW trailhead: N47° 34.907' / W122° 24.232'

**0.1**  Begin stair climb: N47° 35.008' / W122° 24.054'

**0.3**  Top of stair climb: N47° 34.945' / W122° 23.971'

**0.4**  Fifty-second and Hughes Avenues SW (stairs down): N47° 35.050' / W122° 23.922'

**0.5**  Bonair Drive SW and Alki Avenue SW: N47° 35.084' / W122° 23.975'

**0.7**  Alki and 53rd Avenues SW: N47° 35.008' / W122° 24.054'

**1.1**  Fifty-second and Hughes Avenues SW: N47° 35.019' / W122° 23.874'

**1.2**  College Street Ravine: N47° 34.979' / W122° 23.819'

**1.5**  End of College Street Ravine (48th Avenue SW and Southwest Niesz Court): N47° 34.974' / W122° 23.573'

**1.7**  Southwest Admiral Way: N47° 34.866' / W122° 23.537'

**2.1**  Southwest Lander Street and Southwest Admiral Way: N47° 34.743' / W122° 24.030'

**2.5**  Return to trailhead: N47° 34.907' / W122° 24.232'

# Trail Hazards 1

Few plants strike as much horror in people's hearts in the Pacific Northwest as stinging nettle (*Urtica dioica*) and devil's club (*Oplopanax horridus*).

A weedy herbaceous perennial from Europe, stinging nettle grows to 6 feet tall and has soft green leaves with strongly toothed margins. The plant is covered with brittle, hollow hairs that inject a combination of a histamine, acetylcholine, and serotonin into anyone unfortunate enough to brush against them. But the plant is also edible early in the spring, and the ancient Greeks used it as a medicine!

Devil's club is an unusual native plant that often forms impenetrable thickets. Woe the poor hiker who cuts a switchback and stumbles into devil's club. The plant is covered with sharp hairs—even on its large, maplelike leaves—and causes contact dermatitis.

Devil's club

# 3

## Fort Lawton–Discovery Park

*Discovery Park is a 534-acre natural area operated by Seattle Parks and Recreation. At one time it was all part of Fort Lawton, a U.S. Army base. Something curious happened there late one moonless night on August 14, 1944: Private Guglielmo Olivotto, an Italian prisoner of war quartered at Fort Lawton, was found lynched in a ravine above the beach. For African-Americans in that era, a lynching was not unusual. What made this case so peculiar was that three African-America soldiers were charged with the first-degree murder/lynching of Private Olivotto. Another forty black soldiers were accused of rioting on that hot August night and attacking the barracks of Italian POWs.*

**Start:** East parking lot at entrance to Discovery Park Environmental Learning Center
**Distance:** 6.0-mile lollipop (longer or shorter, depending on your interest and time)
**Approximate hiking time:** 2 hours to all day
**Difficulty:** Easy
**Trail surface:** Dirt path, paved, gravel road
**Seasons:** Year-round
**Other trail users:** Bikes, runners, motorcycles, cars
**Canine compatibility:** Leashed dogs permitted
**Land status:** Seattle Parks and Recreation; U.S. Army; some property possibly private in the future
**Nearest town:** Seattle (Magnolia neighborhood)

**Services:** Gas, restaurants, groceries; flush toilets and drinking fountain inside Environmental Learning Center; porta-potties throughout the park
**Northwest Forest Pass:** No
**Maps:** USGS North Seattle
**Trail contacts:** Seattle Department of Parks and Recreation, 100 Dexter Avenue N, Seattle, WA 98109; general parks information: (206) 684-4075; www.cityofseattle.net/parks/; www.cityofseattle.net/parks/Environment/discovpark index.htm. Daybreak Star Cultural Center, United Indians of All Tribes Foundation, Discovery Park, P.O. Box 99100, Seattle, WA 98199; (206) 285-4425; www.united indians.org/daybreak.html
**Special hazards:** Stinging nettle

**Finding the trailhead:**
From anywhere in Seattle, navigate to the Fisherman's Terminal on West Emerson Street and travel west. Turn right (north) onto Gilman Avenue W, which wends its way through the Magnolia neighborhood, eventually becoming

West Government Way and entering Discovery Park. Once inside the park turn left (east) into the Discovery Park Environmental Learning Center (east) parking lot. *Delorme: Washington Atlas and Gazetteer:* Page 79 C-5.

## THE HIKE

After visiting the Discovery Park Environmental Learning Center (open Tuesday through Sunday 8:30 a.m. to 5:00 p.m.; closed holidays), walk through the parking lot to West Government Way. Find the sidewalk, turn left (northwest), and walk up the street for 0.2 mile. Turn right (northeast), pass through a cyclone fence gate, and enter the small Fort Lawton cemetery (closes at dusk) marked with a sign stating, WE HONOR THOSE WHO HAVE MADE THE SUPREME SACRIFICE. Private Olivotto's grave is in the extreme northeast corner of the cemetery.

As a POW, Private Olivotto wasn't buried within the quadrangle of the cemetery where U.S. servicemen and their families were interred. For more than ten years a simple wooden board marked his grave. Then members of Seattle-area Italian-American groups arranged for the current broken-column headstone. Note that Olivotto's given name is incorrectly spelled on the headstone.

Several feet south of the grave is the final resting place of a German POW, Captain Albert Marquardt, who died October 1, 1945, after drinking tainted moonshine. Though the war in Europe had ended May 8, 1945, with Germany's unconditional surrender, Captain Marquardt and many of his countrymen remained in the United States as POWs while awaiting repatriation. The autumn display of bigleaf maples throughout the cemetery is truly stupendous.

Returning to West Government Way and the sidewalk, turn right (northwest) and reach the hilltop after 0.2 mile. Bear left onto Washington Avenue and enter Fort Lawton's historic district, passing a RESTRICTED VEHICLE ACCESS sign. Between 1899 and 1908, twenty-eight buildings were constructed on Fort Lawton's parade ground. Currently the residences of Army and Navy brass, the row of duplexes along Washington Avenue, along with three other buildings below the parade ground, are all that remain of the fort's former architectural glory. The current plan for these "Officers' Row" houses is to turn them over to a private developer, who will renovate the structures and offer them for sale to well-heeled private citizens. By some estimates, each residence is valued at several million dollars.

Walk the length of Washington Avenue beneath century-old London plane trees. At a barbed wire–topped cyclone fence, the big golf ball–looking thing is part of NORAD—a North American aerospace warning system established

# Fort Lawton–Discovery Park

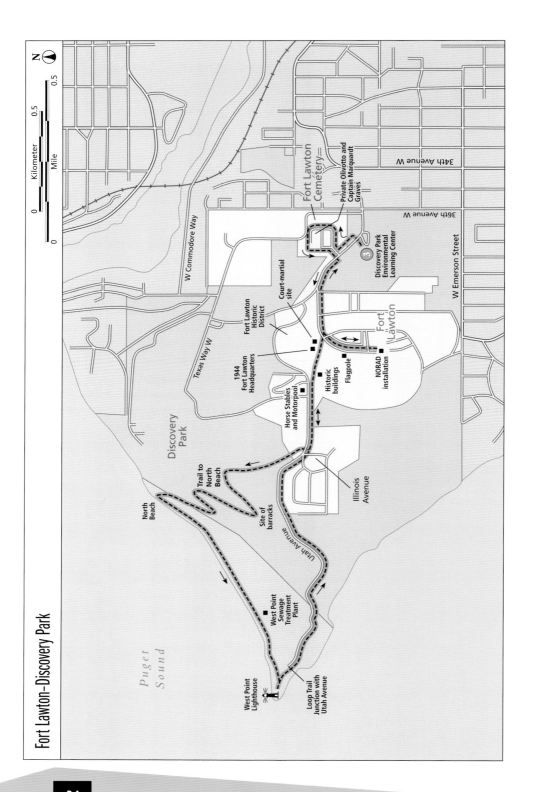

N

Kilometer
0    0.5

Mile
0    0.5

*Puget Sound*

West Point Lighthouse

West Point Sewage Treatment Plant

Loop Trail Junction with Utah Avenue

Utah Avenue

North Beach

Trail to North Beach

Site of barracks

Discovery Park

Horse Stables and Motorpool

Illinois Avenue

1944 Fort Lawton Headquarters

Fort Lawton Historic District

Court-martial site

Historic buildings

Flagpole

NORAD installation

Fort Lawton

Discovery Park Environmental Learning Center

Private Olivotto and Captain Marquardt Graves

Fort Lawton Cemetery

W Commodore Way

Texas Way W

34th Avenue W

36th Avenue W

W Emerson Street

in 1958. Today satellites have supplanted most of its functions. Turn around and retrace your steps, making for a flagpole. Stop and read the interpretive sign, admire the many images by nineteenth-century photographer Asahel Curtis, and enjoy the Olympic Mountain view. A plaque here memorializes Henry M. Jackson, U.S. senator from Washington.

North of the flagpole is a two-story yellow building fronting Utah Avenue that served as Fort Lawton military headquarters in 1944. Situated in the wye created by Utah and Illinois Avenues and immediately east of headquarters is a field given over to straggling alders, Scotch broom, and other ruderal plant life. This is where the court-martial of the forty-three African-American soldiers was held between November and December 1944. After a five-week trial, twenty-eight men were found guilty (including two convicted of manslaughter in the death of Private Olivotto) in the largest and longest army court-martial of World War II.

Walk downhill (west) from the flagpole to Oregon Avenue. The building with raised clusters of pillars supporting a cupola served Fort Lawton as a PX/post gymnasium. Band barracks occupied the two-story house at one time. A brick-yard surrounded the single-storied guardhouse. Chuckanut sandstone was used for building foundations. From the guardhouse front porch it's possible to see jail cells through the windows. At the back is a massive iron door. After examining the buildings, walk north, beyond the bus waiting shelter. Turn left (west) onto a sidewalk beside Utah Avenue.

Pass Montana Circle and a cluster of junior officer homes constructed of brick or clapboard. Less ostentatious than Officers' Row, these homes also lack Olympic views. A row of seven giant sequoia trees towers over a playground. Continue west.

Two long buildings on one side of the street originally served as horse stables. When automobiles replaced horses, the stables became the motor pool. Across the street, a two-story house (notice the foundation is brick, not sandstone) served as a residence for nonmilitary personnel. A beautiful London plane tree graces the front walkway of this house along with an iron light standard.

Utah Avenue continues west, passing Fort Lawton's minimarket. Cross the street (north) at the intersection of Utah Avenue and Hawaii Circle, and walk northwest on an old two-lane asphalt road, formerly Illinois Avenue. Though this area is now field and dense forest, barracks for POWs and African-American soldiers were located here during the 1940s. In 0.1 mile, where the Loop Trail crosses Illinois Avenue, take a moment to look around. This is approximately where the riot began when three American soldiers attacked some POWs. It quickly got out of hand, eventually involving several hundred Americans, although only forty-three were ever charged. All trace of the barracks is long gone.

Turn left (west) at this intersection and walk 0.2 mile to North Beach Trail, turning right (northwest) at a paved road. There is a bench and a portable toilet here. Where the paved road ends, bear left (west) and find a trail signed for North Beach.

West Point Lighthouse

Drop down the bluff on 200 steps and an assortment of bridges and boardwalks, arriving on the shores of Puget Sound. There is good tidepooling here. At low tide it's possible to walk along the beach to West Point.

Should the tide not be cooperating, double back to a wide dirt path and walk above the beach, eventually reaching West Point Lighthouse (access closed to visitors) and a King County sewage treatment plant. The North Beach profile has changed significantly since 1944 due to construction, landslides, and beach erosion. Looking north beyond the extensive facility development, two clumps of tall trees at the top of the bluff mark the approximate location of POW and African-American barracks in 1944. Private Olivotto was found at the bottom of the bluff below that point, where a road once existed. The actual lynching location was destroyed during construction of the West Point facility.

The path changes to asphalt and passes restricted parking and the wastewater treatment facility before ascending Utah Avenue. In 0.2 mile pass a trail junction; continue up for another 0.2 mile and a junction with the Loop Trail. Your choice is to return to the Environmental Learning Center by trail (1.3 miles) or by sidewalk along Utah Avenue (1.0 mile). Or take this opportunity to explore many of the other trails in Discovery Park. An interesting detour is to pass through the North Parking Lot—site of Fort Lawton's rifle range.

> ### 🍃 Green Tip:
> *Keep your dog on a leash unless you are certain it can follow your voice and sight commands. Even then, keep the leash handy and your dog in sight. Do not let it approach other people and their pets unless invited to do so.*

## MILES AND DIRECTIONS

**0.0**   Discovery Park Environmental Learning Center trailhead: N47° 39.467' / W122° 24.367'

**0.4**   Grave of Private Guglielmo Olivotto: N47° 39.638' / W122° 24.291'

**1.4**   Flagpole and plaque: N47° 39.581' / W122° 24.807'

**1.7**   Riot began here August 14, 1944: N47° 39.794' / W122° 25.261'

**1.9**   Site of Italian POW barracks: N47° 39.819' / W122° 25.370'

**3.0**   Approximate site where Private Olivotto was murdered: N47° 39.889' / W122° 25.406'

**3.5**   West Point Lighthouse: N47° 65.851' / W122° 58.431'

**5.0**   Flagpole and plaque: N47° 39.581' / W122° 24.807'

**6.0**   Return to trailhead: N47° 39.467' / W122° 24.367'

**Options:** There are nearly 12 miles of walking/running/biking trails at Discovery Park, including a well-marked loop trail that winds around the park's historic attractions, fields, and forests. Remember, all housing in the park is private and not open to the public.

## HIKE INFORMATION

Discovery Park (open daily 6:00 a.m. to 11:00 p.m.) is one of the darkest places in Seattle, making it ideal for observing owls and nighttime celestial events like meteor showers, planets, and the aurora borealis during the occasional times it comes to town.

Discovery Park is home to the Daybreak Star Cultural Center, a Native American cultural center operated by a parent organization called United Indians of All Tribes. Daybreak Star functions as a conference center, a location for powwows, the location for a Head Start school program, and an art gallery.

# Rush to Judgment?

There was a substantial lack of evidence to support the Army prosecutor's case against any of the black soldiers other than acceptance that a riot had occurred and Private Olivotto, an Italian POW, had been lynched. That didn't stop the lead prosecutor, Leon Jaworski, from pushing ahead—and also denying defense counsel from seeing crucial documents. Jaworski would later become famous as the man who got the goods on Richard M. Nixon. As Jack Hamann, a veteran reporter for PBS, CNN, NBC, and local Seattle television documents in his book *On American Soil,* without this successful prosecution, Jaworski's advancement never would have occurred.

In late 2007 the U.S. Army Board for Correction of Military Records ruled that Jaworski committed an "egregious error" by withholding crucial evidence in the murder and rioting trial of the soldiers. Declaring the trial "fundamentally unfair," the board overturned the forty-three convictions.

It's interesting to speculate why the U.S. government felt such a need to court-martial American soldiers for the death of one man during an incident where little evidence existed (even the murder weapon—a rope—was missing) and eye-witnesses were unreliable. After all, more than four years of world conflict was resulting in the death of tens of millions. One reason may have to do with racism. Another reason could be our country's feelings of obligation to treat prisoners in a responsible and humane manner. The United States saw victory on the battlefield as a way to free Europe and Asia from totalitarian governments while remaining convinced that the people of those countries were not our enemies. Indeed, our opponents from that war are now some of our strongest allies.

Read a full account of the event in *On American Soil* by Jack Hamann (Algonquin Books, 2005), or visit www.jackhamann.com for more information.

Private Olivotto's grave

# Meadowdale County Park

*Even the tramp, tramp, tramp of many feet along this popular route won't detour amblers and walkers from enjoying this fine urban trail. The rewards and pleasures are many—not the least of which are a deep, cool forest and arrival at trail's end on the shores of Puget Sound. Then there is the subtle beauty of a rare (for our area) forest tree and the autumnal arrival of chum salmon (Oncorhynchus keta) in Lunds Gulch Creek. All things considered, Meadowdale County Park is a marvelous treasure.*

**Start:** Parking area in Meadowdale County Park, Lynnwood
**Distance:** 2.5 miles out-and-back
**Approximate hiking time:** 3 hours
**Difficulty:** Easy, with one short, steep pitch
**Trail surface:** Old road
**Seasons:** Year-round
**Other trail users:** Runners
**Canine compatibility:** Leashed dogs permitted
**Land status:** Snohomish County Parks
**Nearest town:** Lynnwood
**Services:** Gas, restaurants, lodging, groceries; unisex portable toilet at trailhead

**Northwest Forest Pass:** No
**Maps:** USGS Edmonds East, Seattle
**Trail contacts:** Snohomish County Parks Department, 3000 Rockefeller Avenue, Everett, WA 98201; (425) 388-3411 or (800) 562-4367; www1.co.snohomish.wa.us/Departments/Parks/. Meadowdale Park, 6026 156th SW, Edmonds, WA 98036. Washington Water Trails Association, 4649 Sunnyside Avenue N #305, Seattle, WA 98103; (206) 545-9161; www.wwta.org; e-mail: wwta@wwta.org
**Special hazards:** No potable water in winter at trailhead or on trail; active railroad line (mostly fenced) parallel to the beach

**Finding the trailhead:**
From Seattle drive north on Interstate 5 to exit 182, Highway 525. Proceed 2.8 miles to Highway 99 S. Follow Highway 99 S 1.8 miles to 168th Street SW. Turn right (west). In 0.4 mile turn right (north) onto 52nd Avenue W at Beverly Elementary School. In 0.5 mile turn left (west) onto 160th Avenue W, following signs to Meadowdale County Park. Turn right in 0.2 mile onto 56th Avenue W, once again following signs to the park. In 0.2 mile turn left (west) onto 156th Street W at another park directional sign. In 0.3 mile, 156th Street W passes through a gate and drops into the park.

The paved parking lot fills quickly on weekends and sunny afternoons. No parking is allowed on 156th Street W. Meadowdale County Park closes at dusk. *Delorme: Washington Atlas and Gazetteer:* Page 9 B-6.

A couple of volunteer trails lead away from the parking lot and into the surrounding residential neighborhood. The actual trailhead is located on the east side of the parking lot. Loop downhill around the large grassy area on an asphalt path. Pass several picnic benches and enter the forest in 0.1 mile.

The wide, seasonally wet and muddy trail descends steeply through a forest of bigleaf maple, Douglas fir, and western hemlock. Benches are placed periodically to aid short-breathed people as they huff and puff up the hill. Don't laugh! You'll be returning this way soon enough!

Halfway down the 1.25-mile trail into Lunds Gulch, the pitch levels out and the trail begins to parallel the stream. Large tree stumps attest to the previous history of Meadowdale County Park.

The trail passes a large Sitka spruce and enters a copse of red alder.

Sitka spruce is an important forest tree throughout its range from Kodiak Island to northern California. The clear-grained wood is highly desired in manufacturing musical instruments because of its high sound-conducting quality. The bark

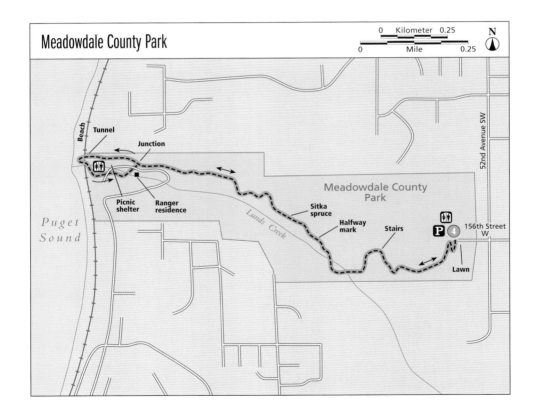

Close to the beach, a quiet respite for hikers

has the appearance of having large cornflakes glued to it; the needles are stiff and sharp and arise from a short peg (sterigma). The third largest of North American conifers, Sitka spruce are beautifully shaped trees with boughs hanging almost all the way down to the ground.

In 0.8 mile reach a trail junction. Go left (southwest) and cross a bridge over Lunds Creek. Make your way by the ingeniously decorated ranger residence (private; please don't disturb), and proceed 0.3 mile toward the beach past a picnic shelter located within a large lawn. Or continue straight ahead (west) 0.3 mile, also toward the beach. Both trails meet at a pair of portable toilets enclosed within an impressively designed rock shelter. Drinking water (not available in winter) can be found at both the picnic shelter and porta-potty shelter. There are picnic tables and trashcans located around the grassy area.

A short tunnel over Lunds Creek passes under the railroad track and onto a sandy beach. There are views northwest to Whidbey Island and west to Kingston on the Kitsap Peninsula. The beach can be walked, especially at low tide, for a short distance in either direction. Beware of passing trains, and keep off the railroad tracks.

This beach is part of the Cascadia Marine Trail, providing campsites to sea kayakers and other nonmotorized watercraft. After enjoying the view, retrace your steps back up the hill to the parking lot.

**Options:** A gated access road leading down to the grassy lawn beside the ranger residence is provided for disabled persons. To apply for access, submit an application form, available by calling (425) 388-6600 or downloading from www. co.snohomish.wa.us/documents/Departments/Parks/MeadowdaleParkingAccess. pdf. Call (425) 745-5111 to make picnic shelter reservations.

## MILES AND DIRECTIONS

**0.0**   Trailhead at east end of parking lot: N47° 51.437' / W122° 18.971'

**0.3**   Stairs: N47° 51.406' / W122° 19.190'

**0.5**   Sitka spruce: N47° 51.483' / W122° 19.450'

**1.0**   Trail junction: N47° 51.594' / W122° 19.911'

**1.2**   Tunnel: N47° 51.601' / W122° 20.073'

**1.2**   Toilet: N47° 51.606' / W122° 20.071'

**1.2**   Beach: N47° 51.598' / W122° 20.092'

**1.25**   Ranger residence (private): N47° 51.568' / W122° 19.927'

**2.5**   Return to trailhead: N47° 51.437' / W122° 18.971'

## HIKE INFORMATION

Lunds Gulch was homesteaded by John Lund in 1878. The property was eventually acquired by the Meadowdale Country Club, which built a clubhouse, manicured lawns, an Olympic-size swimming pool, bathhouses, and a fish hatchery. Problems with road access contributed to the club's closure in the 1960s.

In 1968 the Snohomish County Parks Department acquired the property. Public access was denied from 1979 to 1988 due to the lack of emergency vehicle access. The park was closed again for a year in 1996 due to storm damage.

Lunds Creek supports a small run of chum salmon. They can easily be seen in pools between the bridge and the beach.

> *"Walk and be happy, walk and be healthy.*
> *The best way to lengthen out our days is to*
> *walk steadily and with a purpose."*
> —*Charles Dickens*

# Tree Stories 1

There are many things Douglas fir (*Pseudotsuga menziesii,* or false hemlock) is not: It's not a true fir because the cones are pendent. Also, the scales are not shed while the cone is still attached to the tree. It's not a hemlock because its leaves (needles) don't leave a persistent base when shed.

Conversely, there are many things the Douglas fir is: It's named in honor of David Douglas, the peripatetic early-nineteenth-century botanical collector for the Royal Horticultural Society in London. It is one of the most common forest trees in the Pacific Northwest. It is the most important source of lumber from southern Canada to northern California and from the Rocky Mountains to the Pacific coast. It is a fairly recent arrival to the Northwest, having come on the scene little more than 7,000 years ago. The cones have protruding scales that resemble the hindquarters of little mice a tad too large to fit inside the cone. Trees reach heights of 250 feet with a diameter of 6 feet, and coastal trees attain ages between 200 and 800 years old. The tree is also known affectionately as the Doug fir.

Douglas fir

*During summer, the popular beach at O. O. Denny Park is crowded with people over-dosing on sun while the sylvan trail up Denny Creek lies forlorn and ignored. That's too bad, because along with some good representatives of large standing wood is one Douglas fir with a 26.3-foot circumference, which previous writers have claimed to be 600 years old. But you don't have to be looking for big old trees to enjoy this hike. It's perfect for a jaunt after work when the only other option is cocktails with co-workers whose idea of the outdoors is either a tennis court or a municipal plunge. If you live or work on the east side, make a habit of taking a picnic dinner and walk this lovely trail every week during summer and fall. The path gets a bit too wet the remainder of the year, but it's still worth the effort.*

**Start:** Trailhead in gravel overflow parking lot, across from the beach and picnic area along Holmes Point Drive

**Distance:** 1.6-mile loop with some out-and-back

**Approximate hiking time:** 2 to 3 hours

**Difficulty:** Easy, with several creek crossings and a muddy trail

**Trail surface:** Forested path, gravel, boards

**Seasons:** Year-round

**Other trail users:** Runners

**Canine compatibility:** Leashed dogs permitted

**Land status:** Finn Hill Park and Recreation District

**Nearest town:** Kirkland

**Services:** Gas, restaurants, groceries, lodging; flush toilet at trailhead

**Northwest Forest Pass:** No

**Maps:** USGS Bellevue North

**Trail contacts:** Finn Hill Park Commission, P.O. Box 2792, Kirk-land, WA 98083-2792; www .finnhillparks.net; e-mail: parkinfo@finnhillparks.net

**Special hazards:** Devil's club; creek crossings, wet and slippery boardwalk. No sidewalks along Holmes Point Drive; while driving, keep a careful eye out for pedestri-ans walking along the road

**Finding the trailhead:**
From Seattle cross Lake Washington on either Interstate 90 or Highway 520 to Interstate 405 north. Reaching Kirkland, take exit 20A, NE 116th Street. Turn left (west) at the stoplight. NE 116th Street becomes NE Juanita Drive and then Juanita Drive NE. Turn left (north) onto Holmes Point Drive NE. Continue 1.1 miles and look for the trailhead parking lot on the left (west). A subsidiary gravel parking lot is located on the east side of Holmes Point Drive but may be locked. There is limited street parking on Holmes Point Drive. *Delorme: Washington Atlas and Gazetteer:* Page 79 C-7.

Lake Washington—a prime prehike lunch spot

## THE HIKE

Begin by leaving the paved parking lot and carefully crossing Holmes Point Drive. Walk to the northern end of the gravel overflow parking lot, and find the trail behind a welcoming sign. Trails up the ravine were first constructed in 1926 by the City of Seattle when the park was chosen as a camping site for Seattle children in one of the first outdoor education schools in the United States. The park was upgraded in 1934 by the Civilian Conservation Corps, which improved the trails.

The sometimes muddy trail skirts a wet area on possibly slippery boards and enters a thick forest of Douglas fir and western red cedar. Denny Creek along with

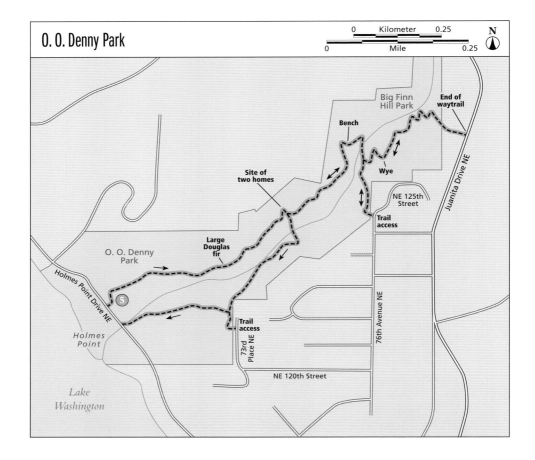

O. O. Denny Park

its anadromous fish population is below on the right (south). Cross more wet areas on a combination of bridges and boards, and in 0.2 mile reach a large Douglas fir.

The trail climbs on steps to avoid the creek, climbs through more wet areas on boardwalks and stairs, and emerges in a long, narrow copse of mature red alder. Light streams in beautiful contrast with the dark, shady regions of the surrounding conifer forest on the upper slopes.

After 0.4 mile stop for a moment at an interpretive sign at the site of two homes built during the 1920s. This property was purchased in 1974 by King County for Big Finn Hill Park. Turn right (south) and walk to a bridge over the creek and another interpretive sign that describes the fish ladder, which was conceived, designed, and built by volunteers in July 2002.

Behind you, the trail continues up the creek (northeast) for another 0.3 mile and involves splashing through the creek several times. Then, passing a bench that affords a nice place to sit and rest, the trail switchbacks steeply up the hill until it forms a wye. At this unmarked trail junction a waytrail extends left (northeast), getting narrower and narrower until it disappears completely. A degree of bushwhacking brings adventurous hikers to the backyards of people living along Juanita Drive NE. This route is not recommended.

Turning right (south) at the wye brings you in 0.1 mile to trail access at the intersection of 76th Avenue NE and Northeast 125th Street.

Returning to the fish ladder and bridge, pass several more interpretive signs. The trail here is actually an old roadbed. Note the occasional decommissioned utility pole. Continue along this old road to another access point at 73rd Place NE. Turn right (north), and descend toward Holmes Point Drive, crossing the street and reaching the paved parking lot.

## MILES AND DIRECTIONS

**0.0**   Holmes Point Drive SE trailhead: N47° 42.584' / W122° 14.994'

**0.2**   Large Douglas fir: N47° 42.637' / W122° 14.763'

**0.4**   Homesite: N47° 42.732' / W122° 14.624'

**0.6**   Bench: N47° 42.833' / W122° 14.478'

**0.7**   Wye split in trail: N47° 42.802' / W122° 14.418'

**0.8**   Trail access at 76th Avenue NE: N47° 42.721' / W122° 14.413'

**1.4**   Trail access at 73rd Place NE: N47° 42.533' / W122° 14.726'

**1.6**   End of trail: N47° 42.551' / W122° 14.975'

**Options:** Bridle Trails State Park, Saint Edward State Park (includes 3,000 feet of shoreline and 316 acres representing the last large piece of intact forest on Lake Washington), Big Finn Hill County Park, and City of Kirkland's Juanita Bay Park are all within a few miles of O. O. Denny Park and offer a wide breath of amenities ranging from secluded wooded paths to horse riding trails to baseball and soccer fields.

🍃 **Green Tip:**
*Minimize the use and impact of fires. Use designated fire spots or existing fire rings (if permitted). When building fires, use small sticks (less than 1.5 inches in diameter) that you find on the ground. Keep your fire small, burn it to ash, put it out completely, and scatter the cool ashes. If you can, it's best to avoid making a fire at all.*

O. O. Denny Park is located in the City of Kirkland, but the property is owned by the City of Seattle. The park was once known as "Klahanie," the country estate of Orion O. Denny, son of Seattle founder Arthur Denny. When the younger Denny died in 1916, his widow willed the property to Seattle. The park is located on Finn Hill and is managed by the Finn Hill Park Commission.

The lake side of the park has a grass lawn, picnic areas with benches, and a gravely beach. O. O. Denny Park closes at dusk. Alcohol beverages, fireworks, and weapons are not allowed. All fires must be in raised park grills only. There is a shelter available by reservation; call (425) 820-4358, or by e-mail easter@totallandscape .net.

No powered watercraft, including personal watercraft, are allowed within 300 feet of the park shoreline. Parking space is limited, so no trailer parking is allowed in either the parking lot or along Holmes Point Drive. Parking along Holmes Point Drive is limited; read signs carefully.

## How Plants Were Named

Blame it all on a guy, fixated on sex, born over 300 years ago in Sweden.

The modern discipline of taxonomy—the art of naming and classifying living things—was invented by Carl Linnaeus, who once declared, "God creates, Linnaeus arranges." Albrecht von Haller, a contemporary of Linnaeus, called the master naturalist "the second Adam," since the biblical Adam had named everything on earth the first time around. He just hadn't thought to use Latin!

The Linnaeus system relied on a binomial nomenclature—what we now refer to as genus + species. He also decided that organisms would be classified based upon their most conservative structures (i.e., those body parts less likely to be modified over time). This meant their sexual structures. In plants that meant flowers. Linnaeus wrote, "Every animal feels the sexual urge," and, "Yes, love comes even to the plants."

This did not endear him to some of his fellows during the late eighteenth century. They called the Linnaeus sexual system of plant classification indecent. One of his detractors, Johann Siegesbeck, called Linnaeus's work "loathsome harlotry," writing, "Who would have thought that bluebells, lilies, and onions could be up to such immorality?"

Indeed.

Keeping hikers' feet dry

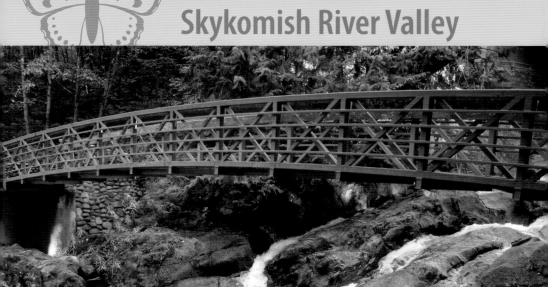

Bridging the creek below upper Deception Falls

Rimmed by water and high mountains, the nineteenth century City Fathers of Seattle were hard-pressed to find a fast and reliable route for imports and exports. When ideas for a rail route were floated, the Great Northern Railroad preferred a route over Stevens Pass to Seattle's idea of Snoqualmie Pass. U.S. Highway 2 through the Skykomish Valley follows much of this pioneering railroad through mountains of stunning beauty and complexity. When hikers and motorists can take their eyes off the peaks, cliffs, and waterfalls, they gravitate toward the Skykomish River. Whitewater kayakers and anglers make the Sky an important recreational river.

Established and dedicated in May 2008, the Wild Sky Wilderness will provide a valuable link between Alpine Lakes Wilderness, other Forest Service wilderness lands, and North Cascades National Park. The Wild Sky protects 106,000 acres of land under the jurisdiction of Mount Baker–Snoqualmie National Forest. The measure has always enjoyed the support of valley residents and businesses along with broad congressional support across party lines.

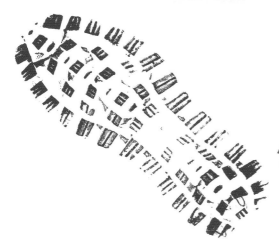

Enjoying the view of Lake Serene

# Wallace Falls State Park

*Wallace Falls marks the entrance to the grand scenery of the Skykomish River Valley. The river is a popular whitewater run, and paddlers know the river as "The Sky." Traveling eastward, every turn of the road reveals another character of The Sky's beauty. As for the falls, within 0.5 mile the Wallace River drops 800 feet, creating nine distinct waterfalls. Like Bridal Veil Falls, some 8 road miles farther upstream, the main cascade of Wallace Falls can be seen from the highway as it gushes, foams, and leaps 265 feet. Walking the trail to the falls takes your breath away—and it isn't solely because it feels like you're heading straight up. This popular trail can be full of people in summer and nearly devoid of hikers in winter—which is a shame, since winter rains make Wallace Falls truly impressive.*

**Start:** Wallace Falls State Park
**Distance:** 6.0 miles out and back
**Approximate hiking time:** 3 to 4 hours
**Difficulty:** Moderate, with many steep pitches
**Trail surface:** Forested path, old railroad bed
**Seasons:** Year-round
**Other trail users:** Mountain bikers
**Canine compatibility:** Leashed dogs permitted
**Land status:** Washington State Parks

**Nearest town:** Gold Bar
**Services:** Gas, restaurants, groceries; flush toilets at trailhead; camping and cabins for rent at Wallace Falls State Park
**Northwest Forest Pass:** No
**Maps:** Green Trails No.142: Index; USGS Index; USDAFS Mount Baker–Snoqualmie National Forest
**Trail contacts:** Washington State Parks and Recreation Commission, 7150 Cleanwater Drive SW, P.O. Box 42650, Olympia, WA 98504-2650
**Special hazards:** Exposure, cliffs

**Finding the trailhead:**
From Seattle drive north on Interstate 405 and then northeast on Highway 522 to Monroe. In Monroe drive 13 miles east on U.S. Highway 2 to the town of Gold Bar. Turn left (north) at First Avenue, following the signs to Wallace Falls State Park. In 0.4 mile turn right (east) onto May Creek Road. In 1.1 miles bear left (northwest) onto Ley Road. Enter the park and pass through a gate. The road ends in 0.2 mile at a large paved parking lot. *Delorme: Washington Atlas and Gazetteer:* Page 80 A-3.

## THE HIKE

There are no fees for hiking in Wallace Falls State Park, although donations are requested. The Woody Trail begins beside the restroom. Pass an information kiosk explaining the history of Wallace Lake and Wallace Falls. Begin walking the wide way underneath power lines, sharing the route with mountain bikes. In 0.2 mile the way veers left (north), away from the humming electricity. Stop and enjoy views eastward up the Skykomish Valley.

Wallace Falls—actually nine distinct waterfalls

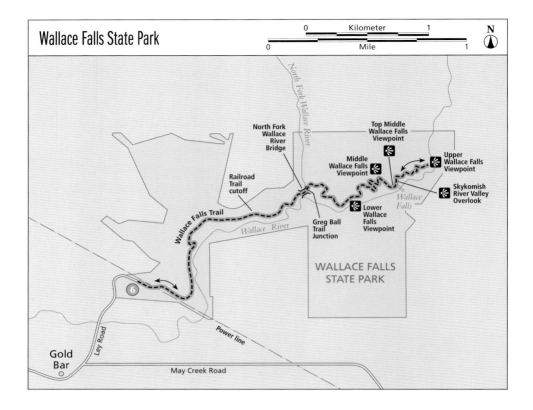

0                  Kilometer          1

0                    Mile              1

In another 0.1 mile reach a trail junction. Left (northwest) is the Railroad Grade Trail, which takes the long way (and the bicyclists) to the Wallace River's north fork. Hikers turn right (northeast) and continue on the Woody Trail. Drop to the river, passing the first of many benches placed to provide rest for the weary and opportunities to appreciate the awesome beauty of nature. Periodic signposts tick off the mileage.

Abruptly the Woody Trail begins to climb steeply—first on switchbacks and then without. After 1.0 mile you reach a junction with a cutoff trail rising back to the Railroad Trail. Continue straight, upstream (north), on the Woody Trail. Another 0.5 mile brings you to the Greg Ball Trail to Wallace Lake. Bear right (east) and keep heading upstream, crossing the North Fork Wallace River on a stout bridge.

The Lower Wallace Falls Viewpoint is reached in 1.8 miles. There is a large picnic shelter with several large, heavy picnic tables. Tired? Hungry? Take a load off your feet and give thanks to the state park staff, who built the shelter and managed to haul the tables to this spot. This is a good opportunity to remember the donation station at the trailhead and pledge liberally. Railings around the viewpoint help restrain the more inquisitive from risking their lives to obtain a better view. Look upstream for a faraway view to the middle falls.

The trail leaves the cliff and climbs as the river drops, but the din of rushing water never diminishes. In 0.5 mile come to the Middle Wallace Falls Viewpoint, followed by the Skykomish River Valley Overlook and trail's end at the Upper Wallace Falls Viewpoint in 3.0 miles from the parking lot. From this point, although maps show a trail leading another 3.0 miles to Wallace Lake, the route is difficult to follow in many places and not recommended. Nearly all visitors to the upper falls use this as an opportunity to turn around and retrace their way back on the Woody Trail to the parking lot.

## MILES AND DIRECTIONS

**0.0** Trailhead at restroom: N47° 52.008' / W121° 40.684'

**1.0** Wallace Falls Trail–Railroad Trail cutoff: N47° 52.293' / W121° 39.950'

**1.5** Wallace Falls Trail–Greg Ball Trail Junction: N47° 52.410' / W121° 39.556'

**1.5** North Fork Wallace River Bridge: N47° 52.446' / W121° 39.535'

**1.8** Lower Wallace Falls Viewpoint: N47° 52.334' / W121° 39.319'

**2.0** Middle Wallace Falls Viewpoint: N47° 52.419' / W121° 39.098'

**2.5** Skykomish River Valley Overlook: N47° 52.414' / W121° 38.964'

**3.0** Upper Wallace Falls Viewpoint: N47° 52.521' / W121° 38.789'

**6.0** Return to trailhead: N47° 52.008' / W121° 40.684'

## HIKE INFORMATION

The lake, falls, and mounts are named "Wallace" for Joe and Sarah Kwayaylsh, members of the Skykomish tribe, who were the first homesteaders in the area. The State of Washington acquired most of the land for the park in 1971 from the Weyerhaeuser Timber Company.

The Wallace Falls State Park Management Area is a 4,735-acre park with shoreline on the Wallace River, Wallace Lake, Jay Lake, Shaw Lake, and the Skykomish River.

Park hours are 8:00 a.m. to dusk. Check-in time for camping (first come, first served) is 2:30 p.m.; quiet hours are 10:00 p.m. to 6:30 a.m. The number of campsites is currently in flux.

There are five cabins adjacent to the trailhead parking. Cabins feature a 6-foot covered front porch, picnic table, fire pit, electric heat and lights, and locking doors.

They are furnished with bunk beds and a full-size futon. Two cabins have two rooms, providing privacy for the bunk beds, and two cabins have an ADA-compliant ramp. Campers must bring their own linen and blankets. Reservations may be made year-round by calling (888) 226-7688.

Wallace Falls State Park is extremely busy on summer days, and the parking lot usually fills by 11:00 a.m. on weekends. Park personnel live on-site.

## The Banana Slug

Our most common denizen of the forest must be the Pacific banana slug (*Ariolimax columbianus*). The slugs are often bright yellow, but green, brown, and white forms also exist. Growing up to 10 inches long, banana slugs are the second-largest species of land slug in the world. Only the European slug (*Limax cinereoniger*) gets longer.

Banana slugs make their living by crawling along the forest floor on their muscular foot, eating detritus. This makes them important decomposers as they process plant material and animal droppings into soil. They apparently also have a fondness for mushrooms. Movement is accomplished by waves of peristalsis—the same motion that delivers food from our mouths to our stomachs. Two pairs of tentacles sense light or movement and detect phero-mones—chemical clues that help the slugs recognize one another. To avoid injury, the tentacles can be retracted.

A coating of slime protects the slug's skin and also provides a slick sur-face that aids in movement across the ground. The slime can also anesthetize any mucous membrane it comes in contact with, such as the lining of a preda-tor's mouth, though not too many critters delight in eating banana slugs. Some of the slug's enemies include raccoons, geese, and ducks. It's possible to experience the numbing feeling caused by the slime by picking up a banana slug and letting it ooze across your fingertips.

Banana slug

# Lake Serene

*Where the North and South Fork Skykomish Rivers come together, passengers in cars motoring along U.S. Highway 2 are treated to an amazing sight. To the south all eyes find it hard to miss the Yosemite-like visual delight of Bridal Veil Falls leaping a thousand feet into space with a series of foamy cataracts from its source in Lake Serene. Visiting the lake during the week or in the off-season, it's a serene experience as well, albeit a tough and exhausting one. But Lake Serene and Bridal Veil Falls are extremely popular places to visit, so hikers must be in a sharing mode on weekends. Once at the lake, be prepared for the jaw-dropping sight of Mount Index towering 3,500 feet above, dominating the scene.*

**Start:** Trailhead for Lake Serene along US 2

**Distance:** 7.5 miles out and back

**Approximate hiking time:** 4 to 5 hours

**Trail number:** USDA Forest Service Trail 1068

**Difficulty:** Difficult; most steep sections surmounted by stairs

**Trail surface:** Sometimes rocky forested path, boardwalk, stairs

**Seasons:** Summer and fall

**Other trail users:** None

**Canine compatibility:** Leashed dogs permitted

**Land status:** USDAFS Skykomish Ranger District

**Nearest town:** Index

**Services:** Gas, restaurants, groceries, lodging; vault toilet at trailhead

**Northwest Forest Pass:** Yes

**Maps:** Green trails No.142: Index; USGS Index; USDAFS Mount Baker–Snoqualmie National Forest, Alpine Lakes Wilderness

**Trail contacts:** Alpine Lakes Protection Society (ALPS): www.alpinelakes.org. Mount Baker–Snoqualmie National Forest, Skykomish Ranger District, 74920 Northeast Stevens Pass Highway, P.O. Box 305, Skykomish, WA 98288; (360) 677-2414; www.fs.fed.us/r6/mbs/about/srd.shtml

**Special hazards:** Loose rock, exposure (stay within guardrails near Bridal Veil Falls); no potable water at trailhead or on trail

**Finding the trailhead:**
From Seattle take Highway 522 to Monroe, turning (left) east onto US 2. Drive US 2 through Gold Bar, passing signs to Wallace Falls State Park at First Avenue. Continue east for another 7.3 miles to Mount Index Road (Forest Road 6020). Turn right (south) onto a wide, potholed unpaved road. Drive 0.2 mile and bear right (south) at a fork onto Forest Road 6020-109. Continue 0.1 mile to a parking area. *Delorme: Washington Atlas and Gazetteer:* Page 80 B-4.

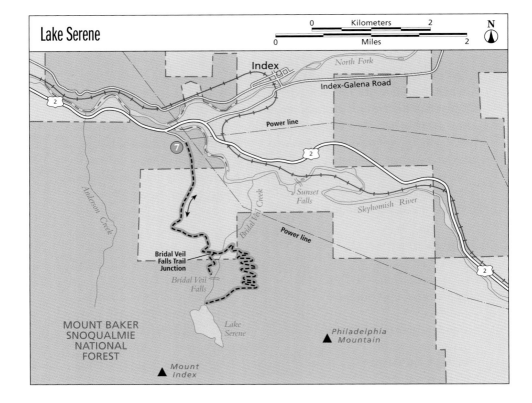

**Lake Serene**

0  Kilometers  2
N
0  Miles  2

Index
North Fork
Index-Galena Road
Power line
7
2
Anderson Creek
Sunset Falls
Skyhomish River
Bridal Veil Creek
Power line
Bridal Veil
Falls Trail
Junction
Bridal Veil
Falls
Lake
Serene
Philadelphia
Mountain
MOUNT BAKER
SNOQUALMIE
NATIONAL
FOREST
Mount
Index
2

## THE HIKE

The current trail to Lake Serene is not the trail that many old-time hikers in the region remember. That thing—hardly a trail at all—was an outrageously extraordinary up-and-down excursion into the fifth dimension across Utah-style slickrock and moon-size tree roots. Enough people were hauled down that old trail, blubbering on the verge of a nervous breakdown, that generations of guidebooks kept Lake Serene out of their pages.

No more. A new trail has changed it all. Not that some of the old trail features have disappeared completely!

The steep trail to Lake Serene seems unending. Especially during the long, hot summer days that periodically sit over the Puget Sound region. Maybe that's why the trail, which feels as if it reaches from the depths of some bottomless hole and into the heavens, is so unbearable to so many people who come equipped for a backyard barbecue versus a strenuous hike.

From the parking area, walk around the gate on what is obviously an old road. After 0.1 mile note the hiker sign and bear right (south). Many of the old volunteer trails still exist—though the yearly renewable flagging is long, long gone. Keep your eyes sharp, and follow the main route to avoid getting off course.

Cross a small creek, and in another 0.3 mile cross it again. Believe it or not, cars used to come this far. After 1.2 miles from the trailhead, another sign directs hikers to the right (south) on a wide, obvious trail. Another fork and another trail sign in 0.1 mile direct hikers left (southeast). In another 0.1 mile the trail bears left (southeast) at another fork. Turning the opposite direction leads to Bridal Veil Falls. It's worth the detour. On a hot day the spray of water is most refreshing. Stay within the guardrails, since the slope is wet and slippery. One false step could be embarrassing, to say the least. Tired hikers stop at the falls, turn around, and head home.

A highway-viewable waterfall flowing from Lake Serene

Returning to the main trail, a series of stairs continues the trail down to a stream, crossing on a sturdy bridge with an even sturdier handrail. After that the trail climbs. And climbs. Switchbacks take the trail west until it reaches a lip below the lake. All of a sudden there it is. Lake Serene. It's difficult to know where to look first. The lake is certainly inviting—especially for hikers flushed in the face from the steep and direct climb. But Mount Index so dramatically overlords the view that it isn't easy to keep one's eyes from drifting toward the sky.

After reaching the lake, boardwalks head out in both directions. People like to swim in the lake on hot days, and it isn't hard to understand why—though the water is very cold. It's all snowmelt, you know.

To return, retrace your steps down the trail—and marvel at how almost vertical it was on the way up. Hopefully a walking stick will slow down the declivitous descent.

## MILES AND DIRECTIONS

**0.0**  Trailhead on FR 6020-109: N47° 48.538' / W121° 34.432'

**1.8**  Bridal Veil Falls: N47° 47.385' / W121° 34.155'

**3.7**  Lake Serene: N47° 47.065' / W121° 34.330'

**7.5**  Return to trailhead: N47° 48.538' / W121° 34.432'

## HIKE INFORMATION

Sunset, Canyon, and Eagle Falls are nearby, located on the South Fork Skykomish River. Wallace Falls State Park, with another very impressive drop of water, is located downstream in the town of Gold Bar.

*Edward Payson Weston made a bet that Abraham Lincoln would lose the 1860 presidential election. Weston's losing bet was to walk from Boston to Washington, D.C., for the inauguration. He completed the 478-mile trip in 10 days, 10 hours—and received a congratulatory handshake from the new president.*

# Barclay and Eagle Lakes

*This is actually two hikes. The first hike, to Barclay Lake, is an easy trail, suitable for young children. It has the added bonus of a lake with a shallow shoreline, large campsites, a designated day-use area, pit toilet, and the possibility of catching fish. The hike to Eagle Lake begins from Barclay Lake and gains nearly 1,500 feet in elevation on a trail that goes straight up. It is recommended only for hikers with experience in route-finding. Even in late spring the upper reaches of the trail in the vicinity of Stone and Eagle Lakes are snow-covered, and a 500-foot ascent through talus may be required.*

**Start:** Trailhead along Forest Road 6024

**Distance:** 4.6 miles out-and-back to upper Barclay Lake; 6.6 miles out-and-back to Eagle Lake (2.0 miles or more round-trip from Barclay Lake, depending on your route-finding skills)

**Approximate hiking time:** 3 hours round-trip to Barclay Lake; 6 to 8 hours round-trip to Eagle Lake

**Trail number:** USDA Forest Service Trail 1055

**Difficulty:** Easy to Barclay Lake; extremely difficult to Eagle Lake, which requires clambering over numerous fallen trees, a steep ascent while route-finding, a stream crossing, and climbing over talus

**Trail surface:** Forested path; rocky

**Seasons:** Summer and fall

**Other trail users:** None

**Canine compatibility:** Leashed dogs permitted

**Land status:** USDAFS Skykomish Ranger District

**Nearest town:** Index (limited services in Baring)

**Services:** Gas, restaurants, groceries, lodging; no toilet at trailhead. An old wooden throne from a privy can be found on a use trail above the parking area. Avoid the temptation to use it; there is no hole beneath it.

**Northwest Forest Pass:** Yes

**Maps:** Green Trails No.143: Monte Cristo; USGS Baring; USDAFS Mount Baker–Snoqualmie National Forest, Alpine Lakes Wilderness

**Trail contacts:** Alpine Lakes Protection Society (ALPS); www.alpinelakes.org. Mount Baker–Snoqualmie National Forest, Skykomish Ranger District, 74920 Northeast Stevens Pass Highway, P.O. Box 305, Skykomish, WA 98288; (360) 677-2414; www.fs.fed.us/r6/mbs/about/srd.shtml

**Special hazards:** Devil's club around lake outlet; snow in early season. Trail to Eagle Lake from Barclay Lake is steep and requires route-finding and climbing over talus; snow in early season along with creek crossing

**Finding the trailhead:**
From Seattle take Highway 522 to Monroe, turning left (east) onto U.S. Highway 2. Drive US 2 through Gold Bar. Five miles east of Index on US 2 is the town of Baring—little more than a whistle-stop for the railroad. Look for a sign announcing FR 6024‡FIRST LEFT. The turn is directly opposite Der Baring Store. Cross the railroad tracks and drive north for 4.4 miles on a good gravel road. Pass Forest Road 310 on the left in 1.5 miles and arrive at the trailhead parking. *Delorme: Washington Atlas and Gazetteer:* Page 81 B-5.

Descending from Eagle Lake to Barclay Lake

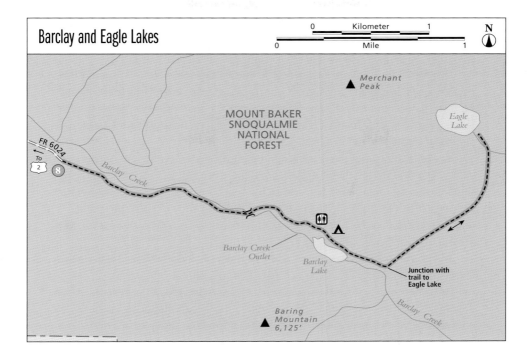

## Barclay and Eagle Lakes

0 — Kilometer — 1
0 — Mile — 1

N

Merchant Peak

MOUNT BAKER
SNOQUALMIE
NATIONAL
FOREST

Eagle Lake

FR 6024

To 2 8

Barclay Creek

Barclay Creek Outlet

Barclay Lake

Baring Mountain 6,125'

Junction with trail to Eagle Lake

Barclay Creek

## THE HIKE

Leaving the parking lot, the trail undulates with very little elevation gain or loss until reaching Barclay Lake. The forest here is mature second-growth, with Douglas fir predominating. The canopy is thick enough to block all views of Baring Mountain and Barclay Creek. Stumps of many large trees line the trail until you reach the bridge crossing the creek.

At 0.7 mile from the trailhead, a split-log walkway helps hikers remain above the wet ground. Look around for flowers and the elephant-ear leaves of the musky-scented skunk cabbage (*Lysichitum americanum*). Similar in construction to calla lilies, the flower is actually the long yellow-green rod you see. It's surrounded by a yellow spathe (a large, showy, solitary bract).

After crossing Barclay Creek on a heavy-duty split-log bridge, the trail gently climbs to the lake. Pass the lake outlet to avoid devil's club and other physical obstructions and continue past the first campsite to the day-use area. If you have no plans to hike farther, this is a good place to stop for lunch or to splash in Barclay Lake. Take a look above you. That's Baring Mountain looming overhead, all but hidden from anywhere on the trail coming in.

A sign directs hikers to an outdoor privy. Campsites are located lakeside and in the trees.

Hikers with experience in route-finding can continue on to Eagle Lake by walking over many fallen trees and passing more campsites to the head of Barclay

Lake. Just past a small wooden bridge at the end of the lake, the Eagle Lake trail branches off to the left. To the right is a small campsite under the trees. Find an old sign marking a missing toilet and you know you're in the right area.

The USGS topo map shows a trail to Eagle Lake. It's more like a game trail, occasionally flagged and ducked. It's not advisable to assume these markings will be there for you unless you leave them yourself for your descent. The route goes straight up the deeply forested hillside, over big logs and through a well-developed shrub layer including devil's club. Ouch.

Keep climbing until you reach around the 3,200-foot elevation mark, and work your way to the stream on your right. Cross the creek below a rock wall, and continue traversing to the right. Signs of an old trail become more frequent; if you're lucky, you'll be able to see it. Ducks are more frequent and helpful at this point. Enter a wide gap in the hillside; follow it up to a snowfield (in early season), and ascend to the left over large talus.

In late summer move up the middle of the drainage between the trees and avoid the talus completely. Views across to Baring Mountain are particularly stunning from here—even more so than from the lake. At the top of the talus the route relents and flattens out. Stone Lake, not much more than a puddle, lies below to your right (east). Traverse above the drainage, around the shoulder of a hill to your left (west), through thin and spotty forest, and finally reach Eagle Lake, which is large and isolated in a beautiful cirque.

Retrace your steps to Barclay Lake; the return trip is easier since you now know the route. From Barclay Lake, retrace your route to the trailhead.

## MILES AND DIRECTIONS

**0.0**  Trailhead on FR 6024: N47° 47.545' / W121° 27.549'

**1.3**  Bridge over Barclay Creek: N47° 47.325' / W121° 26.333'

**1.8**  Barclay Lake campsite: N47° 47.142' / W121° 25.706'

**2.3**  Upper Barclay Lake and start of Eagle Lake Trail: N47° 47.025' / W121° 25.319'. Option: If not continuing to Eagle Lake, retrace your steps to the trailhead.

**3.3**  Eagle Lake: N47° 47.676' / W121° 24.725'

**6.6**  Return to the trailhead: N47° 47.545' / W121° 27.549'

## HIKE INFORMATION

Don't forget to stop at the Reptile Zoo on your way home. It's located in the eastern suburbs of Monroe on the north side of US 2.

# Deception Falls

*Rather than rushing across Stevens Pass, try a side trip to Deception Falls. This short, family-centric walk to some gorgeous waterfalls also provides an abundance of picnic places, a covered picnic area at the parking lot, and several vault toilets—all of which make Deception Falls a nice place for stopping while on a long drive. The waterfalls aren't too shabby either!*

**Start:** Trailhead at Deception Falls Nature Area
**Distance:** 0.5-mile loop
**Approximate hiking time:** 1 hour
**Difficulty:** Easy, with a few short uphill sections
**Trail surface:** Forested path, boardwalk, paved
**Seasons:** Year-round
**Other trail users:** None
**Canine compatibility:** Leashed dogs permitted
**Land status:** USDAFS Skykomish Ranger District
**Nearest town:** Skykomish
**Services:** Gas, restaurants, groceries, lodging; vault toilet at trailhead
**Northwest Forest Pass:** Yes

**Maps:** Green Trails No.176: Stevens Pass; USGS Scenic; USDAFS Mount Baker—Snoqualmie National Forest, Alpine Lakes Wilderness
**Trail contacts:** Mount Baker–Snoqualmie National Forest, Skykomish Ranger District, 74920 Northeast Stevens Pass Highway, P.O. Box 305, Skykomish, WA 98288; (360) 677-2414; www.fs.fed .us/r6/mbs/about/srd.shtml
**Special hazards:** The Tye River and both upper and lower falls are at dangerous levels during spring runoff; stay within barriers. No potable water at trailhead or on trail; potable water available at the Skykomish Ranger Station

**Finding the trailhead:**
From Seattle take Highway 522 to Monroe, turning left (east) onto U.S. Highway 2. Drive US 2 to the Skykomish Ranger Station, and then go another 6.5 miles east on US 2 to Deception Falls Nature Area. Turn left (north) into the large paved parking lot. *Delorme: Washington Atlas and Gazetteer:* Page 81 C-7.

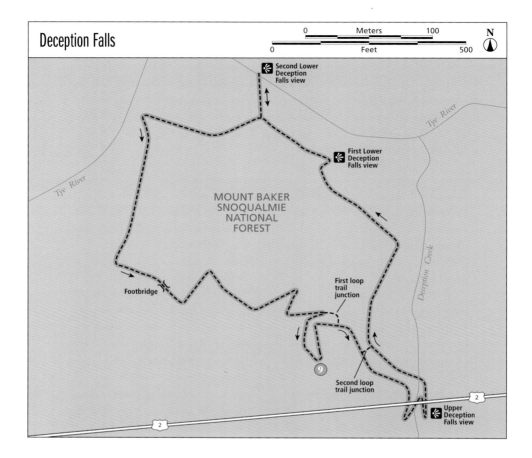

Deception Falls

0    Meters    100

0    Feet    500

N

Second Lower
Deception
Falls view

First Lower
Deception
Falls view

MOUNT BAKER
SNOQUALMIE
NATIONAL
FOREST

Tye River

Tye River

Tye River

Deception Creek

First loop
trail
junction

Footbridge

9

Second loop
trail junction

2

2

Upper
Deception
Falls view

## THE HIKE

From the picnic area, drop down a paved trail for 100 feet to the first of two signed junctions. Go straight ahead, toward the lower falls. For the loop trail, turn left (northwest). In another 100 feet continue straight at a second signed trail junction, toward the upper falls. Turning left (north) is a shortcut to the lower falls and loop trail.

The trail crosses Deception Creek on a footbridge and then leads up stone stairs and under US 2 to a viewing platform. This is upper Deception Falls. The water from Deception Creek tumbles over rocks and is impressive throughout the year—even in late summer during low flows. Take a moment to read the interpretive sign that briefly explains the geologic history of this area.

Retrace your steps under the highway bridge, down the stone steps, and across the footbridge to the second signed junction. Turn right (north) and continue down the loop trail toward Deception Creek, crossing a side channel of the creek that is a seasonally wet area. Don't forget to stop, not only to admire the creek and large trees but also to read the many interpretive signs along the way that explain forest ecology.

Upper Deception Falls

Reach a spur trail and walk down twenty-two stairs to a large viewing platform overlooking the lower falls. Then return to the loop trail, turning right (north), and continue walking. Very soon find a different spur trail on the right (north), and follow it to another viewing platform. This one overlooks the Tye River as it makes an impressive 90-degree turn through bedrock, flowing through a rectangular notch and emerging into a pool below.

Continuing along the loop trail, curve southward, with the Tye River beside you for one last brief moment. Begin to climb up a hill toward the parking area. Cross a subsidiary creek on a nice footbridge—a great spot for a picnic lunch.

Some short, steep stretches of trail eventually lead to the first signed trail junction. Turn right (south) onto the asphalt path, and emerge at the parking lot a hundred feet later.

## MILES AND DIRECTIONS

**0.0**   Deception Falls trailhead: N47° 42.929' / W121° 11.725'

**0.1**   Upper Deception Falls: N47° 42.902' / W121° 11.661'

**0.15**  Cross creek: N47° 42.959' / W121° 11.691'

**0.2**   First lower falls view: N47° 43.013' / W121° 11.717'

**0.3**   Second lower falls view: N47° 43.051' / W121° 11.766'

**0.4**   Footbridge: N47° 42.956' / W121° 11.824'

**0.5**   Return to trailhead: N47° 42.929' / W121° 11.725'

## HIKE INFORMATION

About 4 miles east of Index on US 2 is Eagle Falls (N47° 79.563' / W121° 51.414') along the South Fork Skykomish River. At Milepoint 39, keep your eyes peeled for a parking turnout on the south side of the highway. There are no signs. Volunteer paths lead to a rock formation and spots for viewing the falls, which drop 28 feet. River levels can be dangerously high, and rocks surrounding the falls can be wet and slippery, especially early in the season.

To view Alpine Falls (N47° 71.678' / W121° 22.619'), continue 5.3 miles east of the Skykomish Ranger Station. West of the bridge crossing the Tye River is a turnout on the south side of the road. A short, obvious path leads to a lookout above the falls. Several steep waytrails lead down to the river below the falls, which drop 40 feet. River levels can be dangerously high, and rocks surrounding the falls can be wet and slippery, especially early in the season.

# Surprise Lake

*For such an obscure trailhead, the way up to Surprise Lake (and beyond) gets a lot of foot traffic. This probably has to do with the trail's proximity to Surprise Creek (along with its many waterfalls) and the large number of campsites at the lake. Numerous avalanche chutes provide prime wildflower viewing in spring, and views upcanyon from the lake to cliffs and crags are very impressive. More adventurous hikers can hook up with the Pacific Crest Trail to points farther north or south, create a backpacking loop with Deception Creek (Forest Service Trail 1059), or utilize many other trails on a multiday excursion to reach Salmon La Sac (car shuttle needed).*

**Start:** Surprise Lake trailhead
**Distance:** 8.0 miles out and back
**Approximate hiking time:** 5 to 6 hours
**Trail number:** USDA Forest Service Trail 1060
**Difficulty:** Moderate, with many steep areas
**Trail surface:** Forested path, boardwalk; rocky
**Seasons:** Spring, summer, and fall
**Other trail users:** None
**Canine compatibility:** Leashed dogs permitted
**Land status:** USDAFS Skykomish Ranger District, Alpine Lakes Wilderness Area
**Nearest town:** Skykomish
**Services:** Gas, restaurants, groceries, lodging; camping at Forest Service Money Creek; pit privy with no walls at trailhead
**Northwest Forest Pass:** Yes
**Maps:** Green Trails No.176: Stevens Pass; USGS Scenic; USDAFS Mount Baker–Snoqualmie National Forest, Alpine Lakes Wilderness
**Trail contacts:** Alpine Lakes Protection Society (ALPS): www.alpinelakes.org. Mount Baker–Snoqualmie National Forest, Skykomish Ranger District, 74920 Northeast Stevens Pass Highway, P.O. Box 305, Skykomish, WA 98288; (360) 677-2414; www.fs.fed.us/r6/mbs/about/srd.shtml
**Special hazards:** Devil's club; creek crossing on logs; no potable water at trailhead or on trail

**Finding the trailhead:**
From Seattle take Highway 522 to Monroe, turning left (east) onto U.S. Highway 2. Drive US 2 to Der Baring Store in Baring. Drive 17.6 miles farther east to Milepost 58.7, passing the turnoff to Skykomish Ranger Station, Deception Falls, and Iron Goat Interpretive Center.

Turn right (south) onto an unmarked road. This road crosses the Tye River and some railroad tracks and in 0.1 mile passes through a railroad service yard. Bear right (west), and continue 0.3 mile on a narrow, rough road (Forest Road 840) to a small parking area and the trailhead. *Delorme: Washington Atlas and Gazetteer:* Page 81 C-7.

## THE HIKE

Self-register at the trailhead to enter the Alpine Lakes Wilderness. The trail starts along a power line road. In 0.2 mile reach the Surprise Creek Trail on the left (southwest) and a poorly made trail sign mounted on an equally poorly mounted 4"4 wooden post being consumed by the vegetation around it. Begin climbing gently on a series of old steps and puncheons through deep second-growth forest alongside the creek. After 0.6 mile enter the Alpine Lakes Wilderness Area and delight to the much larger trees.

Meander through the old-growth forest, and at 1.0 mile cross Surprise Creek on a log. The trail steepens but climbs below an avalanche slope and talus field before climbing in earnest. The stream gradient changes as well, making Surprise Creek louder and louder with plenty of small waterfalls. The canyon narrows, and more avalanche slopes appear on both sides.

Devil's club (*Oplopanax horridus*) fills many of these avalanche slopes. This native plant is perfectly adapted to growing in disturbed areas. Spiny leaves discourage plant predators. Brittle stems easily break off the parent plant and take root. Many Northwest Indians included the fruit as part of their pharmacopoeia. Anglos have found the fruit to be poisonous and the remainder of the plant to cause contact dermatitis.

After 3.0 miles, and tired of pussyfooting around alongside the creek, the trail makes a couple of switchbacks to the northeast, getting higher up on the east canyon wall, and then resumes its steep climb. The trail crosses innumerable side channels, kisses the creek one last time, and turns away like a spurned lover. The following switchbacks are numerous, shorter and steeper than the previous ones, and continue for another 0.5 mile. Near the top of the switchbacks, a sign bolted to a tree announces that fires are prohibited past this point.

Sadly for those in hope of rest and respite, the end is not near. The trail continues its steep climb, utilizing a couple more switchbacks before finally flattening out for its final approach to Surprise Lake. During this last 0.5 mile, gentle trail sections alternate with short spurts of steepness. Finally, after one last lung-buster, reach a trail junction with the Pacific Crest Trail (PCT) and a large camping area.

For the PCT turn left (east). To continue on to the lake, bear right (southwest). Soon reach a trail junction. Turn left to continue 1.0 mile to Glacier Lake and far-

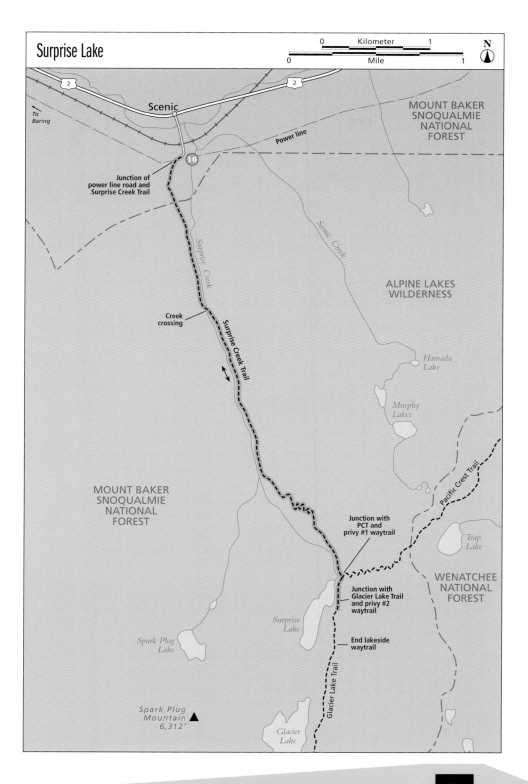

Surprise Lake

0 — Kilometer — 1
0 — Mile — 1

N

US 2

Scenic

US 2

To Baring

Power line

MOUNT BAKER SNOQUALMIE NATIONAL FOREST

10

Junction of power line road and Surprise Creek Trail

Surprise Creek

Scenic Creek

ALPINE LAKES WILDERNESS

Creek crossing

Surprise Creek Trail

Hamada Lake

Murphy Lakes

MOUNT BAKER SNOQUALMIE NATIONAL FOREST

Pacific Crest Trail

Junction with PCT and privy #1 waytrail

Trap Lake

Junction with Glacier Lake Trail and privy #2 waytrail

WENATCHEE NATIONAL FOREST

End lakeside waytrail

Spark Plug Lake

Surprise Lake

Glacier Lake Trail

Spark Plug Mountain 6,312'

Glacier Lake

ther to Surprise Gap. Continue on waytrails past a privy to reach Surprise Lake in 0.1 mile. There are many camping areas alongside the eastern lakeshore as well as another privy. On a promontory, at what looks like the best camping site at Surprise Lake, is a great day-use-only area. The lakeside waytrail passes several other campsites before being lost in the rocks and boulders at the head of Surprise Lake. Remember, no campfires are allowed.

## MILES AND DIRECTIONS

**0.0** Trailhead on FR 840: N47° 42.479' / W121° 09.397'

**0.2** Junction of power line road and Surprise Lake Trail: N47° 42.411' / W121° 09.548'

**0.6** Boundary of Alpine Lakes Wilderness Area: N47° 42.063' / W121° 09.478'

**1.0** Cross Surprise Creek: N47° 41.753' / W121° 09.299'

**4.0** Surprise Lake: N47° 40.136' / W121° 08.316'

**8.0** Return to trailhead: N47° 42.479' / W121° 09.397'

## How to Deal with Blisters

Blisters can feel just awful. How amazing it is that a little bubble of water on your toe can turn a fantastic hiking trip into disaster. Keeping in mind that blisters are caused by friction, the following hints may help to keep your hiking trips in the fun column.

It is said that "you don't break in boots, you break in feet." That's why it's wise to wear boots that fit. Ditto for socks. Padding is a good thing! Wear socks that aren't worn away in the heels and toes. It helps to keep your toenails trimmed too, since this ensures that boots and socks fit properly. One last comment about socks: If your feet sweat a lot, bring an extra pair of socks and switch them out every hour or so. Dry socks won't rub as much.

Remove any pebbles, twigs, or other foreign objects from your shoe ASAP. Pay attention to any signals your feet send to your brain. A "hot spot" likely means rubbing has begun to build a new blister. It can happen fast. Real fast.

If a blister does form, add some padding. If you decide to pop the blister, be aware that infection could set in. Wash your hands and the affected foot, and sterilize a needle. After draining the blister, apply antiseptic. Wrap the blister to keep it clean. Check and change the bandage frequently, keeping it as dry as possible.

## HIKE INFORMATION

Stop at Zekes roadside diner at Milepoint 31.5 on US 2, 2 miles west of Forest Road 62, for root beer floats and their famous big, fat and juicy onion rings. They're not open late, but when they're open, it's great.

Surprise Lake

# Boulder Lake

*The Oxford English Dictionary tells us there are at least a quarter of a million distinct English words, excluding words from technical and regional vocabularies. With that amazing richness, why are so many rocky bodies of water named Boulder River or Boulder Lake? No matter. All is not in a name, as you will discover from this lightly used trail. The rich understory, experienced only in old-growth forests—something you will see in abundance here—is delightfully refreshing. The nine designated campsites (closed from October 15 to June 15) at Boulder Lake have dynamite views of the lake basin and surrounding cirque.*

**Start:** Trailhead along South Shore Road (marked first as Road SL4000 and then Road 61 on the Green Trails map)
**Distance:** 4.8 miles out-and-back
**Approximate hiking time:** 4 to 5 hours
**Difficulty:** Moderate, with some steep areas and possibility of downed trees
**Trail surface:** Forested path; rocky
**Seasons:** Summer and fall
**Other trail users:** None; lake is reported to be fishless with no appeal to anglers
**Canine compatibility:** Leashed dogs permitted
**Land status:** Department of Natural Resources—part of the 6,700-acre Greider Ridge Natural Resources Conservation Area
**Nearest town:** Sultan
**Services:** Gas, restaurants, groceries; vault toilet at trailhead
**Northwest Forest Pass:** No
**Maps:** Green Trails No.142: Index; USGS Mount Stickney; USDAFS Mount Baker–Snoqualmie National Forest
**Trail contacts:** Commissioner of Public Lands, Department of Natural Resources, P.O. Box 47001, Olympia, WA 98504-7001; (360) 856-3500; e-mail: recreation@ wadnr.gov. City of Everett, Public Works, 3200 Cedar Street, Everett WA 98201; (425) 257-8800; e-mail: everettpw@ci.everett.wa.us
**Special hazards:** No potable water at trailhead or on trail

**Finding the trailhead:**
From Seattle drive northeast on Highway 522 to Monroe. Connect with U.S. Highway 2 and drive east to Sultan. Just past Milepost 23, turn left at the traffic signal onto Sultan Basin Road. Avoid diverting onto the many smaller side roads. The pavement ends at 10.5 miles, becoming wider and hard packed, with occasional clusters of potholes. At 13.5 miles bear right at the fork onto South Shore Road.

Stop at the self-registration station, marked prominently by a sign that reads: ALL VEHICLES MUST CHECK IN. After registering, drive on, passing numerous fishing access points to Spada Reservoir. Stop at Bear Point and appreciate the reservoir view.

The road character now begins to change, becoming increasingly narrower and rockier. Pass the Greider Lakes trailhead at 20.7 miles, where the road continues to narrow. Although the road is rocky and the potholes are more frequent and deeper than before, the way is still passable for passenger cars. Drive another 1.3 miles and park at the Boulder Lake trailhead. *Delorme: Washington Atlas and Gazetteer:* Page 80 A-4.

## THE HIKE

B egin by the large sign announcing camping, driving, shooting, and dumping restrictions—and the lack of sanitary facilities at the lake. Ascend a rocky, abandoned road through an area clear-cut in the 1960s and replanted in 1970. Older guidebooks mention the open character of the country, but after nearly fifty years the forest has experienced significant regeneration. See? It does come back. Early in the season it's possible to hear the roar of Boulder Creek, but it remains hidden and unknown behind green mansions until you reach a bridge in 0.1 mile.

Stopping on this bridge to admire the creek is *de rigueur* because the cascades, pools, and waterfalls are so impressive. Old-growth forest lovers will also want to take a peek at how this bridge was constructed.

The road is no longer much of a road and quickly devolves into a trail that makes a low traverse of Greider Ridge. It's amazing to contemplate that this small area receives 100 to 180 inches annual precipitation. It's no wonder the city of Everett decided to build its domestic water supply along the Sultan River and collect some of the precious fluid.

After about a mile the traverse ends and—Boom!—enter an old-growth forest and begin switchbacking up the hill. The nicely graded trail alternates with stairs reinforced with cedar planking. The steps are tall and deep and will have you panting for breath in no time. In 1.6 miles the trail crosses a sizable marsh along a boardwalk of split cedar rounds—designed both to keep your feet dry and to protect this sensitive area from trampling. Watch for skunk cabbage (*Lysichitum americanum*), marsh marigold (*Caltha* sp.), shooting star (*Dodecatheon* sp.), red columbine (*Aquilegia formosa*), and other wildflowers. Mosquitoes, too. The marsh rim is covered with huckleberries (*Vaccinium* sp.).

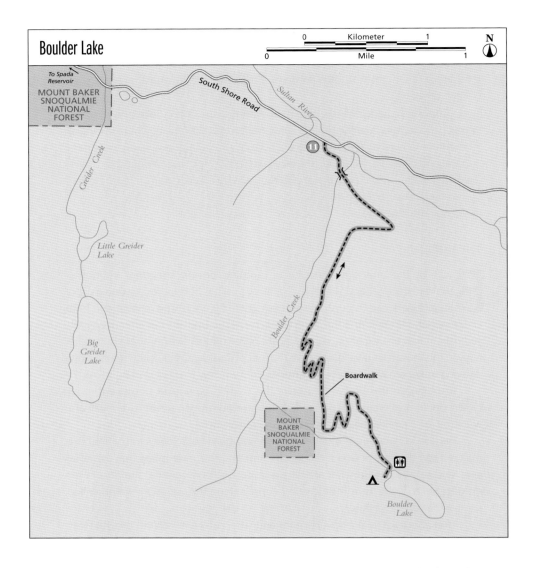

## Boulder Lake

To Spada Reservoir

MOUNT BAKER SNOQUALMIE NATIONAL FOREST

South Shore Road

Sultan River

Greider Creek

Little Greider Lake

Big Greider Lake

Boulder Creek

Boardwalk

MOUNT BAKER SNOQUALMIE NATIONAL FOREST

Boulder Lake

The boardwalk provides a swell place to stop and look around. The forest has become much more interesting. The trees are not all the same age and size. There are plenty of big holes in the canopy, and a highly developed understory of herbs and shrubs is evident. Observe the number of fallen trees and snags (standing, dead trees). This is what old-growth habitat looks like—so different from what we become accustomed to by hiking in places with a history of human impact.

At 2.4 miles cross a bridge below the log-jammed outflow of Boulder Lake. There are nine numbered campsites either along the lakeshore or above it. Each has a fine view of the lake, a fire pit with a useless barbecue grill, and a roughly hewn bench. If you're here to camp (June 15 through October 15; the lake is closed to camping the remainder of the year), haul out all your trash. Behind Campsite 5 is a privy with a limited-capacity portable vault toilet. Don't rely on the vault being empty and the privy operational.

Boulder Lake is situated in a narrow chasm with rocky crags high above. Directly across from the campsites is an immense talus slope, which no doubt gives the lake its descriptive name. The far end of the lake disappears around a forested corner, and adventurous souls will want to explore to see what there is to see.

The trail ends here. Had enough of azure waters, stark horizons, and a subalpine forest? Turn around and retrace your route back to the parking lot.

Negotiating an old boardwalk in an even older forest

## MILES AND DIRECTIONS

**0.0** Boulder Lake trailhead: N47° 58.226' / W121° 33.438'

**1.6** Boardwalk: N47° 56.966' / W121° 33.446'

**2.4** Boulder Lake: N47° 56.755' / W121° 33.017'

**4.8** Return to trailhead: N47° 58.226' / W121° 33.438'

**Options:** The trail to Little and Big Greider Lakes provides a lower, shorter, easier, and more popular (i.e., more crowded) route.

## HIKE INFORMATION

Spada Reservoir, operated by the City of Everett Public Works Department for domestic consumption, was formed in 1965 when Culmback Dam was built. The dam was raised in 1983 to increase water storage capacity and to construct a hydropower project, which is operated by the Snohomish Public Utility District. Today the reservoir covers nearly 1,900 acres and has 17 miles of shoreline. The reservoir is named for John Spada, an original Snohomish County PUD Commissioner and organizer of the Snohomish Soil Conservation District.

To maintain the water's high quality, recreational activities on the reservoir are limited. Gas-powered engines, swimming, and fishing with bait are prohibited. Both the watershed and the reservoir are patrolled daily, and access to the reservoir is restricted after sundown.

Kayakers consider the Sultan River, below Spada Reservoir, to be one of our region's premiere whitewater runs. American Whitewater is working to improve flows and public access on the Sultan River for the benefit of fish, wildlife, and recreation as part of relicensing the Jackson Hydroelectric Project and Culmback Dam on this river.

> **Green Tip:**
> *Keep to established trails as much as possible. If there aren't any, stay on surfaces that will be least affected, like rock, gravel, dry grasses, or snow.*

# Iron Goat Trail–Martin Creek to Wellington

*A mostly level walk though thick second-growth forest on the old Great Northern Railroad route is the prime reason for hiking the Iron Goat Trail. But there are also dazzling displays of wildflowers during spring, extensive views up and down the Skykomish River Valley, and a rich human history replete with great tragedy—all of which contributes to bring people to the trail. There are also many opportunities for loop hikes, but this particular hike makes a one-way trip from Martin Creek to the Wellington townsite and trailhead, requiring a car shuttle. Stopping at the Iron Goat Trail Interpretive Site at Milepoint 58.3 on U.S. Highway 2 is a requirement for understanding the trail, the railroad, and the people who made both happen.*

**Start:** Trailhead at Martin Creek
**Distance:** 6.0-mile point-to-point shuttle
**Approximate hiking time:** 4 to 5 hours
**Trail number:** USDA Forest Service Trail 1074
**Difficulty:** Easy, nearly level path
**Trail surface:** Forested path, boardwalk, old railroad bed; rocky
**Seasons:** Spring, summer, and fall
**Other trail users:** Runners
**Canine compatibility:** No dogs allowed
**Land status:** USDAFS Skykomish Ranger District
**Nearest town:** Skykomish
**Services:** Gas, restaurants, groceries, lodging; camping at USDAFS Money Creek; vault toilet at trailhead

**Northwest Forest Pass:** Yes
**Maps:** Green Trails No. 176: Stevens Pass; USGS Scenic; USDAFS Mount Baker–Snoqualmie National Forest, Alpine Lakes Wilderness
**Trail contacts:** Volunteers for Outdoor Washington (VOW), Iron Goat Trail, 8511 15th Avenue NE, Room 206, Seattle, WA 98115; (206) 517-3019; www.irongoat.org; www.trailvolunteers.org. Mount Baker–Snoqualmie National Forest, Skykomish Ranger District, 74920 Northeast Stevens Pass Highway, P.O. Box 305, Skykomish, WA 98288; (360) 677-2414; www .fs.fed.us/r6/mbs/about/srd.shtml
**Special hazards:** Stinging nettle, devil's club; no potable water at trailhead or on trail

**Finding the trailhead:**
From Seattle take Highway 522 to Monroe, turning left (east) onto US 2. Drive US 2 through Gold Bar to Der Bering Store in the town of Baring. Continue east on US 2 for 14 miles. Pass the turnoff to Skykomish and the Skykomish Ranger Station, continuing east to Milepoint 55 and Northwest Old Cascade Highway (Forest Road 67). Turn left (north). Proceed 2.3 miles on a narrow, well-paved

asphalt road to a junction with Forest Road 6710 and turn left (northwest) and travel 1.4 miles on a narrow, well-graded gravel road to the small parking lot. A picnic bench and garbage can are beside the toilet.

Passing the turnoff to Martin Creek trailhead, the Old Cascade Highway continues for another 2 miles to the Iron Goat Interpretive Site.

To reach the Wellington trailhead and townsite, continue east on US 2 toward Stevens Pass. At 23.6 miles from Der Baring Store (Milepoint 64.4), continue past the Old Stevens Pass Highway on the left (north). It is unsafe to make the turn from this part of US 2, so drive on for 0.3 mile to Stevens Pass. Turn around at the pass and head west to the Old Stevens Pass Highway. Turn right (east, curving to north, then west) onto a rough and poorly paved asphalt road with plenty of Seattle-size potholes. After 2.9 miles turn right (northwest) at the junction with Forest Road 050 onto a good gravel road to reach a large parking area in 0.3 mile. There are picnic tables, a garbage can, vault toilets, and a saddleback-style bicycle rack at Wellington. *Delorme: Washington Atlas and Gazetteer:* Page 81 C-7.

## THE HIKE

Cross FR 6710 at the Martin Creek trailhead to an information kiosk to find benches and a boardwalk. Follow the ADA-accessible boardwalk for 100 yards onto a wide gravel path. Soon reach an interpretive sign and self-registration station where you can sign in and pick up an Iron Goat Trail brochure.

Continue east through a copse of mature red alder. These trees live not much longer than sixty years, so it's instructive to contemplate how this area appeared before World War II. Destructive logging practices during the late nineteenth and early twentieth centuries contributed to the avalanche problems encountered by the Great Northern Railroad.

Immediately past these trees is a signed junction with the Martin Creek Crossover, which continues the ADA-accessible trail to the Iron Goat Interpretive Site along US 2. Bear left (north) and climb some switchbacks to the old railroad grade, passing the ruins of a collapsed snow shed. Snow sheds were built to protect trains and tracks from avalanches and rockslides.

In 0.5 mile reach the first of several tunnels. This tunnel and the ones that follow have not been maintained since the route was closed in 1929. Rockfalls, cave-ins, and other hazards make these tunnels unsafe for exploration. Keep out, but by all means look inside to see that the roof has collapsed and there is no way to get out the other side. Afterward make use of the bypass trail on the right (south).

Come to Milepoint 1716; the marker was placed there by Iron Goat Trail workers to help walkers know how far it is to the end of the old Great Northern line in

# Iron Goat Trail–Martin Creek to Wellington

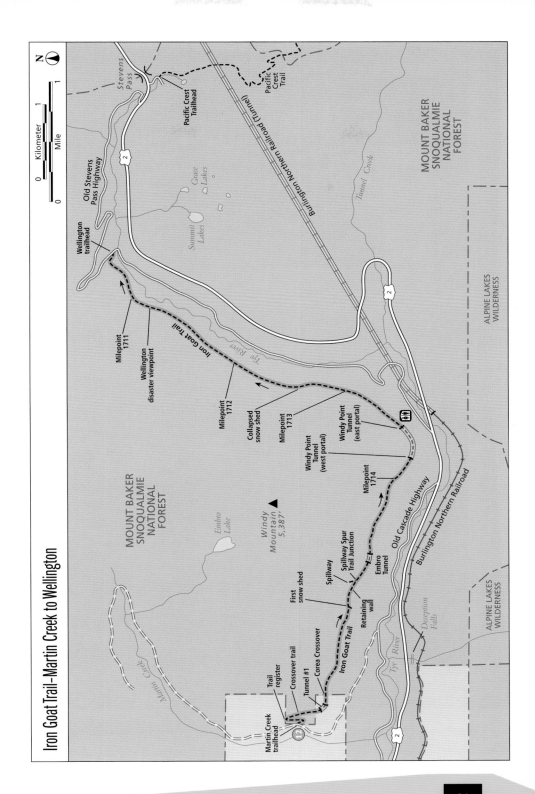

N

| Kilometer | 0 | 1 |
| Mile | 0 | 1 |

Stevens Pass

Pacific Crest Trailhead

Pacific Crest Trail

Old Stevens Pass Highway

Wellington trailhead

Milepoint 1711

Wellington disaster viewpoint

Iron Goat Trail

Summit Lakes

Grace Lakes

Burlington Northern Railroad (Tunnel)

Tunnel Creek

MOUNT BAKER SNOQUALMIE NATIONAL FOREST

ALPINE LAKES WILDERNESS

Tye River

Milepoint 1712

Collapsed snow shed

Milepoint 1713

Windy Point Tunnel (west portal)

Windy Point Tunnel (east portal)

Milepoint 1714

Embro Tunnel

Old Cascade Highway

Burlington Northern Railroad

Embro Lake

Windy Mountain 5,387'

MOUNT BAKER SNOQUALMIE NATIONAL FOREST

First snow shed

Spillway

Spillway Spur Trail Junction

Retaining wall

Iron Goat Trail

Corea Crossover

Tunnel #1

Crossover trail

Trail register

Martin Creek trailhead

Martin Creek

Deception Falls

Tye River

ALPINE LAKES WILDERNESS

1 mile down—1,716 more to go!

St. Paul, Minnesota. It also helps in ticking off the trail miles to the railroad's eastern terminus in Wellington. Steep grades, horrendous weather that routinely brought 35 feet of snow every winter, and avalanches made this stretch of track incredibly difficult to build and maintain. On occasion it could take up to twenty-four hours to make the trip from Wellington to Martin Creek. In 1910 two stranded trains that had spent eight days trying to get through were swept away by a half-mile-wide avalanche. Ninety-six people died.

A signed junction for the Corea Crossover (to the lower grade) lies just beyond, switchbacking downhill for 0.5 mile. It's possible to loop back to Martin Creek from here. Our trail continues straight ahead.

Ruins of a second snow shed are reached a mile later at Milepoint 1715. All that can be seen is a pile of large, rough-cut lumber where the collapsed shed used to be. The trail now passes a long retaining wall, a good 25 feet tall. It, like the others that follow, was built to hold back the hillside from spilling out onto the tracks. In places, erosion of the concrete has revealed the massive amount of steel reinforcement used in its construction. On the far side of the wall, reach the Spillway Spur.

A short side trail leads hikers up fifty-five steps to the top of the wall and thence to a reservoir and timber spillway built across a branch of the Tye River in 1910 as part of the Great Northern's fire protection system. The spillway and reservoir were completely lost to history until discovered in 1991 by trail workers attempting to find a solution to drainage problems along the route.

After 1.8 miles reach the Embro Tunnel and skirt around on the pretunnel grade—the amount of fallen rock in the tunnel underscores how dangerous it is to enter. Beside Embro's west portal, stand atop a huge pile of rock excavated by tunnel construction. More than 100 feet long and 30 feet tall, the rock pile resembles the terminal moraine of a mountain glacier. The east portal is impressive when compared with the west since it retains its concrete archway, but rockfall has completely sealed the opening.

Leaving the east portal, come to several more sections of retaining wall, scenic visits, and a forest of vine maple and red alder. The dense second-growth that covers the hillsides and roadbed makes it difficult to comprehend the avalanche dangers encountered by the Great Northern. Most of the timber below Windy Mountain and beneath Delberts Ridge was logged off to provide railroad ties; fuel to feed the engines' boilers; and construction materials for bridges, trestles, and tunnel shoring. Lots of timber was shipped down to Puget Sound, where it was turned into houses. Historical photographs from a hundred years ago show that the heavily forested slopes of today were denuded of their cover. Without this clear-cutting there wouldn't have been issues with avalanches. The problem with sliding snow was solved—impermanently—by wall and tunnel construction.

Another long retaining wall begins around Milepoint 1714 and continues to Windy Point. The concrete-lined tunnel here is in better shape than any of the preceding ones, but it's still unsafe to travel. Great Northern trains crossing Stevens

Pass between 1892 and 1913 had to crawl around Windy Point because the curve was so sharp. Trains risked derailment if they traveled faster than 5 miles per hour. Passengers on one side faced a rock face; those on the other side looked into a deep abyss falling into the Tye River. The 0.25-mile Windy Point Tunnel reduced track curvature, allowed speedier travel, and shielded trains from avalanches.

Walk around the tunnel and come to a signed junction for the Windy Point Crossover Trail, dropping 1.0 mile south on switchbacks to the Iron Goat Trail Interpretive Site. Then quickly arrive at a signed spur trail to a portable vault toilet. Whether you use the facilities of not, there is a nice view across the valley to Surprise Lake, US 2, and the Burlington Northern–Santa Fe train tracks leading through the 7.8-mile tunnel between Scenic and Berne. The same view, with an interpretive sign but without the privacy, can be had at a viewpoint 100 feet east of the spur trail.

Following the east portal is another long retaining wall. Leading up to Milepoint 1713, start looking upslope; you'll notice many railroad spikes poking up out of the ground. The ties rotted away long ago. They're in clusters, resembling bunches of rust-colored toadstools. Pass another collapsed snow shed at Milepoint 1712.57, constructed in 1910. It was 256 feet long and made with 12- by 12-inch roof timbers. It looks like a big wooden blanket draped over the hillside.

More retaining walls lead up to a concrete snow shed built after the 1910 Wellington disaster. A double row of pillars on 10-foot centers hold up the roof. Midway through is a viewpoint with interpretive signs explaining the March 1, 1910, Wellington avalanche disaster and memorializing the ninety-six people who were swept to their deaths.

It's now possible to see rotted railway ties in small patches; the rails having been salvaged for scrap when the line was abandoned. At Milepost 1711 the east portal of the all-concrete snow shed is reached along with another hiker register. Cross a footbridge, pick up a wide gravel path, and follow it to the Wellington trailhead parking lot and your shuttle vehicle.

## MILES AND DIRECTIONS

**0.0**    Martin Creek trailhead: N47° 43.746' / W121° 12.409'

**0.5**    First railroad tunnel: N47° 43.512' / W121° 12.246'

**1.6**    Spillway junction: N47° 43.237' / W121° 10.809'

**1.8**    Embro Tunnel: N47° 43.167' / W121° 10.649'

**3.0**    Windy Point Tunnel (west portal): N47° 42.851' / W121° 09.536'

**3.1**    Toilet/Windy Point Crossover: N47° 42.860' / W121° 09.244'

**3.2**   Windy Point Tunnel (east portal): N47° 42.892' / W121° 09.208'

**5.5**   Concrete snow shed (west portal): N47° 44.415' / W121° 08.099'

**5.7**   Wellington disaster viewpoint: N47° 44.656' / W121° 07.855'

**6.0**   Reach Wellington trailhead and your shuttle: N47° 44.830' / W121° 07.658'

**Options:** At the Iron Goat Trail Interpretive Site (Milepoint 58.3 on US 2, 17.3 miles east of Der Baring Store), there are vault toilets, a restored caboose, and interpretive displays. A 1.0-mile spur trail climbs steeply on several switchbacks to Windy Point. An ADA-accessible trail also leaves from here and leads to Martin Creek.

**HIKE INFORMATION**

A seventy-two-page guidebook to the Iron Goat Trail is available from Volunteers for Outdoor Washington. Write to them at the address listed above, or call (206) 517-3019.

More about the history and aftermath of the Wellington avalanche is available from Robert Kelly, 18722 Southeast Lake Youngs Road, Renton, WA 98058; www.home1.gte.net/mvmmvm/index.html; e-mail: mvmmvm@gte.net.

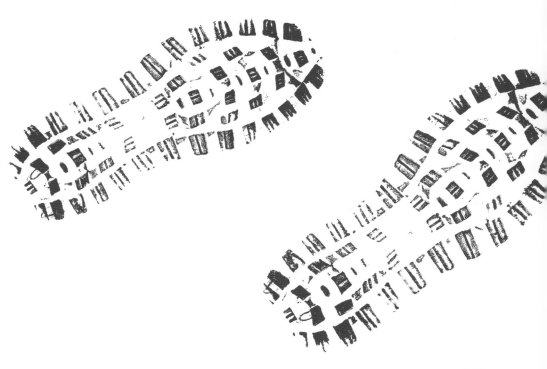

Lake Twenty-two

The South Fork of the Stilly, as the Stillaguamish River is affectionately known, has always provided challenges to people. In the early days of Anglo settlement around Puget Sound, loggers and miners had a devil of a time getting the fruits of their labor to market. Road builders couldn't find any flat spots. Railroads, following the river through Robe Valley, were constantly washed away by floods. This historical lack of access continues to this day. The Mountain Loop Highway is closed by snow every winter; it's even occasionally washed away by winter storms.

Hiking next to the rushing river in Robe Canyon

# Robe Canyon Historic Park–Lime Kiln Trail

*The Lime Kiln Trail provides hiker access to a portion of the historic Everett–Monte Christo Railroad. Built in 1892–93, it was abandoned in 1933. The rock-and-mortar limekiln was built in 1900 and produced anhydrous lime, used as a whitening agent at the Lowell paper mill and as a flux agent at the smelter in Everett.*

*Like many towns west of the Cascades, Granite Falls was once much larger than it is today, servicing smaller towns like Robe, along the banks of the South Fork Stillaguamish River. In the boom days of mining, logging, and the railroads, Granite Falls was an economic engine. Transportation, construction, and service industry jobs are the main employers today.*

*Though resource extraction doesn't register stronger than a blip these days, it does create historical interest for people walking along the Lime Kiln Trail. A tetanus booster is recommended for those who choose to wander off-trail; rusted artifacts from the region's logging and railroad past lie hidden in the forest duff. Relicts have been gathered by past hikers and placed on display along the trail and at the kiln. Leave them where they are for other people to enjoy.*

**Start:** Trailhead along Waite Mill Road
**Distance:** 6.0 miles out and back
**Approximate hiking time:** 4 hours
**Difficulty:** Easy
**Trail surface:** Forested path, gravel road, historic railroad grade
**Seasons:** Spring, summer, and fall
**Other trail users:** Runners
**Canine compatibility:** Leashed dogs permitted
**Land status:** Snohomish County Parks; private property
**Nearest town:** Granite Falls
**Services:** Gas, restaurants, groceries, lodging; vault toilet at trailhead
**Northwest Forest Pass:** No
**Maps:** Green Trails No. 109: Granite Falls; USGS Granite Falls; USDAFS Mount Baker–Snoqualmie National Forest
**Trail contacts:** Snohomish County Department of Parks and Recreation, 3000 Rockefeller Avenue, Everett, WA 98201; (425) 388-3411 or (800) 562-4367; TTY: (425) 388-3700. Mount Baker–Snoqualmie National Forest, Skykomish Ranger District, 74920 Northeast Stevens Pass Highway, P.O. Box 305, Skykomish, WA 98288; (360) 677-2414; www.fs.fed.us/r6/mbs/about/srd.shtml
**Special hazards:** Stinging nettle, devil's club; no potable water at trailhead or on trail; Stillaguamish River not suitable for swimming

**Finding the trailhead:**
From Seattle take Interstate 5 north through Everett to U.S. Highway 2 exit 194 east. At the eastern end of the Hewlett Avenue trestle, follow signs directing you to Highway 204 and Lake Stevens. The high volume of subdivision development in the Lake Stevens area, which services Everett, will undoubtedly lead to widening roads and additional stoplights along with increased traffic and eliminate current landmarks, so it is best to follow directions and highway signs.

Where Highway 204 meets Highway 9, turn left (north). At Highway 92 turn right (east) and proceed to Granite Falls. Pass through town and turn right onto South Alder Avenue. Turn left at a T intersection onto East Pioneer Street. Pioneer becomes Mendel Lake Road. In about 1 mile turn left onto Waite Mill Road. Follow this for a short distance; after passing a schoolbus turnaround, bear left at the wye and follow a gravel road uphill to the Robe Canyon Historic Park parking lot and trailhead. *Delorme: Washington Atlas and Gazetteer:* Page 96 D-1.

## THE HIKE

The wide, well-marked Lime Kiln Trail takes off from the Robe Canyon Historic Park parking lot and gently ascends a small hill through second- and third-growth Douglas fir forest. This first stretch is an easement through private property. Please respect the property owners by not wandering off-trail, even though the depth of slash and dense undergrowth are serious impediments to travel.

At the T intersection, turn right (south). Leaving private property behind, the trail narrows into a forest path. The trees feel older and taller now as the canopy closes in. Stumps of moderate-size trees pop out of underbrush dominated by sword fern, thimbleberry, and salmonberry.

Cross a large, well-built bridge at Hubbard Creek. Appreciate the beauty of the scene by taking advantage of a rustic bench. Hubbard Lake lies upstream of the bridge. Shortly after the bridge, the trail drops onto a forest path on the left (north). Continuing straight ahead is a maze of logging roads capable of keeping any mountain biker occupied for years.

Stinging nettle loves this part of the trail. Early in the season, when the stinging hairs are still soft and pliable, it's possible to get by with only a warning while brushing the plant. By April this is no longer so, and even a gentle touch can lead to day-long self-recriminations.

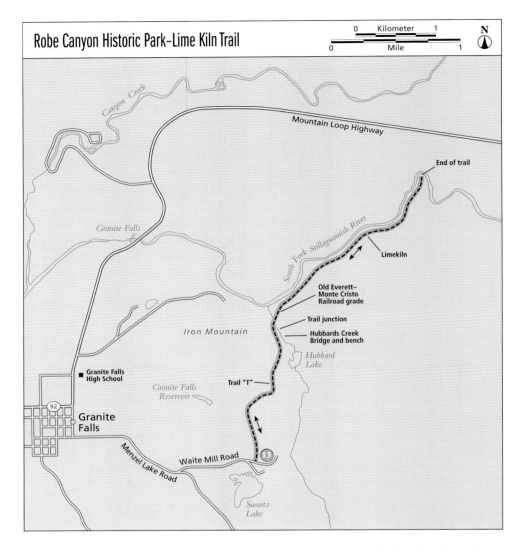

0    Kilometer    1

0         Mile         1

N

Canyon Creek

Mountain Loop Highway

End of trail

Granite Falls

South Fork Stillaguamish River

Limekiln

Old Everett–
Monte Cristo
Railroad grade

Iron Mountain

Trail junction

Hubbards Creek
Bridge and bench

Hubbard
Lake

Granite Falls
High School

Granite Falls
Reservoir

Trail "T"

92

Granite
Falls

Menzel Lake Road

Waite Mill Road

13

Swartz
Lake

The trail quickly drops onto the old Everett–Monte Cristo Railroad grade and starts paralleling the river. The overstory forest of Sitka spruce with moss- and fern-covered trunks is as beautiful as it is odd. Sitka spruce is highly uncommon so far inland. Early in spring, watch for the nodding pink flowers of bush gooseberry. Vine maples are also prevalent through here.

The drainage ditch on the uphill side of the trail serves to keep water off the grade. Keep your eyes open for a spot where runoff is channeled beneath the grade to a V-shaped notch carved some 6 feet through the bank.

Around about this time you're probably wondering where the limekiln is that gives the trail its name. Old pieces of rusted iron have begun to appear along with broken pieces from circular saw blades. Come around a slight bend in the trail and there it is—the limekiln. It's a tall, squat structure built of native rock. Ferns and other epiphytic plants cover the kiln. It's possible to climb up the hill and around the kiln and see it from all angles. Take nothing but pictures—all artifacts are protected by law.

After another mile, a sign announces the end of the trail and also points to a short loop that plunges down to the river. Walk to the end of the trail first and look several hundred feet down to the water. Through shrubs and trees you can also look across to the opposite bank and see a concrete pillar—all that remains of a railroad bridge that once crossed the Stillaguamish here.

Retrace your steps to the loop trail, and drop steeply to the river. This is a nice place for lunch. Upstream and around the corner, the river is wide and placid, but a particularly nasty rapid is just downstream. Avoid the temptation to play or swim here.

For the return trip, retrace your steps to the parking lot.

The limekiln

## MILES AND DIRECTIONS

**0.0**    Lime Kiln trailhead: 48° 04.641' / W 121° 55.957'

**0.7**    Trail "T": N48° 05.103' / W121° 55.919'

**1.0**    Hubbard Creek Bridge and bench: N48° 05.455' / W121° 55.693'

**2.0**    Trail junction: N48° 05.496' / W121° 55.711'

**2.7**    Limekiln: N48° 06.160' / W121° 54.931'

**2.8**    End of trail: N48° 06.543' / W121° 54.236'

**3.0**    Loop trail to South Fork Stillaguamish River: N48° 06.535' / W121° 54.325'

**6.0**    Return to trailhead: 48° 04.641' / W 121° 55.957'

**Options:** The town of Granite Falls is named for an amazing waterfall, and a trip there is *de rigueur*. On your return to town from the hike, from the intersection of South Alder and Stanley, drive north 1.5 miles past Granite Falls Middle School and High School. The road becomes Mountain Loop Highway. After passing a plant nursery on the left, the road bends right. Before the highway bridge, spot the parking lot on your left or the large turnout on the right. Walk down the stairs to the Granite Falls viewpoints and fish ladder.

## HIKE INFORMATION

The entrance to Robe Canyon Historic Park is on the left, marked by a tasteful and colorful sign. Park in the large gravel lot. Use the portable toilet, and read the extensive history of Robe Canyon and the story of acquiring the park property at the information kiosk. Don't miss the many historic photos on the back of the kiosk.

Robe Canyon is one of Washington's most difficult whitewater kayak runs. During this hike you'll be able to see some of the "easier" rapids at the bottom end of the run. To the inexperienced eye, these rapids look scary—and they are—so just imagine the difficulty of rapids lying upstream! Kayakers refer to the Stillaguamish as "the Stilly," most likely facetiously because the water is anything but still!

Ancient Egyptians, Greeks, and Babylonians used limekilns in the production of quicklime from limestone to make the mortar that held their building blocks together. Hence the pyramids were built.

Snohomish County Department of Parks and Recreation has a Web page devoted to the Lime Kiln Trail and Robe Canyon Historic Park. Navigate to www1. co.snohomish.wa.us/Departments/Parks/Park_Information/Park_Directory/ Regional_Parks/Robe_Canyon.htm.

# Robe Canyon

*Over a hundred years ago some entrepreneurs with more cash than brains decided to build a railway through Robe Canyon. It didn't occur to them that they couldn't keep a route open through several miles of vertical canyon prone to landslides and flooding. It was a good try but they failed—miserably and monumentally. The railroad builders left us with a challenging and exciting walk that will have you stumbling over and slipping into and through history with nearly every step. This is the upper section of Robe Canyon Historic Park and part of the Monte Cristo Railroad grade built in 1893.*

*Hanging gardens above the trail are great places to look for wildflowers. Adventurous hikers will delight in passing through three defunct railroad tunnels. Many parts of the trail have either washed away or been carried off by slides, so one false step could send you careening down into life-threatening whitewater. It's worthwhile to make a detour to the Lime Kiln Trail on the other side of the river to read the complete history of the Monte Cristo Railroad and its construction through Robe Canyon.*

**Start:** Old Robe Canyon sign on south side of Highway 92, the Mountain Loop Highway
**Distance:** 3.4 miles out and back
**Approximate hiking time:** 3 hours
**Difficulty:** Strenuous, with uneven surfaces and lots of downed trees; trail washed out in many places; not recommended for children or the faint of heart
**Trail surface:** Forested path, old railroad bed; rocky
**Seasons:** Year-round
**Other trail users:** None
**Canine compatibility:** Leashed dogs permitted. A sign at the trailhead states the area is hazardous to unleashed dogs
**Land status:** Snohomish County Department of Parks and Recreation

**Nearest town:** Granite Falls
**Services:** Gas, restaurants, groceries; no toilet at trailhead
**Northwest Forest Pass:** No
**Maps:** Green Trails No. 109: Granite Falls; USGS Granite Falls; USDAFS Mount Baker–Snoqualmie National Forest
**Trail contacts:** Snohomish County Department of Parks and Recreation, 3000 Rockefeller Avenue, Everett, WA 98201; (425) 388-3411 or (800) 562-4367
**Special hazards:** Loose and slippery rock, exposure, cliffs; trail washed out and missing; no potable water at trailhead or on trail; flashlight advised for those hikers attempting to pass through Tunnel 6

**Finding the trailhead:**
From Seattle take Interstate 5 north through Everett to U.S. Highway 2 exit 194 east. At the eastern end of the Hewlett Avenue trestle, follow signs directing you to Highway 204 and Lake Stevens. The high volume of subdivision development in the Lake Stevens area, which services Everett, will undoubtedly lead to widening roads and additional stoplights along with increased traffic and eliminate current landmarks, so it is best to follow directions and highway signs.

Where Highway 204 meets Highway 9, turn left (north). At Highway 92 turn right (east) and proceed to Granite Falls. Follow East Stanley Street through downtown Granite Falls to South Alder. Turn left (north). Pass Granite Falls Junior and Senior High Schools. At the stop sign, South Alder becomes the Mountain Loop Highway.

Drive 7 miles to the trailhead, passing Granite Falls (the waterfall) after 1.4 miles and crossing the South Fork Stillaguamish River. Continue on the Mountain Loop Highway until you spot the sign for Old Robe Canyon on the right (south) side of the highway. In 2007 the wooden sign announcing the trailhead had been defaced and was barely readable. The brickwork surrounding the sign resembles a two-dimensional old-fashioned wood-burning bread oven. It appears to be perpetually vandalized. *Delorme: Washington Atlas and Gazetteer:* Page 96 D-2.

## THE HIKE

Keeping the railroad track open through this stretch of narrow canyon was an impossible task. Once you hike down from the trailhead and enter Robe Canyon, you'll wonder why anyone wanted to put a railroad through here in the first place. The hillsides move and slide so often they may as well be alive.

From the trailhead along the Mountain Loop Highway, drop rapidly on switchbacks, passing a picnic area and warning signs, to the South Fork Stillaguamish River and the old railroad grade. Even in winter the Stilly is wide here, with large gravel banks. A quick gaze downstream reveals canyon walls rising precipitously.

The first hint the trail is not a common route occurs at the river when hikers stumble upon a slab of concrete embedded with railroad ties. In order to keep the roadbed from washing away during winter floods and spring runoff, the Monte Cristo Railroad was blasted out of the Stilly's rock walls and "stabilized" in this novel manner. It didn't work. What landslides and fallen trees couldn't extinguish, the river carried away.

While you're admiring the ingenuity of the road builders, don't forget to admire the fierce beauty of the river. Where the canyon begins, the river looks dangerous. If this impresses you, then farther downstream the canyon will frighten you to death.

After 1.2 miles the official trail ends. At 1.4 miles, if the first indications of danger (wiped-out trails and steep detours ending in abrupt drops into the river) have you considering turning back, do so now at Tunnel 6. The route not only deteriorates from here, but it does so quickly. Before reaching Tunnel 5 downstream, the route stops resembling a trail altogether.

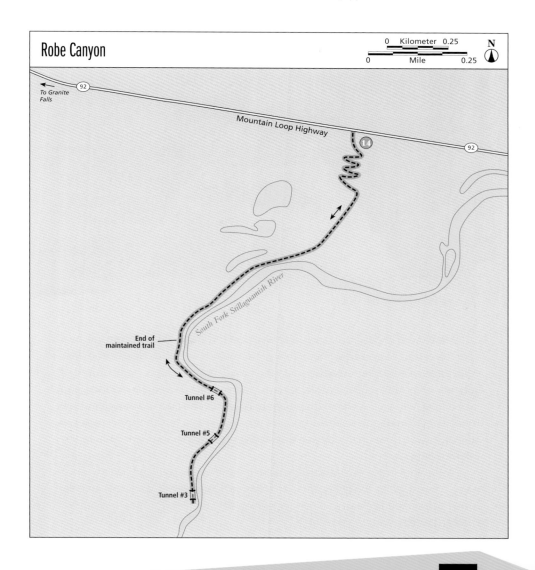

Robe Canyon

Crossing above Hole-in-the-Wall

Should you choose to extend your hike past this point, the highlight will be a spot the extreme kayakers who run this section of river known as Hole-in-the-Wall. After years of watching the Stilly claim their road, the engineers came up with a solution. They built retaining walls to push the river back, paved the roadbed, and embedded railroad ties within thick slabs of concrete. The river didn't even notice. It not only claimed the roadbed but also washed away a few of the sextuplet of tunnels carved through the canyon walls to allow trains to pass unencumbered by geology or hydrology.

As for Hole-in-the-Wall, the river undercut the retaining wall, and slides washed away the rest. What today appears like a Roman causeway or viaduct is actually a wall suspended like a glacial hanging valley. At 1.6 miles from the trailhead, it marks a perfect turnaround point.

On the other hand, not a few folk have seized their courage by the throat and ventured across the causeway to be finally stymied by Tunnel 3 and the official end of the unofficial trail.

## MILES AND DIRECTIONS

**0.0**  Robe Canyon trailhead on Highway 92: N48° 06.587' / W121° 51.378'

**0.7**  South Fork Stillaguamish River: N48° 06.473' / W121° 51.352'

**1.2**  End of official trail: N48° 06.103' / W121° 51.971'

**1.4**  Tunnel 6: N48° 05.973' / W121° 51.830'

**1.5**  Tunnel 5: N48° 05.871' / W121° 51.861'

**1.7**  Tunnel 3: N48° 05.730' / W121° 51.909'

**3.4**  Return to trailhead: N48° 06.587' / W121° 51.378'

**Options:** The town of Granite Falls is named for an amazing waterfall, and a trip there is de rigueur. On your return to town from the hike, from the intersection of South Alder and Stanley, drive north 1.5 miles past Granite Falls Middle School and High School. The road becomes Mountain Loop Highway. After passing a nursery on the left, the road bends right. Before the highway bridge, spot the parking lot on your left or the large turnout on the right. Walk down the stairs to the Granite Falls viewpoints and fish ladder.

## HIKE INFORMATION

Hikers along the Robe Canyon Trail can see why extreme kayakers—"hair boaters"—consider this stretch of the Stilly one of the most challenging and dangerous rivers in North America. It isn't the easiest patch of ground to walk on either! The trail follows the old railroad grade in all its wonders. It is washed out and obliterated by slides more often than not. Maintained by a cadre of volunteers, the Robe Canyon Trail is as difficult to keep open for foot traffic as it was for trains. Nature knows no bounds.

Despite all the caveats for danger, this is one of the most interesting, intriguing, and beautiful trails in the area. If you are tough enough to meet its challenges, hiking Robe Canyon is as rewarding as running it in a kayak.

The Snohomish County Department of Parks and Recreation has a Web page devoted to Robe Canyon Historic Park. Navigate to http://www1.co.snohomish.wa.us/Departments/ Parks/Park_Information/Park_Directory/Regional_Parks/ Robe_Canyon.htm.

*"Of course there are people entirely indifferent to the sight of flowers or of meadows in spring, or, if not indifferent, at least preoccupied elsewhere. They devote themselves to ball-games, to drinking, gambling, money-making, popularity-hunting."*

**—John Ray, seventeenth-century English naturalist**

Surveying the river from an old railroad tunnel

# Heather Lake

*The very popular walk to Heather Lake is short, but it's a classic: old-growth and mature second-growth forest, perennial creeks, peekaboo views, and a lake situated in a beautiful setting. Mount Pilchuck towers above, and a long ribbon of water falls into the lake. Midsummer swimming is always a possibility, and anglers are known to frequent the lake nearly year-round. Wildflower displays along the rocky shoreline are usually pretty good, as is berry picking in the fall.*

**Start:** Heather Lake trailhead alongside Pilchuck Road (Forest Road 42)
**Distance:** 6.1-mile lollipop, including a circuit around the lake
**Approximate hiking time:** 3 to 4 hours
**Trail number:** USDA Forest Service Trail 701
**Difficulty:** Moderate
**Trail surface:** Forested path, boardwalk; rocky
**Seasons:** Spring, summer, and fall
**Other trail users:** Runners
**Canine compatibility:** Leashed dogs permitted
**Land status:** USDAFS Darrington Ranger District
**Nearest town:** Granite Falls
**Services:** Gas, restaurants, groceries, lodging; unisex vault toilet at trailhead

**Northwest Forest Pass:** Yes
**Maps:** Green Trails No. 109: Granite Falls; USGS Verlot; USDAFS Mount Baker–Snoqualmie National Forest, Alpine Lakes Wilderness
**Trail contacts:** Alpine Lakes Protection Society (ALPS); www.alpinelakes.org. Middle Fork Snoqualmie; www.midforc.org. USDA Forest Service Darrington Ranger District, 1405 Emens Street, Darrington, WA 98241; (360) 436-1155; www.fs.fed.us/r6/m bs/about/drd.shtml. USDA Forest Service Verlot Public Service Center, 33515 Mountain Loop Highway, Granite Falls, WA 98252; (360) 691-7791
**Special hazards:** Stinging nettle, devil's club; loose rock; no potable water at trailhead or on trail

**Finding the trailhead:**
From Seattle take Interstate 5 north through Everett to U.S. Highway 2, exit 194 east. At the eastern end of the Hewlett Avenue trestle, follow signs directing you to Highway 204 and Lake Stevens. The high amount of subdivision development in the Lake Stevens area, which services Everett, will undoubtedly lead to widening roads and additional stoplights along with increased traffic and eliminate current landmarks, so it is best to follow directions and highway signs.

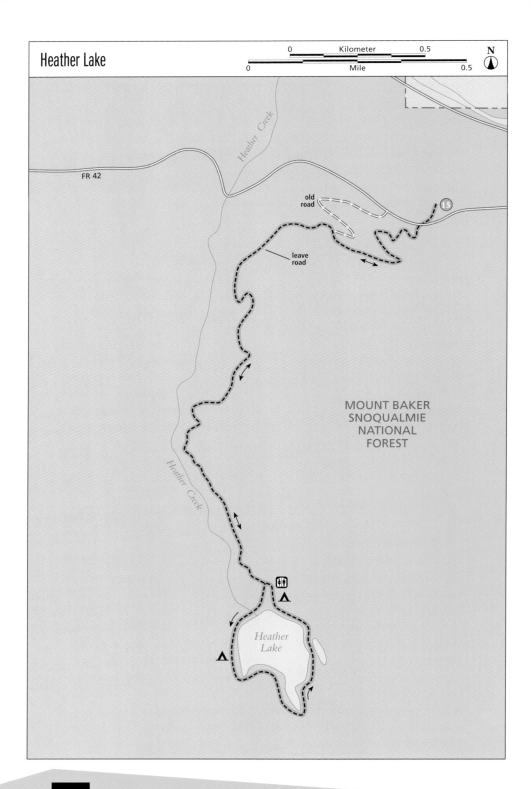

Heather Lake

0 Kilometer 0.5
0 Mile 0.5

N

FR 42

Heather Creek

old road

leave road

15

MOUNT BAKER
SNOQUALMIE
NATIONAL
FOREST

Heather Creek

Heather Lake

Where Highway 204 meets Highway 9, turn left (north). At Highway 92 turn right (east) and proceed to Granite Falls. Follow East Stanley Street through downtown Granite Falls to South Alder. Turn left (north). Pass Granite Falls Junior and Senior High Schools. At the stop sign, South Alder becomes the Mountain Loop Highway (Highway 92).

Pass Granite Falls (the waterfall) in 1.4 miles; cross the South Fork Stillaguamish, and continue upstream. In 11 miles east of the town of Granite Falls, reach the USDA Forest Service Verlot Public Service Center on the north side of Highway 92. After another 1 mile, turn right (south) onto the Pilchuck Road (Forest Road 42). In 0.2 mile the road turns to gravel. In 1.3 miles reach a wide spot in the road on the right (north) with parking for a dozen or so cars. *Delorme: Washington Atlas and Gazetteer:* Page 96 D-2.

## THE HIKE

Cross FR 42 (south) and find the trailhead marked by a sign and reader board. Walk a bit up the trail and self-register. The forest here is dense—a mix of old-growth and mature second-growth trees. Some of the tree stumps are stupendous. The notches seen on these giants allowed early loggers to work from platforms higher above the ground, where the tree's circumference was less.

Amble up a rocky trail beside a creek; after 0.5 mile merge with an old road and descend a wide path crowded with young trees. The old road allows more light to penetrate the thick forest canopy and encourages more growth than directly under the trees.

After 0.7 mile from the trailhead, leave the road and return to a rocky, root-strewn trail. Begin a constant, but not horribly steep, uphill climb. This is real old-growth forest. Some of the trees are massive in size and shape.

In 1.4 miles cross a small creek; Heather Creek thunders unseen to the right (west). Start some steep, short switchbacks. The last 0.3 mile to Heather Lake is more or less a level ramble through the forest.

Reach the lake after 2.0 miles. Pass a sign announcing the toilet on the left (east). A side trail leads to the right (southwest) on a circumnavigation of Heather Lake. Cross Heather Creek on a long, elaborate wooden bridge.

You soon reach a campsite. Camping is very poor at Heather Lake. The sites are less than level, there are no views, and the forest is damp, even in summer. However, plenty of opportunities exist for getting down to the lake, and there are a plethora of fine lunch spots.

Below Mount Pilchuck, a long ribbon waterfall dives into a jumble of talus before working its way to Heather Lake. Wildflowers are normally plentiful in this area. Scattered small copses of yellow cedar grow along the lakeshore, but most of the trees are mountain hemlock.

Evidence of past logging practices

Finishing the trail around the lake, come to another campsite and the toilet. Find the trail back down to the trailhead and retrace your steps.

## MILES AND DIRECTIONS

**0.0**	Trailhead on Pilchuck Road (FR 42): N48° 04.963' / W121° 46.443'

**0.5**	Old road: N48° 04.941' / W121° 46.802'

**0.7**	Leave road: N48° 04.902' / W121° 46.979'

**1.0**	Creek crossing: N48° 04.640' / W121° 47.092'

**2.0**	Heather Lake: N48° 04.162' / W121° 47.006'

**2.4**	Campsite: N48° 04.058' / W121° 47.063'

**3.0**	Campsite: N48° 04.189' / W121° 46.941'

**3.1**	Toilet: N48° 04.211' / W121° 46.906'

**6.1**	Return to trailhead: N48° 04.963' / W121° 46.443'

## HIKE INFORMATION

The stunning peak that overlooks Heather Lake is Mount Pilchuck—most likely among the "long ridge of snowy mountains" sighted by Captain George Vancouver during the Englishman's 1792 voyage to western North America. There is a challenging 3.0-mile trail to the summit. From 1957 to 1980 Washington State Parks administered a ski area on the slopes of Mount Pilchuck, but it was closed due to poor annual snow accumulations. Atop the peak's 5,324-foot summit is a Forest Service lookout, still managed by Washington State Parks but maintained by the Everett Mountaineers. The lookout, built in 1918, is available to the public for overnight trips on a first-come, first-served basis. *Pilchuck* is a Native American name meaning, "red water," probably for a creek in the area.

## 15

## Vegetation on the West Slope Cascade Mountains

The first Europeans to reach our shores were blown away by the size and age of the conifers they found and the paucity of arboreal angiosperms. Relatively nutrient-rich soils along with ample rainfall, an absence of catastrophic fire, and extended drought were the main reasons for this. Our dry summers and our topography (leading to cold and snowy winters, especially in the mountains) also precluded the vast deciduous forests of eastern North America and of Europe.

In the early twentieth century, when the science of ecology was young, it was believed that plant communities developed in orderly steps much like the historic succession of kings and queens or presidents and prime ministers. "Succession" is convenient when thinking of community development as predictable, but reality doesn't work that way. One set of species isn't replaced by another set in anything resembling predictability. Today we realize that a number of outcomes, or "seres," are possible depending on factors such as type, size, and duration of disturbance.

The vegetation type of the Cascade Mountains' west slope is Lowland Coniferous Forest. Up to 2,000 feet in elevation, the dominant woody vegetation is Douglas fir transitioning to western hemlock/western red cedar. Above that elevation is Pacific silver fir, with mountain hemlock and western red cedar. "Old-growth" is not a vegetation type. It denotes a forest where trees have reached their biological maturity after a long period with no major natural or human disturbance.

Old-growth

# Lake Twenty-two

*Lake Twenty-two has a well-justified reputation for being the most popular trail in the Stillaguamish Valley. It's loved by all kinds of hikers, from families with small children through mountaineers, because of its accessibility. Because of this heavy use, the trail shows constant evidence of being upgraded with new switchbacks, water bars and boardwalks—especially around the lake perimeter. Clearly, what makes this hike exciting is the nice forest, high quality of boardwalks, and the ability to walk all the way around Lake Twenty-two and stare up the steep walls comprising the basin.*

**Start:** Trailhead along Highway 92, Mountain Loop Highway
**Distance:** 5.4 miles out and back, with optional 1.3-mile walk around the lake
**Approximate hiking time:** 4 to 5 hours
**Trail number:** USDA Forest Service Trail 702
**Difficulty:** Moderate due to steepness of the trail
**Trail surface:** Forested path, boardwalk; rocky
**Seasons:** Summer and fall
**Other trail users:** None
**Canine compatibility:** Leashed dogs permitted
**Land status:** USDAFS Darrington Ranger District
**Nearest town:** Granite Falls
**Services:** Gas, restaurants, groceries; unisex vault toilet at trailhead; camping at three close-by Forest Service campgrounds: Turlo, Verlot, and Gold Basin
**Northwest Forest Pass:** Yes
**Maps:** Green Trails No. 109: Granite Falls and No. 110: Silverton; USGS Verlot; USDAFS Mount Baker–Snoqualmie National Forest, Alpine Lakes Wilderness
**Trail contacts:** USDA Forest Service Darrington Ranger District, 1405 Emens Street, Darrington, WA 98241; (360) 436-1155; www.fs.fed.us/r6/mbs/about/drd.shtml. USDA Forest Service Verlot Public Service Center, 33515 Mountain Loop Highway, Granite Falls, WA 98252; (360) 691-7791
**Special hazards:** No potable water at trailhead or on trail

**Finding the trailhead:**
From Seattle take Interstate 5 north through Everett to exit 194 east (U.S. Highway 2). At the eastern end of the Hewlett Avenue trestle, follow signs directing you to Highway 204 and Lake Stevens. The high volume of subdivision development in the Lake Stevens area, which services Everett, will undoubtedly lead to widening roads and additional stoplights along with increased traffic and eliminate current landmarks, so it is best to follow directions and highway signs.

Where Highway 204 meets Highway 9, turn left (north). At Highway 92 turn right (east) and proceed to Granite Falls. Follow East Stanley Street through downtown Granite Falls to South Alder. Turn left (north). Pass Granite Falls Junior and Senior High Schools. At the stop sign, South Alder becomes the Mountain Loop Highway (Highway 92).

Pass Granite Falls (the waterfall) in 1.4 miles; cross the South Fork Stillaguamish, and continue upstream. In 11 miles east from the town of Granite Falls reach the USDA Forest Service Verlot Public Service Center on the north side of Highway 92. In another 2.2 miles reach the trailhead for Lake Twenty-two. Turn right (south), and proceed 0.1 mile to the trailhead parking lot. On heavy-use days you will see cars parked on both sides of this short access road and also along Highway 92. *Delorme: Washington Atlas and Gazetteer:* Page 96 D-2.

## THE HIKE

Find the trailhead 50 feet west of the toilet. Walk 100 feet and come to a trail register kiosk and, 20 feet after that, a sign announcing the Lake Twenty-two Research Natural Area (RNA), established January 14, 1947. The big trees you see along the way predate any legal, scientific, or educational RNA protection.

Parents with very small children may elect go no farther than here, since they will still enjoy a gravel path accompanied by a gurgling creek. The Mountain Loop Highway is close and all but invisible through a deep and shady forest.

Choosing to go on, soon cross a creek on a new bridge. The trail starts to climb on switchbacks that won't end until you reach the lake. There was a time when Lake Twenty-two epitomized a place overused and loved to death. The trail was beaten down and eroded. Several years of labor have cured most of that past misuse. Help minimize our impact in this beautiful forest; resist the temptation to cut switchbacks and step off any boardwalks that span damp ground.

Throughout its climb to Lake Twenty-two, the trail crosses many places where moisture is weeping out of the rocks. In season, these are perfect places to find wildflowers, and the soil remains moist throughout summer.

In 0.8 mile take the opportunity to admire a large waterfall on Twenty-two Creek. Reach a talus slope and leave the forest behind. On hot and sunny summer

> 🌿 **Green Tip:**
> *Go out of your way to avoid birds and animals that are mating or taking care of their young.*

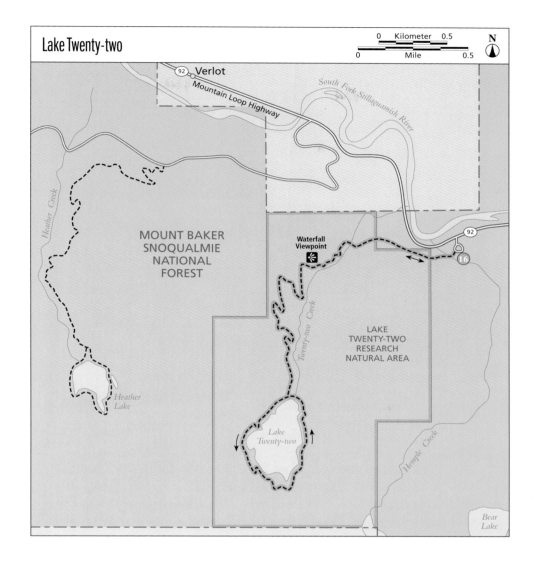

0   Kilometer   0.5

0   Mile   0.5

N

Verlot

Mountain Loop Highway

South Fork Stillaguamish River

92

MOUNT BAKER
SNOQUALMIE
NATIONAL
FOREST

Waterfall
Viewpoint

Heather Creek

Twenty-two Creek

LAKE
TWENTY-TWO
RESEARCH
NATURAL AREA

Heather
Lake

Lake
Twenty-two

Hemple Creek

Bear
Lake

days, this section of trail has hikers yearning for shade. Nevertheless, it's excellent habitat for wildflowers, pikas, and birds so keep your eyes open! Views up or across the Stillaguamish Valley to jagged mountain peaks are impressive.

Ducking back into the forest, the trail begins its final climb in shade to Lake Twenty-two. You know when you're almost there when the trail drops alongside the outflow creek. Views upward toward the lake reveal massive cliffs leading to Mount Pilchuck's summit. At the lake be greeted by a long bridge spanning Twenty-two Creek and an even longer boardwalk. It's possible to circumnavigate the lake in either direction: your choice.

Great views from a bridge over the lake's outlet

Lunch spots and views abound. So do damp areas—be careful where you step and sit. Camping or open fires are prohibited at the lake. Due to its popularity, Lake Twenty-two is a perfect place to remember your outdoor manners. Pick up after yourself and leave no trash—including lunch leftovers. The food is not only bad for the critters and birds but also presents an unsightly mess for the next person who chooses to eat lunch in the same spot.

## MILES AND DIRECTIONS

**0.0**   Trailhead along Highway 92: N48° 04.610' / W121° 44.747'

**0.8**   Waterfall view: N48° 04.540' / W121° 45.613'

**2.7**   Lake Twenty-two: N48° 04.020' / W121° 45.748'

**5.4**   Return to trailhead: N48° 04.610' / W121° 44.747'

## 16

**Options:** Four miles east of Verlot turn right (south) onto Forest Road 4020. In 2.5 miles turn right (west) onto Forest Road 4021 for another 3 miles to reach the trailhead for a short, easy walk to Bear Lake. Continue 2 miles farther on the trail to Pinnacle Lake.

## HIKE INFORMATION

The Lake Twenty-two Trail passes through a research natural area (RNA), public land established primarily for scientific and educational purposes under the Organic Administration Act of 1897. Principally located within national forests, RNAs exemplify typical or unique vegetation, geological, or aquatic features and preserve representative samples of ecological communities.

> *"Walking is man's best medicine."*
> *—Hippocrates*

Cedar Butte from Rattlesnake Mountain

Tiger, Cougar, and Rattlesnake Mountains and the Snoqualmie Valley lowlands are some of the most popular places for hiking within an hour of Seattle. If the term "Issaquah Alps" for the Tiger Mountain Natural Resources Conservation Area sounds pretentious at first blush, consider that appearances are often 100 percent of the reason that legislators set aside parklands and sanctify wilderness. There are no high, glacially sculpted peaks; alpine fell fields; and deep, azure lakes here. Still, these mountains are stupendous.

> **Proximity to a vast urban area makes places like Tiger Mountain a glorious, and convenient, escape into wildness.**

Lake Sammamish

# De Leo Wall

*Take a walk on the wild side—trail that is! The way to De Leo Wall and an outstanding view toward Mount Rainier, Renton, and bits of Lake Washington begins with a challenging array of trail junctions. A good map gets you through the worst of it and leads to everything that makes Cougar Mountain special: quiet and solitude; trails that eschew the up, up, and away nature of Cascade Mountain trails; and, at De Leo Wall Viewpoint, some unusual drier habitat with distinctive flora. All this, plus it's close to town and easily accessible.*

**Start:** Red Town trailhead along Lakemont Boulevard SE
**Distance:** 4.5-mile lollipop
**Approximate hiking time:** 3 to 4 hours
**Trail Numbers:** Cougar Mountain Regional Wildland Park Trails W1 (Wildside Trail), W6 (Marshall's Hill Trail), and W9 (De Leo Wall Trail)
**Difficulty:** Moderate due to slippery trail and confusing trail junctions
**Trail surface:** Forested path
**Seasons:** Year-round
**Other trail users:** Horses (in some sections), runners
**Canine compatibility:** Leashed dogs permitted
**Land status:** King County Parks and Recreation
**Nearest town:** Issaquah (Interstate 90) or Renton (Interstate 405)
**Services:** Gas, restaurants, groceries, lodging; unisex portable toilet at trailhead

**Northwest Forest Pass:** No
**Maps:** Green Trails No. 203S: Cougar Mountain–Squak Mountain; USGS Issaquah, Renton, Maple Valley; USDAFS Mount Baker–Snoqualmie National Forest
**Trail contacts:** King County Parks and Recreation Division, 201 South Jackson Street, Suite 700, Seattle, WA 98104; (206) 296-8687; www .metrokc.gov/parks/parks/. For emergencies either dial 911 or call King County Police at (206) 296-3311. Download a map of Cougar Mountain Regional Wildland Park from www.metrokc. gov/gis/vmc/Recreation.htm#CM
**Special hazards:** Stinging nettle, devil's club; many trail junctions during the first 0.5 mile; no potable water at trailhead or on trail

**Finding the trailhead:**
From Seattle drive east on I-90. Take exit 13, and drive uphill (south) on Lakemont Boulevard SE for 3.1 miles. Look for entrance to the Red Town trailhead on the left side.

From I-405 take exit 10 and follow Coal Creek Parkway SE 2.4 miles to the shopping center. Turn left at the light onto Southeast 72nd Place and then left again at Newcastle–Coal Creek Road. Follow Newcastle–Coal Creek Road for 1.9 miles. Look for the Red Town trailhead on the right side of the road. *Delorme: Washington Atlas and Gazetteer:* Page 63 A-8.

## THE HIKE

It's impressively easy to get lost on Cougar Mountain because of the network of conjoining trails, so maps are necessary. The Red Town trailhead is particularly confusing: Four trails essentially take off from the same place, including the Military Road Trail (N2), which begins east of the large gravel parking lot. At the southeast corner of the lot are two adjacent service gates. Choose the left (easternmost) one, and stop to read the notices posted on an information kiosk. These include admonishments for hikers to remain out of mine shafts that were dug for coal extraction when Puget Sound settlement was young. A thinking person would have no trouble understanding the dangers. In rainy weather the kiosk also serves as the last dry place before entering Cougar Mountain Regional Wildland Park.

The trail forks immediately after the kiosk. On the left (easternmost trail) is the Red Town Trail (W2) and the sole portable toilet available to hikers. Turn right (west) and proceed 100 feet to the start of the Wildside Trail (W1), which leads to De Leo Wall Viewpoint.

The wide trail takes off straightaway into a thick forest of vine and bigleaf maple, western red cedar, and Douglas fir. Drop to an intersection with the Bagley Seam Trail (W10). Turn right (south) and remain on W1. Notice a 25-foot-tall, 4-inch pipe ventilation shaft on the left (north) —a leftover from the mining days.

W1 crosses the creek on a fine, stout bridge and 100 feet later joins with the Rainbow Town Trail (W3). Turn left (south); in 50 feet W1 splits from W3 and passes through a log turnstile designed to keep horseback riders off the trail. In yet another 50 feet, reach the junction of W1 and the Steam Hoist Trail (W4). Bear right (southwest), remaining on W1. Climb a short distance and encounter the Lazy Porcupine Trail (W11). Bear left (southeast) and continue on W1. Walk downhill 50 feet and intersect W4 once again. Keep right (south) and remain on W1. Surmount a little rise, drop to the creek, and cross on a bridge with a single handrail.

You've hiked only about 0.5 mile from the trailhead, with enough trail junctions to last a lifetime. Fortunately there are only a few more to De Leo Wall, and they don't come with such rapidity. The trail now weaves and undulates through thick, shady forest in summer; cool and damp in winter. Pass through another wooden stile and pass Marshall's Hill Trail (W6) on the right (south).

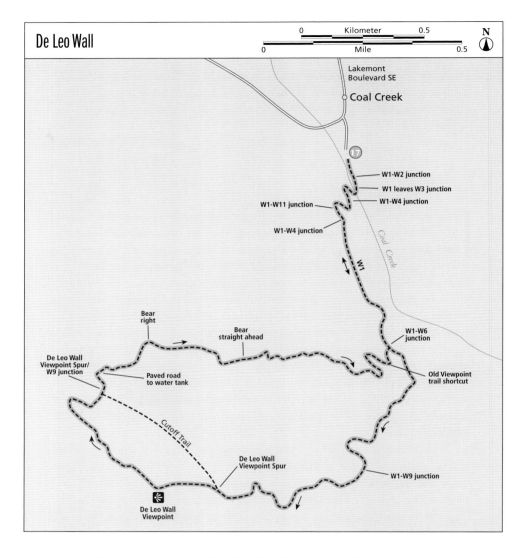

Continue ahead (southeast) on W1. Pass through a small grove of western red cedar, then begin a steep but short climb that turns into a steep, longer descent. The trail resumes its winding nature. After 1.3 miles, reach De Leo Wall Trail (W9) and turn right (southwest). Start to climb, level off, then drop before beginning an earnest climb. Reach the spur trail to De Leo Wall and bear left (west) as W9 continues uphill. The viewpoint is in 0.2 mile.

If it's late enough when you reach De Leo Wall, stop and enjoy lunch while also enjoying fine views (weather and season dependent) south and west. The shaggy-barked trees all around are Pacific madrona—more common to southern Oregon and California. Other plants indicative of drier habitat that can be found around the viewpoint include snowberry, serviceberry, wild rose, strawberry, honeysuckle, and two small stands of Garry oak.

Pressing on, the trail is a narrow cut in the hillside. Climb briefly but steeply, reaching the spur trail junction with W9 and then crossing a narrow asphalt road. For a brief and uninteresting detour, turn right (southeast) on this road, and in 0.1 mile reach a water tank (no public access). Otherwise, cross the road, negotiate a log turnstile and join the trail, which becomes Marshall's Hill Trail (W6). Begin a gentle 1.1-mile drop past homes in the China Creek development (visible through the trees). Bypass a shortcut trail on the right (east) between W6 and W1, and rendezvous with W1.

Turn left (north) onto W1 and retrace your steps back to Red Town. Remember at every junction to take the turn that keeps your feet on W1, the Wildside Trail. And that's it: Your walk on the wild side!

Madrone

**0.0** Red Town trailhead on Newcastle–Coal Creek Road: N47° 32.041' W122° 07.696'

**0.8** Junction of Wildside Trail (W1) and Marshall's Hill Trail (W6): N47° 31.629' W122° 07.566'

**2.3** De Leo Wall Viewpoint: N47° 31.293' / W122° 08.353'

**2.7** Asphalt road: N47° 31.538' / W122° 08.499'

**3.8** Junction of W1 and W6: N47° 31.629' / W122° 07.566'

**4.5** Return to trailhead: N47° 32.041' / W122° 07.696'

## Trail Hazards 2

The animals in our region are more afraid of us than we are of them and most often cause problems when their habitat gets in the way of our development or recreation. They don't cause much trouble, but American black bears (*Ursus americanus)* and mountain lions (*Felis concolor*) garner a lot of concern among hikers. Generally speaking, there's nothing to worry about from either unless you look like a dead animal or a steak.

Black bears are omnivorous, shy, and retiring. They like to eat insects, fruits and berries, the occasional root or two, and carrion if it's available. Bears get in trouble because people in the suburbs leave pet food outside or don't cover their garbage. If they weren't looking for a free meal, bears would never be seen.

Once hunted nearly to extinction, mountain lion populations are rebounding throughout the West. Mountain lions have been known to attack people, and ten fatal attacks in the United States between 1890 and 1998 have been documented. Pets have more to worry about than people, but it's still important to be aware of any lion sightings in your area when going for a hike.

# Cougar Mountain

*What a beautiful place! And so close to town! So unbelievably quiet, too. Adminis-tered by METRO-King County, Cougar Mountain Regional Wildland Park has 35 miles of wooded trails. There are lots of turns on this excursion, so keep your map and these instructions handy. It's not easy to get lost, even though the trails on this part of Cou-gar Mountain seem to go in every direction. If you're confused, simply turn around and head back the way you came. Every walk here is a great walk, even if you end up seeing it from both directions. Be aware that several of the trails on this route have similar names.*

**Start:** Bear Ridge trailhead on Renton-Issaquah Road SE (High-way 900)
**Distance:** 6.2-mile lollipop
**Approximate hiking time:** 4 hours
**Trail numbers:** Cougar Mountain Regional Wildland Park Trails E3 (Bear Ridge Trail), E1 (Shangri-La Trail), E2 (Surprise Creek Trail), N7 (Anti-Aircraft Ridge Trail), N8 (Cou-gar Pass Trail), N9 (Tibbetts Marsh Trail), and E10 (West Tibbetts Creek Trail)
**Difficulty:** Moderate due to con-stant map reading and ease of getting lost
**Trail surface:** Forested path
**Seasons:** Year-round
**Other trail users:** Horses (on some sections), runners
**Canine compatibility:** Leashed dogs permitted
**Land status:** Cougar Mountain Regional Park (King County); private
**Nearest town:** Issaquah

**Services:** Gas, restaurants, grocer-ies, lodging; no toilet at Bear Ridge trailhead; portable toilet at Anti-Aircraft Peak trailhead
**Northwest Forest Pass:** No
**Maps:** Green Trails No. 203S: Cou-gar Mountain–Squak Mountain; USGS Issaquah; USDAFS Mount Baker–Snoqualmie National For-est; King County-METRO Cougar Mountain Regional Wildland Park
**Trail contacts:** King County Parks and Recreation Division, 201 South Jackson Street, Suite 700, Seattle, WA 98104; (206) 296-8687; www .metrokc.gov/parks/parks/. For trail emergencies either dial 911 or call King County Police at (206) 296-3311. Download a map of Cougar Mountain Regional Wild-land Park from www.metrokc.gov/ gis/vmc/Recreation.htm#CM
**Special hazards:** Stinging nettle, devil's club; no potable water at trailhead or on trail

**Finding the trailhead:**

Drive east from Seattle on Interstate 90 to exit 15. Turn right (south) at the signal, and cross Northwest Gilman Boulevard. Proceed on Renton-Issaquah Road SE (Highway 900) for 1.5 miles, passing the Talus subdivision. The parking lot is on your right (west), a tiny (space for three to four cars) and easily missed. Signal your turn well in advance! Look for Southeast 83rd Place, a private road, opposite the parking area. Don't be intimidated by people behind you flashing their lights, honking their horns, and gunning their engines. There can also be a huge amount of truck traffic on this highway. Be careful!

If you should miss the parking area, don't jam on your brakes! Continue up the road a few miles to the traffic signal at Southeast May Valley Road, turn around, and return. Once again, signal your turn well in advance (look on the right for Southeast 83rd Place)—you will be making a left turn across dangerous cross-traffic.

This parking area is prone to car clouts, and judging by the amount of broken glass in the parking lot, it is wise to pay attention to the warning signs at the trailhead. Take all valuables with you on the trail. *Delorme: Washington Atlas and Gazetteer:* Page 79 D-8.

## THE HIKE

Begin on the Bear Ridge Trail (E3), which gently ascends from the parking area through a section of the Cougar Mountain–Squak Mountain Corridor. Pass a trail sign for Bear Ridge Trail. After 0.8 mile enter the Cougar Mountain Regional Wildland. Stop and read the rules—all four are very reasonable. The noise of the highway is far behind, and all you hear are twittering birds, the gurgle of West Fork Tibbetts Creek, and breezes through the trees.

In another 100 feet come to the famous "Fantastic Erratic" glacier boulder. Huge swaths of ground lying under our feet in the Puget Sound region were pushed here long ago by the continental glacier moving south out of Canada. In fact, it's possible to see where the terminus of that glacier was when driving through Olympia on Interstate 5. And when the Cascades were deeply covered by frozen water, this boulder was transported from some place far away. It came to rest here, to be covered by ferns and moss and cause curious hikers to stop and appreciate its beauty. Because the rock type of the boulder is different from the bedrock it rests upon, it's called a "glacial erratic." There are views down Tibbetts Creek drainage from the boulder's summit.

Reach a junction with Tibbetts Creek Trail (E10) and turn right (north). This junction is unmarked on older Green Trails maps. Continue along the Bear Ridge

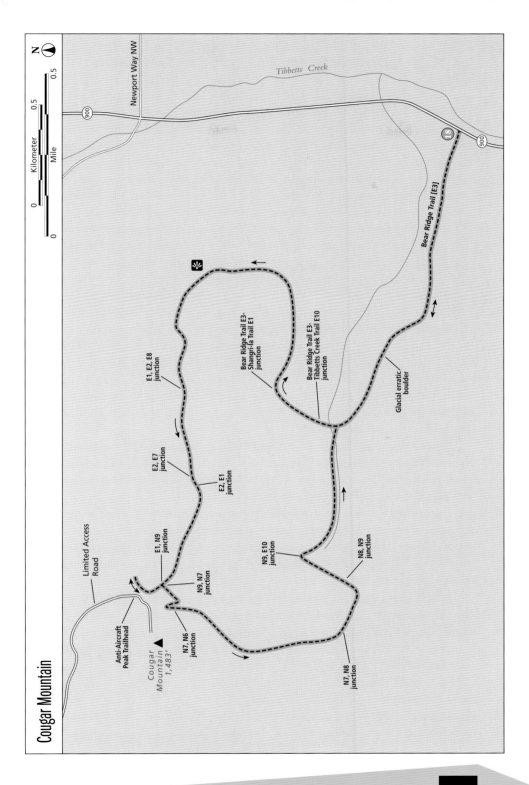

Cougar Mountain

N

Kilometer
0        0.5

Mile
0        0.5

Newport Way NW

*Tibbetts  Creek*

900

Bear Ridge Trail [E3]

900

Bear Ridge Trail E3-
Shangri-la Trail E1
junction

Bear Ridge Trail E3-
Tibbetts Creek Trail E10
junction

E1, E2, E8
junction

Glacial erratic
boulder

E2, E7
junction

E2, E1
junction

E1, N9
junction

N9, E10
junction

N8, N9
junction

Limited Access
Road

N9, N7
junction

Anti-Aircraft
Peak Trailhead

N7, N6
junction

N7, N8
junction

*Cougar
Mountain
1,483'*

Trail for 0.2 mile to another trail junction. Turn right (east) onto the Shangri-La Trail (E1).

The E1 trail begins to drop and circles around the east side of Cougar Mountain, temporarily leaving the park and crossing private property above the Talus subdivision. There are views into the subdivision as well as north to the Sammamish Plateau development, Mount Si and Mount Baker, and east to the western flank of Tiger Mountain, Stevens Pass, and Snoqualmie Pass. Lake Sammamish lies below.

The trail begins to climb again, regaining all its lost elevation; passes an unmarked waytrail; reenters the park; and 0.5 mile after the viewpoint reaches a junction with the Surprise Creek (E2) and No Name (E8) Trails. Go straight (west) for 0.3 mile. At the next junction turn left (west), continuing on E2 toward Anti-Aircraft Peak, ignoring the Goodes Corner Trail (E7) to Issaquah Reservoir. Reach another junction after a scant 0.1 mile, and turn right (west) back onto the Shangri-La Trail (E1). Confused yet? Pay attention—and don't put away that map!

The trail here is very wide and enters a lovely copse of red alder. After 0.5 mile reach yet another junction—this one with the Tibbetts Marsh Trail (N9); remain on E1, straight ahead (northwest). Reach the Anti-Aircraft Peak trailhead in 0.1 mile. The building you see belongs to the Cougar Mountain maintenance office. There is a community trail maintenance station here. If you want to do your part, read the instruction sign.

Turn to your right (north), ignoring the road that goes down to the west, and walk past the portable toilet to reach a couple of picnic benches. There is a view of Lake Sammamish and points north.

Retrace your steps to the E1–N9 trail junction, and turn right (southwest) onto the Tibbetts Marsh Trail (N9). Very quickly come to the junction with the Anti-Aircraft Ridge Trail (N7) and turn right (west). In 100 yards come to the Lost Beagle Trail (N6); turn left (south) to remain on N7.

The trail meanders through a maturing forest with an extensive and impressive grove of understory sword ferns along with big patches of Oregon grape and red huckleberry. Stop and appreciate how big these ferns are! This forest is an excellent example of the differences between an overstory of red alder and one of western hemlock and Douglas fir.

After 0.7 mile reach yet another trail junction, the Cougar Pass Trail (N8), and turn left (southeast). N8, in turn, meets up again with Tibbetts Marsh Trail (N9) in 0.2 mile for a left (northeast) turn. Cross Tibbetts Creek on a boardwalk and fallen log. After 0.2 mile N9 reaches the junction with the upper end of West Tibbetts Creek Trail (E10), where the turn is to the right (east). Descend 0.5 mile along Tibbetts Creek to Bear Ridge Trail (E3); turn right (southeast) and follow the trail back to the parking lot in 1.1 miles.

Using walking sticks to help reduce impact to knees and legs

## MILES AND DIRECTIONS

**0.0**  Bear Ridge trailhead (E3): N47° 31.627' / W122° 03.831'

**0.8**  Enter Cougar Mountain Regional Wildland Park: N47° 31.806' / W122° 04.744'

**1.1**  Tibbetts Creek Trail (E10): N47° 31.978' / W122° 05.117'

**1.3**  Junction with Shangri-La Trail (E1): N47° 32.119' / W122° 04.915'

**2.4** Junction with Surprise Creek (E2) and No Name (E8) Trails: N47° 32.353' / W122° 04.945'

**2.7** Junction with Surprise Creek (E2) and Shangri-La (E1) Trails: N47° 32.316' / W122° 05.350'

**3.0** Junction with Shangri-La (E1) and Tibbetts Marsh (N9) Trails: N47° 32.399' / W122° 05.727'

**3.1** Anti-Aircraft Peak trailhead: N47° 32.460' / W122° 05.772'

**3.2** Junction with Anti-Aircraft Ridge (N7) and Lost Beagle (N6) Trails: N47° 32.379' / W122° 05.806'

**3.9** Junction with Anti-Aircraft Ridge (N7) and Cougar Pass (N8) Trails: N47° 31.924' / W122° 05.917'

**4.1** Junction with Cougar Pass (N8) and Tibbetts Marsh (N9) Trails: N47° 31.892' / W122° 05.739'

**4.4** Junction with Tibbetts Marsh (N9) and West Tibbetts Creek (E10) Trails: N47° 32.039' / W122° 05.608'

**4.9** Junction with West Tibbetts Creek (E10) and Bear Ridge (E3) Trails: N47° 31.978' / W122° 05.117'

**6.2** Return to Bear Ridge trailhead (E3): N47° 31.627' / W122° 03.831'

## HIKE INFORMATION

The Talus subdivision of Issaquah is a master-planned community designed to exploit a mix of housing configurations and densities with the topography and open space of Cougar Mountain. It comprises 626 acres, with 387 acres dedicated to open space. When complete it could contain up to 2,000 dwelling units, along with significant amounts of commercial retail space. To learn more visit www.ci.issaquah.wa.us/Page.asp?NavID=77 and www.talusliving.com.

# Wilderness Peak

*There is no view from the summit of Wilderness Peak, but the trail up and back is still very nice. Even better, the trail is less than 20 miles from Seattle. That makes it a perfect after-work hike year-round. The mixed forest of maturing Douglas fir, red alder, mountain hemlock, western red cedar, and maples form a rich mosaic of vegetation. The interplay of sky and sunshine filtering through the many shades of green is immensely pleasing to the eye. For these reasons it's easy to comprehend why the trails of Cougar Mountain are so popular. But as popular as this hike is, the small size of the parking lot will always limit the number of people you see until reaching Shy Bear Pass. From there, access to a large complex of Cougar Mountain trails is possible.*

**Start:** Wilderness Creek trailhead along Highway 900

**Distance:** 5.7-mile lollipop (including the waytrail on summit); 3.7-mile loop without waytrail

**Approximate hiking time:** 2 to 3 hours

**Trail numbers:** Cougar Mountain Regional Wildland Park Trails: E6 (Wilderness Creek Trail), E5 (Wilderness Cliffs Trail), E4 (Wilderness Peak Trail)

**Difficulty:** Moderate, with long, steep sections

**Trail surface:** Forested path

**Seasons:** Year-round

**Other trail users:** Runners

**Canine compatibility:** Leashed dogs permitted

**Land status:** Cougar Mountain Regional Park (METRO–King County)

**Nearest town:** Issaquah

**Services:** Gas, restaurants, groceries, lodging; portable toilet at trailhead

**Northwest Forest Pass:** No

**Maps:** Green Trails No. 203S: Cougar Mountain/Squak Mountain; USGS Issaquah, Renton, Maple Valley

**Trail contacts:** King County Parks and Recreation Division, 201 South Jackson Street, Suite 700, Seattle, WA 98104; (206) 296-8687; www .metrokc.gov/parks/parks/. For emergencies either dial 911 or call King County Police at (206) 296-3311. Download a map of Cougar Mountain Regional Wildland Park from www.metrokc.gov/ gis/vmc/Recreation.htm#CM

**Special hazards:** Stinging nettle, devil's club; no potable water at trailhead or on trail

**Finding the trailhead:**
Drive east from Seattle on Interstate 90 to exit 15. Turn right (south) at the signal, cross Northwest Gilman Boulevard. Proceed on Renton-Issaquah Road

SE (Highway 900 west) for 3.2 miles, passing a large blue sign on your right at 2.7 miles for Cougar Mountain–Squak Mountain. The turnoff for the trailhead is on your right and plainly marked Cougar Mountain Regional Wildland Park. There is plenty of truck and commuter traffic on this highway. Be patient. Don't speed, and signal your turn well in advance.

The parking area is small and paved, and it's possible to miss both the entrance and the exit. If this should happen, don't jam on your brakes! Drive another 0.9 mile to the traffic signal at Southeast May Valley Road, where you can turn around safely. Once again, signal your turn well in advance (look for the Issaquah Highlander Recreation Club on the right), as you will be making a left turn across dangerous cross-traffic.

This parking area is prone to car clouts (note the sign) and is subject to video surveillance (note the sign). Be wise—take all valuables with you on the trail. *Delorme: Washington Atlas and Gazetteer:* Page 63 A-8.

## THE HIKE

Pass the small information kiosk welcoming hikers to King County Parks, and begin ascending the steep E6 trail along Wilderness Creek. Cross the creek on a sturdy bridge in 100 feet. Occasionally it's possible to pick up photocopied maps of Cougar Mountain Regional Wildland Park here.

Except for the most egregious sounds intruding on the solitude of the trail, you quickly leave behind the highway noise. Science has discovered a reliable way of measuring how much air pollution a forest can remove; it would be interesting to develop a technique doing the same with noise. If that sort of information was known, there might be greater respect for trees.

In 0.5 mile turn right (east) toward Wilderness Peak on the Wilderness Cliffs Trail (E5). In 400 feet, turn left (north) continuing on E5 and bypassing the Squak Mountain Connector Trail (E11). Note the stumps of very large trees. This maturing second-growth forest still has a long way to go.

After a heart-thumping mile, the trail relents briefly, dropping into the basin of an ephemeral stream before resuming its upward climb. After 1.7 miles, reach the intersection with the Wilderness Peak Trail (E4). Turn right (east) and reach the summit of Wilderness Peak in 0.1 mile.

Don't expect a view from the summit—there are too many trees! Now is a good time to catch your breath, contemplate your sweat equity, and decide what to do. Someone has thoughtfully built a log bench (slowly returning its nutrients to the soil) and bolted a trail register to a tree. Sign it or not, but do read the amusing things previous hikers have written.

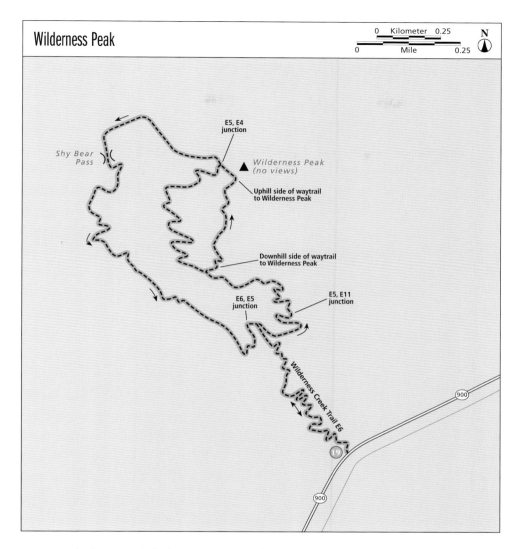

At the summit find a narrow waytrail, unmarked on maps, that drops steeply for a 1.0-mile shortcut to meet the E5 trail. If you choose this route, turn left (southeast) to return to the trailhead.

Cougar Mountain's many crisscrossing trails—most junctions marked, some not—guarantee that every year or so an inattentive hiker or jogger gets lost. Don't laugh. If you do, it's an indication that you are one of those inattentive types. Keep your eye on your map, and read every trail junction closely to make sure you've chosen the right one.

If you're not using the shortcut, retrace your steps to the E5-E4 junction and continue straight ahead (west) for 0.3 mile to Shy Bear Pass. Several choices are

Log pathway crisscrossing a boggy spot

presented. To the right (west) Trail S2 leads to Far Country Viewpoint or Anti-Aircraft Peak. To the left (west), Trail S4 leads to Long View Peak. Also to the left (south) is the Wilderness Creek Trail (E6) and the way home, completing this loop.

Drop steeply, cross a wet area on split logs, and soon meet the E6-E5 junction. Bear right (southeast) and cross the creek on a stout bridge. The noise of the highway soon signals the impending end of the trail and return from the wilderness to civilization.

## MILES AND DIRECTIONS

**0.0**  Wilderness Creek trailhead along Highway 900: N47° 30.603' / W122° 05.228'

**0.7**  Squak Mountain Connector Trail: N47° 30.870' / W122° 05.407'

**1.7**  E5 and E4 trail junction: N47° 30.866' / W122° 05.486'

**1.8**  Wilderness Peak: N47° 31.156' / W122° 05.551'

**3.1**  Waytrail intersection with E5: N47° 30.957' / W122° 05.611'

**4.2**  Shy Bear Pass: N47° 31.203' / W122° 05.916'

**5.7**  Return to trailhead: N47° 30.603' / W122° 05.228'

**Options:** The Squak Mountain Connector Trail (E11) leads back down to Highway 900, crossing the highway and connecting with the West Access Trail (W1) in Squak Mountain State Park. It leaves the Wilderness Cliffs Trail (E5) about 400 feet after the E5-E6 junction.

## HIKE INFORMATION

Cougar Mountain Zoological Park is dedicated to increasing the understanding and appreciation of the earth's wildlife and the role of humanity in nature through education, research, captive breeding, conservation, exhibition, and recreation. Returning from Wilderness Peak on Highway 900, turn left (west) onto Newport Way just prior to reaching I-90. Turn left (south) up the hill on Southeast 54th Street at the Zoo Landmark sign. The Zoological Park is located approximately 0.25 mile up Southeast 54th Street. For more information check the Web at www. cougarmountainzoo.org.

# 20

## South Tiger Mountain

*Unlike the Tiger Mountain trails along Interstate 90, South Tiger Mountain hardly ever sees the bottom of a boot. Along the route can be found some unusual native Washington plants as well as great representatives of the usual suspects. There are amazing views to the Olympic Mountains and south Puget Sound. For such an easily accessible hike, this place is rare, precious, and beautiful. This loop incorporates the southern terminus of Tiger Mountain Trail, a 16.0-mile traverse that wends its way past or over all six Tiger Mountain peaks.*

**Start:** Tiger Mountain trailhead along Tiger Mountain Road SE
**Distance:** 7.3-mile lollipop
**Approximate hiking time:** 4 to 5 hours
**Difficulty:** Moderate
**Trail surface:** Forested path, road
**Seasons:** Year-round
**Other trail users:** Runners, horses
**Canine compatibility:** Leashed dogs permitted
**Land status:** Washington State Department of Natural Resources, Tiger Mountain State Forest
**Nearest town:** Issaquah
**Services:** Gas, restaurants, groceries, lodging; no toilet at trailhead
**Northwest Forest Pass:** No
**Maps:** Green Trails No. 204S: Tiger Mountain–Taylor Mountain; USGS Fall City, Hobart; USDAFS Mount Baker–Snoqualmie National Forest

**Trail contacts:** Middle Fork Snoqualmie: www.midforc.org. Issaquah Alps Trail Club, P.O. Box 351, Issaquah, WA, 98027; www.issaquahalps.org/. Washington Department of Natural Resources, South Puget Sound Region, 950 Farman Avenue N, Enumclaw, WA 98022-9282; (360) 825-1631; www.dnr.wa.gov. Washington Native Plant Society, Puget Sound Chapter, 6310 Northeast 74th Street, Suite 215E, Seattle, WA 98115; (206) 527-3210; www.wnps.org/cps/index.html; e-mail: wnps@blarg.net
**Special hazards:** Stinging nettle, devil's club, blackberry; no potable water at trailhead or on trail

**Finding the trailhead:**
From Seattle drive east to Issaquah on I-90 and get off at exit 17, Front Street. Turn right (south) at the signal and drive slowly through town; they get very upset at speeders. Front Street becomes Issaquah-Hobart Road. In 4.8 miles pass Southeast Tiger Mountain Road on the left (east). After 8.2 miles, just before reaching Highway 18, turn left (northeast) onto Tiger Mountain Road SE.

In 0.25 mile is a blind curve with a wide shoulder on the left (west) and a School Bus Stop Ahead sign on the right (east). Drive another 0.1 mile to Southeast 175th Place. Turn around and return to park on the wide shoulder. *Delorme: Washington Atlas and Gazetteer:* Page 64 A-1.

## THE HIKE

Cross from the shoulder on Tiger Mountain Road SE and find the trailhead, 50 feet south of the school bus sign, for Tiger Mountain Trail–South Tiger Traverse Trail. This section of Tiger Mountain Trail has seen a lot of volunteer labor to control its perpetually muddy character. The work has helped, as is plain to see, but mud remains in many places. The trail is sporadically marked "TMT" with small handpainted wooden signs nailed onto trees.

In 1.0 mile, reach a trail junction that is not marked on older Green Trails maps. Right (northeast) is a horses-only trail. Continue straight (north) on the hikers-only Carkin's Cliff Trail. This narrow route meets the horses-only trail at Hobart Gap 0.3 mile later. Tiger Mountain Road SE and Highway 18 are never far away, and occasionally the passing of a semi–trailer truck or barking of neighborhood dogs can be heard through the thick forest.

At Hobart Gap note the old road on the left (west). Turn right (east) above the horse trail to continue on the TMT. The way through here is mostly level or with gentle uphill sections. Cross a creek, and in 0.8 mile from Hobart Gap reach the South Tiger Powerline Trail. Turn right (northeast), walk under the power lines for 0.1 mile, and turn left (north) onto a gravel road. Walk a few hundred feet, reenter the woods, and spot the actual TMT. Turn right (northeast).

The trail makes lazy dipsy-doodles, crosses a couple of creeks, and in 1.2 miles reaches a trail junction with the South Tiger Traverse. To continue on to Otter Lake and some botanical curiosities, continue straight ahead (northwest) on the old gravel road. In 0.1 mile—before meeting the wide, gravel West Side Road—pass through a gate, which may or may not be closed. Short of the gate is a waytrail on the left (west) signed ATTENTION. THIS IS NOT A TRAIL by the DNR and threatening prosecution for trespassing.

Turn left (west) onto West Side Road and proceed about 0.1 mile, passing a continuation with TMT in 10 feet on the right (north). Where the road begins to rise and curve away from the drainage, find a medium-size western red cedar and a waytrail that leads down to Otter Lake on the left (south). This route obviates the need to walk on the trail that DNR has closed.

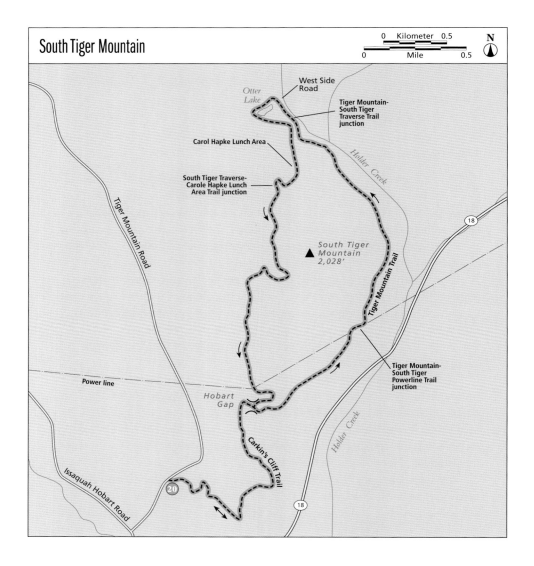

Otter Lake isn't really a lake; it's more of a pond. In midsummer during dry years, the pond becomes a wetland. In all times of year Otter Lake sports some unusual vegetation, including a forget-me-not (*Myosotis laxa*) that is found only in the Issaquah Alps. There is also a bed of simple-stem bur-reed (*Sparganium emersum*), lens-fruited sedge (*Carex lenticularis*), and several other species in the sedge family.

Return to the TMT–South Tiger Traverse junction, turn right (southwest) onto a gravel road and begin to climb the only truly steep portion of this entire trip. In 1.0 mile find a hand-routed sign announcing the Carole Hapke Lunch Area. Turn right (north) and climb a narrow horse trail that meanders 0.1 mile through thick brush to the top of a knoll, where a sign bolted to a tree says this lunch area is in memory of Carole Hapke. Climb a nearby stump for fine views that encompass most of Tiger Mountain State Forest and all of the Olympics. The informal lunch area includes a hitching post and rough benches.

After this detour, come back at the main trail and cross the road (south) to resume South Tiger Traverse. According to signs, this area is slated for logging; but as of 2007, no cutting has occurred. At times like these it's worthwhile to recall that Tiger Mountain State Forest is a "working" forest, and monies generated from timber sales help fund public institutions like schools, prisons, and county governments. To avoid road building and reduce erosion, helicopters will be used when this area is eventually logged, and some trail closures may occur. DNR worked with the Tiger Mountain Advisory Committee and the Issaquah Alps Trails Club on the harvest plan.

Tiger Mountain Trail marker

After 1.0 mile of hiking down the south flank of the mountain, the trail pops out at South Tiger Powerline Trail. Views to the right (west) include an amazing vantage of the Olympic Mountains and lower Puget Sound. Continue straight (south) underneath power lines to find the trail and continue dropping. A homemade routed sign points out the way. At the bottom of a steep switchback, find an old road and jog left (east) and in 20 feet arrive at Hobart Gap. From here retrace your steps down the trail to Tiger Mountain Road SE.

## MILES AND DIRECTIONS

**0.0**   Trailhead along Tiger Mountain Road SE: N47° 26.588' / W121° 58.617'

**1.0**   TMT–Carkin's Cliff Trail junction: N47° 26.660' / W121° 58.018'

**1.3**   Hobart Gap: N47° 26.893' / W121° 58.049'

**1.5**   Cross creek: N47° 26.991' / W121° 57.816'

**2.1**   TMT–South Tiger Powerline Trail junction: N47° 27.249' / W121° 57.453'

**3.3**   TMT–South Tiger Traverse Trail junction: N47° 28.168' / W121° 57.818'

**3.4**   West Side Road: N47° 28.256' / W121° 57.895'

**3.5**   Otter Lake: N47° 28.217' / W121° 58.008'

**4.8**   South Tiger Traverse–Carole Hapke Lunch Area Trail junction: N47° 27.877' / W121° 57.909'

**6.0**   Hobart Gap: N47° 26.893' / W121° 58.049'

**7.3**   Return to trailhead: N47° 26.588' / W121° 58.617'

> **WEATHER LORE:**
> *Red sky at morning,*
> *sailor take warning.*
> *Red sky at night,*
> *sailor's delight.*
> *If the moon rises*
> *haloed round,*
> *Soon you'll tread on*
> *deluged ground.*

# Tiger Mountain–High Point Trail

*This forest ramble is a good rainy-day trip when Tiger Mountain is shrouded in clouds, and since you're going to get wet anyway, you won't be bothered by wet vegetation along the overgrown sections of trail. It's a wonderful summer hike as well, because it stays away from the more popular places in an already very popular place.*

**Start:** High Point trailhead at West Tiger Mountain Natural Resources Conservation Area, Issaquah

**Distance:** 6.3-mile lollipop

**Approximate hiking time:** 4 to 5 hours

**Difficulty:** Moderate, with faint trails and overgrown vegetation sometimes obscuring the trail

**Trail surface:** Forested path; rocky, wet

**Seasons:** Year-round

**Other trail users:** Runners

**Canine compatibility:** Leashed dogs permitted

**Land status:** Washington State Department of Natural Resources

**Nearest town:** Issaquah

**Services:** Gas, restaurants, groceries, lodging; no toilet at trailhead

**Northwest Forest Pass:** No

**Maps:** Green Trails No. 204S: Tiger Mountain; USGS Fall City, Hobart; USDAFS Mount Baker–Snoqualmie National Forest

**Trail contacts:** Middle Fork Snoqualmie: www.midforc.org. Issaquah Alps Trail Club, P.O. Box 351, Issaquah, WA, 98027; www.issaquahalps.org/. Washington Department of Natural Resources, South Puget Sound Region, 950 Farman Avenue N, Enumclaw, WA 98022-9282; (360) 825-1631; www.dnr.wa.gov.

**Special hazards:** Stinging nettle, devil's club; confusing trail junctions; no potable water at trailhead or on trail

**Finding the trailhead:**
From Seattle drive east on Interstate 90 to exit 20, High Point Way. At the end of the off-ramp, bear right onto 270th Avenue SE, and then immediately turn right (west) onto Southeast 79th Street and park. There are usually many cars already parallel parked along the street, so join them! *Delorme: Washington Atlas and Gazetteer:* Page 80 D-1.

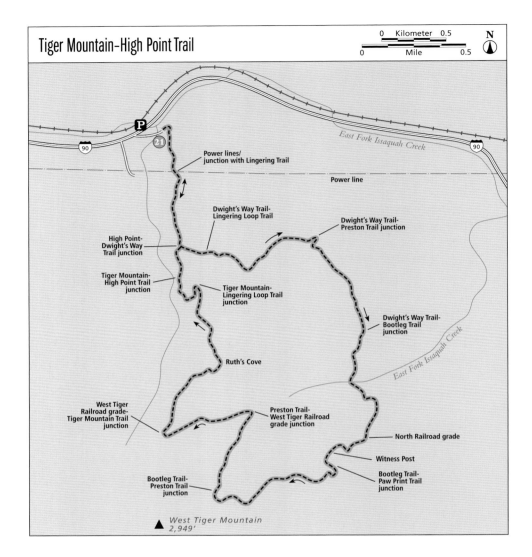

# Tiger Mountain–High Point Trail

0    Kilometer    0.5

0    Mile    0.5

N

**P**

21

90    90

East Fork Issaquah Creek

Power lines/
junction with Lingering Trail

Power line

Dwight's Way Trail-
Lingering Loop Trail

Dwight's Way Trail-
Preston Trail junction

High Point-
Dwight's Way
Trail junction

Tiger Mountain-
High Point Trail
junction

Tiger Mountain-
Lingering Loop Trail
junction

Dwight's Way Trail-
Bootleg Trail
junction

East Fork Issaquah Creek

Ruth's Cove

West Tiger
Railroad grade-
Tiger Mountain Trail
junction

Preston Trail-
West Tiger Railroad
grade junction

North Railroad grade

Witness Post

Bootleg Trail-
Preston Trail
junction

Bootleg Trail-
Paw Print Trail
junction

▲ West Tiger Mountain
2,949'

## THE HIKE

From the street parking along Southeast 79th, walk east, crossing 270th Avenue SE, to a heavy-duty metal gate blocking the street. Walk around the gate and continue along the asphalt road for 0.2 mile to the trailhead. Walk around another metal gate, and pass through a turnstile constructed of log poles to the High Point Trail. Start walking northeasterly to avoid High Point Pond, and then curve right (south), beginning a steep 0.3-mile ascent to some power lines.

High Point Trail passes under power lines to a junction with Lingering Trail. Continue straight ahead (south), passing two defunct high-voltage switching boxes; they give an indication of how this area was not always geared towards recreation. Climb 0.4 mile to Dwight's Way Trail, turning left (east) and continuing up. In 0.1 mile meet Lingering Trail Loop; remain straight (east) on Dwight's Way Trail. The trail levels out (more or less) and meanders through the forest. Upon reaching Preston Trail, turn right (south).

Begin a steep climb; after 0.5 mile meet Bootleg Trail and bear left (southwest). This section of trail is narrow and faint in many places—keep a sharp eye! Cross the East Fork Issaquah Creek (which can be seasonally high) and traverse around the south end of the drainage. Start a sharp ascent of the east side of Tiger Mountain. As you huff and puff up the hill, note the ample evidence that this has not always been hiking heaven.

Reach a faintly delimited trail junction in 2.7 miles, with homemade signs marking this as the way to East Tiger on the North Railroad grade. The route is narrow, faint, and heavily overgrown and is not marked on any map.

Continue up on Bootleg Trail, cross a creek, and notice the witness post (T23N R7E S6) marking the NRCA (Natural Resources Conservation Area) boundary. A

Tiger Mountain trail signs

hundred yards later, Bootleg Trail meets up with the Paw Print Connector. Turn right (west). No longer faint and overgrown, this section of Bootleg Trail maintains its long climb towards West Tiger 1.

Meet again with the Preston Trail in 0.8 mile. A turn to the left (west) leads to Hiker's Hut Viewpoint in 0.5 mile. If this is a rainy-day hike, no views will be forthcoming, so turn right (east). Drop down for 0.5 mile and turn left (west) onto West Tiger Railroad grade. After 0.4 mile of wide and level, turn right (north) onto Tiger Mountain Trail.

Cross a branch of High Point Creek on a wooden bridge. Keep your eyes sharp to spot three old power line poles, still with their ceramic insulators. Cross the creek on a plank bridge. An amateur sign marks this spot as Ruth's Cove. Tiger Mountain Trail meets with Lingering Loop Trail after 0.9 mile. Turn left (west) for 0.1 mile and reach the junction between Tiger Mountain Trail and High Point Trail, turning right (north).

Follow this wide trail for 0.2 mile until it hits Dwight's Way Trail. Turn left (northwest) and in 0.4 mile reach the trailhead. Walk the asphalt road back to Southeast 79th Street.

## MILES AND DIRECTIONS

**0.0**   Trailhead on Southeast 79th Street: N47° 31.933' / W121° 58.542'

**0.3**   Power lines and junction with Lingering Trail: N47° 31.765' / W121° 58.472'

**0.7**   High Point Trail junction with Dwight's Way Trail: N47° 31.392' / W121° 58.439'

**0.8**   Dwight's Way Trail junction with Lingering Loop Trail: N47° 31.385' / W121° 58.291'

**1.5**   Dwight's Way Trail junction with Preston Trail: N47° 31.452' / W121° 57.588'

**2.0**   Dwight's Way Trail junction with Bootleg Trail: N47° 31.015' / W121° 57.298'

**2.7**   North Railroad grade to East Tiger: N47° 30.557' / W121° 57.362'

**3.0**   Witness post: N47° 30.493' / W121° 57.501'

**3.0**   Bootleg Trail junction with Paw Print Trail connector: N47° 30.434' / W121° 57.467'

**3.8**   Bootleg Trail junction with Preston Trail: N47° 30.340' / W121° 58.206'

**4.3**   Preston Trail junction with West Tiger Railroad grade: N47° 30.689' / W121° 57.988'

**4.7**   West Tiger Railroad grade junction with Tiger Mountain Trail: N47° 30.598' / W121° 58.503'

**5.0**  Ruth's Cove: N47° 30.880' / W121° 58.234'

**5.5**  Tiger Mountain Trail junction with Lingering Loop Trail: N47° 31.238' / W121° 58.344'

**5.6**  Tiger Mountain Trail junction with High Point Trail: N47° 31.276' / W121° 58.436'

**6.3**  Return to trailhead: N47° 31.933' / W121° 58.542'

> 🍃 **Green Tip:**
> *Pass it down—the best way to instill good green habits in your children is to set a good example.*

A blend of past use and a recovering forest

# 22

# Cedar Butte

*An easy-to-moderate half-day walk along the old Milwaukee Railroad grade, which ends with a dynamic view up the Middle Fork Snoqualmie River Valley. The trail is a combination of old railroad grade and forest path. The mix of deep Douglas fir and western hemlock forest with sun breaks and red alder thickets creates good opportunities for bird-watching. This great early- or off-season hike is always accessible, even when snow covers every other trail in the area.*

**Start:** Cedar Falls trailhead, John Wayne Pioneer Trail in Iron Horse State Park
**Distance:** 3.7-mile lollipop
**Approximate hiking time:** 2 hours
**Difficulty:** Moderate
**Trail surface:** Forested path, old railroad bed
**Seasons:** Year-round
**Other trail users:** Bikes, horses, runners
**Canine compatibility:** Leashed dogs permitted
**Land status:** Iron Horse State Park; City of Seattle Cedar River Municipal Watershed Ecological Preserve
**Nearest town:** North Bend
**Services:** Gas, restaurants, groceries, lodging; vault toilet at trailhead
**Northwest Forest Pass:** No
**Maps:** Green Trails No. 205S: Rattlesnake Mountain; USGS North

Bend; USDAFS Mount Baker–Snoqualmie National Forest
**Trail contacts:** Seattle Public Utilities, Cedar River Watershed, 19901 Cedar Falls Road SE, North Bend, WA 98045; www.seattle.gov/util/About_SPU/Water_System/Water_Sources_&_Treatment/Cedar_River_Watershed/index.asp. Washington State Parks, Iron Horse State Park, P.O. Box 42650, Olympia, WA 98504-2650; (360) 902-8844 (open 8:00 a.m. to 5:00 p.m. Monday through Friday); www.parks.wa.gov/parkpage.asp?selectedpark=Iron%20Horse; e-mail: infocent@parks.wa.gov. Milwaukee Road Historical Association, P.O. Box 307, Antioch, IL 60002-0307; www.mrha.com/; e-mail: office@mrha.com
**Special hazards:** No water at trailhead

### Finding the trailhead

Drive from Seattle on Interstate 5 east to North Bend. Take exit 32 (436th Avenue SE) for Iron Horse State Park and the John Wayne Pioneer Trail. Turn right (south) at the stop sign. Pass the Cascade Golf Course, where 436th Avenue SE becomes Cedar Falls Road. In 2.7 miles reach the Rattlesnake Lake

Recreation Area boundary, administered by Seattle Public Utilities in cooperation with Washington State Parks and King County Parks System. In 0.1 mile is a small parking lot for Rattlesnake Ledge. Pass this lot, bearing left at the wye. Follow the paved road to a large sign announcing CEDAR FALLS TRAILHEAD, and park. *Delorme: Washington Atlas and Gazetteer:* Page 64 A-2.

Trilliums lining the trail in the spring

## THE HIKE

At the Cedar Falls trailhead are two clean, well-maintained, wheel-chair accessible vault toilets in bright orange buildings; many picnic tables; and an overbuilt reader board with brief descriptions covering history of the old Milwaukee Railroad grade that forms the first mile of the Cedar Butte Trail. Take a moment to read what little is posted. This first section of trail is but a whisper in the long line that once stretched across the country as the Chicago, Milwaukee, St. Paul, and Pacific Railroad. Afterward, easily locate a wide gravel path, immediately crossing an abandoned paved road that once went to the town of Cedar Falls.

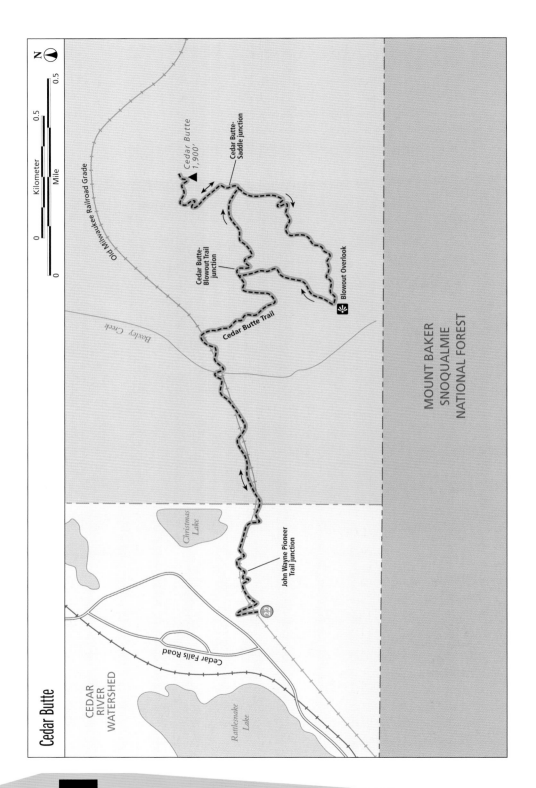

Cedar Butte

N

0    Kilometer    0.5
0    Mile    0.5

Old Milwaukee Railroad Grade

Boxley Creek

*Cedar Butte*
▲ *1,900'*

Cedar Butte-
Saddle Junction

Cedar Butte-
Blowout Trail
junction

Cedar Butte Trail

Blowout Overlook

CEDAR
RIVER
WATERSHED

*Christmas
Lake*

Cedar Falls Road

*Rattlesnake
Lake*

John Wayne Pioneer
Trail Junction

22

MOUNT BAKER
SNOQUALMIE
NATIONAL FOREST

In 0.3 mile reach the John Wayne Pioneer Trail; turn left (east), passing a trail sign to Snoqualmie Tunnel (18.0 miles). This old railroad grade is a popular year-round mountain bike route, but most traffic is confined to weekends. Directly before you is a Keep Out sign prohibiting access to the Cedar River Watershed—part of Seattle's domestic water supply.

In 1.0 mile pass a waytrail on the left (north) and cross Boxley Creek on an old trestle. Below, on the right (south), is a USGS stream gauge. A hundred yards past the creek is a stack of early-twentieth-century cedar railroad ties overgrown with sword fern and blackberry. In another 100 feet come to the Cedar Butte Trail on your right (south). In most years there is a sign nailed to a red alder tree here. The forest path climbs steeply in a maturing second-growth forest with a well-developed understory of salal, gooseberry, blackberry, sword fern, mahonia, huckleberry, and buttercup.

At the trail junction, marked by an ankle-high Blowout sign, bear left. You will be returning by this other trail.

Climb some more, and enter a dark forest where the understory thins out. After one last steep push, reach Saddle Junction and a trail sign bolted to a Douglas fir. This spot marks the official end to where horses and bikes are allowed on the trail. The trail splits in three. To the right (west) is the top end of the Blowout Trail. Straight head the sign directs hikers to the South Side Trail. Do not take this route. After dropping into the drainage, the trail narrows, grows fainter, and then runs up a tree and disappears into a knothole.

To the left is the summit route. Switchbacks climb steeply, with an occasional view across the watershed to Rattlesnake Mountain. From the summit of Cedar Butte are views up the Middle Fork Snoqualmie River to Mount Si, Mount Tenerife, Mailbox Peak, and others. Below the butte are glimpses of a few McMansions tucked into the trees along with Interstate 90.

Once finished with the view, eat lunch on the small log bench. Then retrace your steps back to Saddle Junction.

Rather than turning right (north) and continuing down the main trail, walk straight ahead (west) on the Blowout Trail. Snake around without losing much elevation. The blowout is marked by a small Overlook sign bolted to a tree. There isn't anything to see here except a thick forest of spindly trees, but on Christmas Eve 1918 there was a lot happening. A break in the north bank of the Masonry Dam upstream on the Cedar River caused flooding that washed away the town of Edgewick, 2 miles downstream. The city eventually paid more than $300,000 in damages.

Continue downhill until reaching the main Cedar Butte Trail. Turn left (north) and finally reach the John Wayne Trail again. Turn left (west), cross Boxley Creek again, and return to the trailhead.

## MILES AND DIRECTIONS

**0.0**   Cedar Falls trailhead: N47° 25.886' / W121° 45.897'

**0.7**   Boxley Creek: N47° 25.965' / W121° 45.131'

**1.1**   Blowout Trail junction: N47° 25.912' / W121° 44.810'

**1.4**   Saddle Junction: N47° 25.921' / W121° 44.538'

**1.6**   Cedar Butte: N47° 26.038' / W121° 44.494'

**1.8**   Saddle Junction: N47° 25.921' / W121° 44.538'

**2.3**   Blowout overlook: N47° 25.721' / W121° 44.914'

**2.6**   Blowout Trail junction: N47° 25.912' / W121° 44.810'

**3.0**   Boxley Creek: N47° 25.965' / W121° 45.131'

**3.7**   Return to trailhead: N47° 25.886' / W121° 45.897'

## HIKE INFORMATION

As of this writing, there are no fees at Iron Horse State Park except for overnight backcountry camping. Those fees are $6 per vehicle (paid at trailhead) and $5 per campsite per night (paid at the campsite).

The Cedar River Watershed provides 70 percent of the water for 1.3 million people living in the greater Seattle Area. A side trip to the Cedar River Watershed Visitor Center is well worth the time. Managed by Seattle Public Utilities, the center has interpretive displays and historical material and sells natural history and hiking books.

A walk around the Rain Drum Court, designed by Dan Corson, is a musical and educational experience of the finest kind! A short nature walk, with identification labels for native plants, begins in the parking area. Spur trails provide access to the shore of Rattlesnake Lake. Pick up maps of Rattlesnake Lake and a bird list at the visitors center (open Monday through Thursday 8:00 a.m. to 5:00 p.m.

> *"I have two doctors, my left leg and my right."*
> —*George M. Trevelyan,*
> *English historian*

# Rattlesnake Mountain–East Peak

*Rattlesnake Mountain is far from any rattling reptiles, and that's OK. Challenging but not overly so, the mountain's combination of trails, former logging roads, utility access roads, plus dramatically exposed views of the Snoqualmie Valley make it a popular destination on sunny weekends. Low elevation and proximity to the ameliorating influences of Puget Sound keep it practically snow-free through all but the most monstrous of winter storms. Managed jointly by the Washington State Department of Natural Resources and King County Park and Recreation Department, East Peak Trail in the Rattlesnake Mountain Scenic Area is a popular destination. But once you're past the three ledges, public use drops off in a major way.*

**Start:** Rattlesnake Ledge trailhead
**Distance:** 9.0 miles out and back, with a mini-lollipop near East Peak
**Approximate hiking time:** 4 to 6 hours
**Difficulty:** Moderate
**Trail surface:** Forested path
**Seasons:** Year-round
**Other trail users:** Runners
**Canine compatibility:** Leashed dogs permitted
**Land status:** Rattlesnake Mountain Scenic Area; City of Seattle Cedar River Municipal Watershed Ecological Preserve; Mount Baker–Snoqualmie National Forest; Washington State Department of Natural Resources; Weyerhaeuser Corporation
**Nearest town:** North Bend
**Services:** Gas, restaurants, groceries, lodging; wheelchair-accessible portable toilet at trailhead
**Northwest Forest Pass:** No
**Maps:** Green Trails No. 205S, side A: Rattlesnake Mountain; USGS North Bend; USDAFS Mount Baker–Snoqualmie National Forest

**Trail contacts:** King County Department of Parks and Recreation, 201 South Jackson Street, Suite 700, Seattle, WA 98104; (206) 296-8687; www.metrokc.gov/parks/openspace/rattlesnake.html. Mountains to Sound Greenway Trust, 911 Western Avenue, Suite 523, Seattle, WA 98104; (206) 382-5565; www.mtsgreenway.org/; e-mail: info@mtsgreenway.org. Middle Fork Snoqualmie: www.midforc.org. Mount Baker–Snoqualmie National Forest, Snoqualmie Ranger District, North Bend Office, 42404 SE North Bend Way, North Bend, WA 98045; (425) 888-1421; www.fs.fed.us/r6/mbs/recreation. Department of Natural Resources, South Puget Sound District, 950 Farman Street N, P.O. Box 68, Enumclaw, WA 98022-6381; (360) 825-1631
**Special hazards:** Stinging nettle, devil's club; cliffs and exposure, with danger of falling; no potable water at trailhead or on trail

**Finding the trailhead:**

Drive from Seattle on Interstate 5 east to North Bend. Take exit 32 to 436th Avenue SE to Iron Horse State Park and the John Wayne Pioneer Trail. Turn right (south) at the stop sign. Pass the Cascade Golf Course, where 436th Avenue SE becomes Cedar Falls Road. In 2.7 miles reach the Rattlesnake Lake Recreation Area boundary, administered by Seattle Public Utilities in cooperation with Washington State Parks and King County Parks System. In 0.1 mile is a small parking lot for Rattlesnake Ledge. Pass this lot, bearing left at the wye, and park in the gravel lot. *Delorme: Washington Atlas and Gazetteer: Page 64 A-2.*

## THE HIKE

Walk back to the road from the parking lot. Cross and find the trail sign for Rattlesnake Ledge. Walk around the closed gate on an elevated pathway past a trail sign announcing the east trailhead for the Rattlesnake Mountain Trail (RMT). Follow this access road for 0.2 mile, with Rattlesnake Lake viewable on the left (west). Expect to see families, dogs, and trail. Reach a large grassy area with porta-potties, trash and recycling receptacles, and a bike rack. Begin ascending the trail to Rattlesnake Ledge.

Dog and human interactions, both positive and negative, are common along this stretch of trail, as are positive and negative interactions between leashed and unleashed pets. In 0.1 mile cross a wide, old road that leads eastward to Cedar Falls Road SE. It has been blocked on either side by rocks and brush. Continue straight ahead (west). The path is wide, allowing two-way traffic walking abreast and the occasional passing lane. There are even a few turnouts.

In 0.4 mile encounter a trail leading up the hill. The trail is blocked by a pole fence. Older sections of trail like this are occasionally encountered, although non-use is quickly covering them with fallen trees and other woody debris. When it doubt, stay on the main pathway. The RMT is a work in progress and has been rerouted to avoid roads, control erosion, or reduce the grade.

After 2.0 miles of steady uphill hiking, reach a trail junction. Turn right (northeast), and walk 100 yards to Rattlesnake Ledge. Space on the ledge can be crowded on busy weekends with adults, children of all ages, and frolicking dogs. All the good and safe spots can be taken. There are no handrails, and careless behavior could have disastrous results. Keep little children and dogs on a tight leash.

After taking in the view, return to the trail junction and continue straight ahead (northwest), passing an interpretive sign. Rattlesnake Ledge is actually three separate ledges. Each enjoys dynamic vistas of the entire Snoqualmie Valley. From the lower ledge, continue higher to waytrails leading to ledges 2 and 3, taking the same

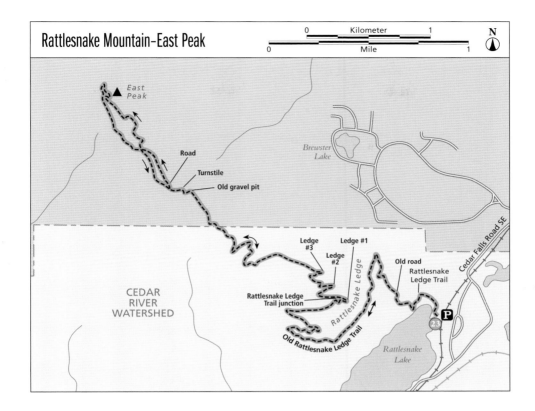

precautions as before. The RMT stays close to the cliff rim for some time afterward, but dense tree growth obscures all views. The RMT now changes significantly—becoming narrower and less peopled. Good-bye, crowds; hello, peace and quiet!

Four miles from the parking lot is an old gravel pit, followed by a turnstile made of poles. A hundred feet farther is an access road used to reach communication antennas atop East Peak. Straight across (west) locate the RMT sign steering hikers to Snoqualmie Point. Instead turn right (northwest) onto the old gravel road. In 0.2 mile cross the trail but remain on the road. Cross the trail one last time as the road makes a hairpin turn, passes two benches, and leads to East Peak and a communication tower. To the south, through a rapidly growing young forest, is a nice view of Mount Rainier (on clear days).

> ### 🌿 Green Tip:
> **Recycle your old gear by giving it to someone or an organization that will reuse it.**

Rattlesnake Ledge

From the hairpin turn it's entirely possible to continue northwest on the RMT for another 6.1 miles to the west trailhead at Snoqualmie Point, with access from exit 27 on Interstate 90. In recent years, more than 40,000 hours of volunteer and trail crew labor with $650,000 from the legislature have converted heavily logged land into a route that connects both trailheads.

For now, double back to the hairpin turn. Ignore the access road this time, and turn left (northeast) to get onto the RMT. Follow this newer section of trail, crossing the road twice. Once at the junction between the RMT and the access road, retrace your steps past the ledges and down the mountain to the parking lot.

## MILES AND DIRECTIONS

**0.0**  Rattlesnake Ledge trailhead: N47° 26.069' / W121° 46.081'

**2.5**  Rattlesnake Ledge 1: N47° 26.165' / W121° 46.713'

**3.5**  Old gravel pit: N47° 26.656' / W121° 47.707'

**4.5**  East Summit, Rattlesnake Mountain: N47° 27.071' / W121° 48.222'

**9.0**  Return to trailhead: N47° 26.069' / W121° 46.081'

## HIKE INFORMATION

Rattlesnake Lake is popular for picnicking throughout the summer. Anglers are frequent visitors as well. The lake was created by water seeping out from under Howard Hanson Dam and Chester Morse Reservoir and is also fed by runoff from Rattlesnake Mountain. A side trip to the Cedar River Watershed Visitor Center is well worth the time. Managed by Seattle Public Utilities, the center (open Monday through Thursday 8:00 a.m. to 5:00 p.m.) has interpretive displays and historical material and sells natural history and hiking books.

> *"Walking is man's best medicine."*
> *—Hippocrates*

*In winter and spring, Weeks Falls is an incredible display of cascading water. Located in Olallie State Park, on the South Fork Snoqualmie River, it is also one of the most accessible waterfalls in our region. If you're looking for an introductory hike for children, river views, fishing access, or a place to stretch your legs after a summer picnic, Weeks Falls is the place. Downstream of the falls is a hydrogenerating facility. It's a great lesson in how electrical generation need not be a negative impact on the landscape.*

**Start:** Overlook Trail trailhead in Olallie State Park
**Distance:** 1.0 mile out and back
**Approximate hiking time:** 1 hour
**Difficulty:** Easy
**Trail surface:** Forested path
**Seasons:** Year-round
**Other trail users:** None
**Canine compatibility:** Leashed dogs permitted
**Land status:** Washington State Park
**Nearest town:** North Bend
**Services:** Gas, restaurants, groceries, lodging; no toilet at trailhead; toilets located in nearby picnic area at state park entrance
**Northwest Forest Pass:** No

**Maps:** Green Trails No. 206S, side B: Mount Si NRCA and No. 206: Bandera; USGS Chester Morse Lake; USDAFS Mount Baker–Snoqualmie National Forest
**Trail contacts:** Washington State Parks and Recreation Commission, 7150 Cleanwater Drive SW, P.O. Box 42650, Olympia, WA 98504-2650; (360) 902-8844 (open 8:00 a.m. to 5:00 p.m. Monday through Friday); www.parks.wa.gov/parks/; e-mail: infocent@parks.wa.gov
**Special hazards:** No potable water at trailhead or on trail; cold, swift river. Water levels in the pool below the power plant can vary dramatically; avoid the temptation to enter the water here

**Finding the trailhead:**
From Seattle drive east on Interstate 90 to exit 38 west. At the stop sign turn right (south). The road curves to the left, joining the approximate route of the Snoqualmie Pass Wagon Road (completed in 1869) and the historic Sunset Highway (old Snoqualmie Pass Highway). Pass a sign for Olallie State Park, Twin Falls State Park, and a gravel road to the east trailhead for Twin Falls. In 0.6 mile pass a wide spot on the left. In 0.2 mile reach a turnoff for Olallie State Park on your left (north). The intersection is not marked.

Enter the park; drive past a large picnic area (toilets) and the ranger residence. Turn left into the parking area. There is also a large picnic area here.

The trailhead for the Weeks Falls/Overlook Trail begins in the northwest corner of the parking lot by a fee-collection (voluntary as of 2007) station. *Delorme: Washington Atlas and Gazetteer:* Page 64 A-3.

## THE HIKE

A s easily seen from the size of the parking lot, this is a popular place. And no wonder! The short trail stays by the river and in deep shade all the way to Weeks Falls—which are stupendous during winter and spring and merely impressive the rest of the year.

Begin by the fee-collection station and a plea from State Parks to make a contribution. As of 2007 all fees in state parks are voluntary. What a sad state of affairs when our parks must beg for the funding the state is obligated to provide. Next will probably come bake sales at picnic grounds and trailheads. Straight ahead (north) is a waytrail that ends at the South Fork Snoqualmie River. The Weeks Falls Trail takes off to the right (east) on an asphalt road, which quickly becomes a forest path without losing any of its width.

Walk upstream along the river, passing frequent opportunities to stray on waytrails to river overlooks and angling sites on the south bank. This is also a nature trail, and there are several large interpretive signs for you to stop and read, learn, and appreciate. There is an occasional bench to rest your weary bones and aching feet.

The trail meanders through the forest, crossing a creek on a quaint wooden bridge. When the trail splits, bear right and soon encounter an amazing sight: a huge Douglas fir. This tree is easily 30 feet in circumference at ground level and is the biggest, tallest thing around. It makes the few large western red cedars in the same grove appear puny by comparison. But they themselves are impressive.

Passing a sign for Olallie State Park, the trail pops out into bright sunshine, reaching a gravel access road and a unisex vault toilet. No parking is allowed here.

Immediately before you is the Weeks Falls Hydroelectric Project and beyond that, Weeks Falls. Stop for a moment to read the interpretive sign explaining the hydro project—commissioned June 5, 1987. Something that makes this hydropower plant different from many others is there isn't a dam. Upstream of the falls is a low, adjustable weir across the river. Water that pools behind the weir is withdrawn into a 600-foot-long underground tunnel, which connects to the powerhouse beside you. If water is flowing out of the concrete channel below the powerhouse, electricity is being generated. If not, then there probably isn't enough water in the river to both generate power and protect the fish. Within the turbine building, 5 megawatts of electricity is produced—enough power for 800 homes.

Move on 100 feet to an observation deck and Weeks Falls. Many fallen trees, along with wet and slippery rocks, make going any farther a dangerous operation. Don't forget to keep an eye on any small children.

Returning from the falls, find where the trail splits and bear right, walking close by the river. Many access points for admiring the view are available. The trail meets up with the main trail and shortly reaches the parking lot.

## MILES AND DIRECTIONS

**0.0**   Overlook Trail trailhead: N47° 26.192' / W121° 39.250'

**0.3**   Big Douglas fir: N47° 26.037' / W121° 38.987'

**0.5**   Weeks Falls: N47° 26.011' / W121° 38.882'

**1.0**   Return to trailhead: N47° 26.192' / W121° 39.250'

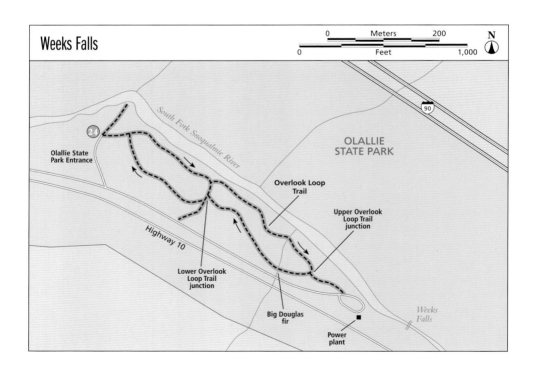

Weeks Falls

# Twin Falls

*A dramatic series of waterfalls along the South Fork Snoqualmie River, a high bridge over an impressive gorge, and an observation deck aerie are the biggest draws for hiking the Twin Falls Trail. It's a popular route, especially from the west trailhead, but beginning from the east allows hikers to appreciate a short section of the old Milwaukee Railroad grade and views both up and down the Snoqualmie Valley. Though the trail is wide below the falls, there are no passing lanes. Solitude seekers are advised to begin at the east trailhead, where few venture. Twin Falls is not the only allure to this trail. Anglers will find plenty of waytrails down to the river below the falls.*

**Start:** East trailhead in Twin Falls State Park; west trailhead for reverse hike

**Distance:** 8.0 miles out and back or 4.0-mile shuttle

**Approximate hiking time:** 5 to 6 hours

**Difficulty:** Moderate, with some steep sections

**Trail surface:** Forested path, old railroad grade

**Seasons:** Year-round

**Other trail users:** Runners, bikes (for a short while on the Milwaukee Railroad grade)

**Canine compatibility:** Leashed dogs permitted

**Land status:** Washington State Park

**Nearest town:** North Bend

**Services:** Gas, restaurants, groceries, lodging; unisex vault toilet at both east and west trailheads

**Northwest Forest Pass:** Yes at west trailhead; no at east trailhead

**Maps:** Green Trails No. 206S, side B: Mount Si NRCA and No. 206: Bandera; USGS Chester Morse Lake; USDAFS Mount Baker–Snoqualmie National Forest

**Trail contacts:** Washington State Parks and Recreation Commission, 7150 Cleanwater Drive SW, P.O. Box 42650, Olympia, WA 98504-2650; (360) 902-8844; www.parks.wa .gov/parks/; e-mail: infocent@ parks.wa.gov; open 8:00 a.m. to 5:00 p.m. Monday through Friday

**Special hazards:** Exposed cliff sections (protected by handrails) on lower trail; no potable water at trailhead or on trail; cold and swift South Fork dangerous for swimming

**Finding the trailhead:**
For the east trailhead, from Seattle drive east on Interstate 90 to exit 38 west. At the stop sign turn right (south). In 0.2 mile the road curves to the left, joining the approximate route of the Snoqualmie Pass Wagon Road (completed

in 1869) and the historic Sunset Highway (old Snoqualmie Pass Highway). In 0.1 mile pass a sign for Olallie State Park and Twin Falls State Park. A good, wide gravel road on your right (west) signals the east trailhead for Twin Falls. Turn right. In 0.2 mile pass a gated vehicle access road to the John Wayne Pioneer Trail on your left and park.

For the west trailhead, from Seattle drive east on I-90 to exit 34, 468th Avenue SE. Turn right (east) and drive 0.6 mile. Before crossing a bridge over the South Fork Snoqualmie River, turn left (east) onto Southeast 159th Street. After 0.3 mile pass through a small residential community and reach the parking lot where the road ends. *Delorme: Washington Atlas and Gazetteer:* Page 64 A-3.

## THE HIKE

Begin on the south side of the east trailhead parking lot and ascend a short, narrow trail to the access road, which leaves from the parking lot. Turn right (west) and continue to the John Wayne Pioneer Trail, bearing right. This is the old Milwaukee Railroad grade, marked with a large Olallie State Park sign. Turn right (west). Even though you're walking on a wide gravel road to the sound of I-90 traffic, this is still a pleasant jaunt. A deep, dark forest is on one side and beautiful Snoqualmie Valley views are on the other.

Walk for 0.5 mile, passing the unmarked Mount Washington trail on the left (south) and find the Twin Falls trail. Turn right (north) and begin dropping toward the South Fork Snoqualmie River. Continue on the John Wayne Pioneer Trail for 500 feet, and arrive at the Twin Falls Substation—a fine detour for those intrigued by the generation of electricity.

This section of the trail is limited to foot traffic and is blocked by a gate that allows human passage only. Maybe because it sees less use than the trail below the falls, expect to see less maintenance for the next 0.5 mile. Fallen trees across the trail show evidence of many-years-old detours. This upper stretch is narrow, but not too narrow—overgrown, but not too overgrown. There are thimbleberries in season and sword ferns all the time.

Cross a culvert that keeps Washington Creek from washing away the trail. The route flattens, then drops in earnest on switchbacks to the increasing roar of falling water. Your first inkling of anything stupendous is a bench, some stairs, and then a handrail. At a sharp corner in the trail, look upstream (east) and see the upper falls.

**Green Tip:**
*Pack out what you pack in, even food scraps because they can attract wild animals.*

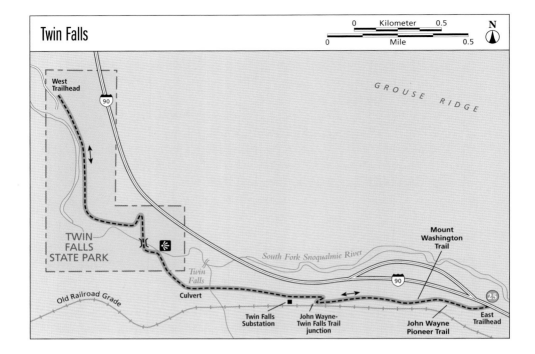

Continue dropping lower and lower on stairs to reach, at 1.7 miles, an impressive bridge spanning the South Fork gorge. Look upstream at the lower reaches of the upper falls—a twin falls in itself. Immediately below is the lip of lower Twin Falls. The rocky reaches of the South Fork stretch below. Sharp eyes can spot the observation aerie for the lower falls on the river-right canyon wall.

Crossing the bridge, the trail climbs on stairs and crosses a creek. Don't bother with a waytrail that circumvents the river side of the handrail. It doesn't lead to any view of the falls.

Continue to a side trail after 2.0 miles—really another series of steps, which drop steeply to an observation platform that clings to the gorge like an eagle's aerie. From here a dramatic view of the lower falls fills the eye. This is no leaping fall of water. Rather the river slides down the rock, splayed into many channels and ends in a deep pool. Standing upon the viewing platform gives observers the distinct feeling of being in a treehouse. Return up the steps—all 106 of them—to the trail. You *have* been practicing your stair climbs, haven't you?

Once on the main trail, keep heading downhill. Leave the sound of falling water and return to the sound of highway traffic. Human traffic on the trail begins to pick up too. After 4.0 miles, reach the west trailhead. Along the way, you'll pass many opportunities to approach the river. Bear in mind at all times, and during all seasons, that the South Fork is swift and cold—which makes it suitable for salmon and unsuitable for swimming.

Twin Falls

Use the vault toilet and pick up your shuttle vehicle, or turn around and retrace your steps to the east trailhead.

## MILES AND DIRECTIONS

**0.0**  East Twin Falls trailhead: N47° 26.521' / W121° 40.360'

**0.3**  John Wayne Pioneer Trail: N47° 26.534' / W121° 40.559'

**0.8**  Twin Falls Trail: N47° 26.534' / W121° 41.168'

**1.7**  Upper Twin Falls and bridge: N47° 26.732' / W121° 41.939'

**2.0**  Lower Twin Falls view, observation aerie N47° 26.672' / W121° 41.850'

**4.0**  West trailhead; shuttle or turnaround point: N47° 27.191' / W121° 42.317'

**8.0**  Return to east trailhead: N47° 26.521' / W121° 40.360'

**Options:** A car shuttle from the east to the west trailhead is an alternative but leaves a larger "carbon footprint."

# Little Si

*Under the shadow of its bigger brother, Little Si is so tiny, so close. Whether you need a quickie in the forest after a hard day at the office or an interesting walk with young children, Little Si is a perfect fit. Its accessibility to Seattle makes it more of an urban walk than a wilderness hike, and this popularity is reflected by a wide and beaten down track and a thirty-car parking area with a lot of turnover—and not of the pastry kind. Nevertheless, this is still a very pretty route to take, and views from the top are just as good as from Mount Si—and much less work!*

**Start:** New trailhead parking lot along Southeast Mount Si Road
**Distance:** 3.0 miles out and back
**Approximate hiking time:** 2 hours
**Difficulty:** Easy. The trail is wide and easy to follow. There are some steep places but nothing a six-year-old can't handle if given enough time. There are an adequate number of places to stop and rest and numerous diversions (bridges, ephemeral streams, banana slugs, rocks to climb, etc.) for children.
**Trail surface:** Forested path; rocky
**Seasons:** Year-round
**Other trail users:** Runners; rock climbers
**Canine compatibility:** Leashed dogs permitted

**Land status:** Washington Department of Natural Resources
**Nearest town:** North Bend
**Services:** Gas, restaurants, groceries, lodging; unisex vault toilet at trailhead
**Northwest Forest Pass:** No
**Maps:** Green Trails No. 206S, side A: Mount Si NRCA; USGS North Bend; USDAFS Mount Baker–Snoqualmie National Forest
**Trail contacts:** Middle Fork Snoqualmie: www.midforc.org. Mount Si: www.mountsi.com. Department of Natural Resources, South Puget Sound District, 950 Farman Street N, P.O. Box 68, Enumclaw, WA 98022-6381; (360) 825-1631
**Special hazards:** Exposure; no potable water at trailhead or on trail

**Finding the trailhead**

Take Interstate 90 from Seattle to exit 32, 436th Avenue SE in North Bend. This avoids the main North Bend exit (exit 31) and traffic congestion caused by the outlet stores and other traveler services. Also, you won't have to drive through downtown North Bend.

At the stop sign at end of the off-ramp, turn left onto 436th Avenue SE. Dead ahead is the summit of Little Si. Drive 0.6 mile, passing the flashing yellow lights, to a stop sign at Southeast North Bend Way. Note that cross-traffic does not stop. Turn left (northwest). After 0.3 mile turn right (north) onto Southeast Mount Si Road.

In 0.3 mile cross the Middle Fork Snoqualmie River Bridge and 434th Avenue SE, the old access to Little Si. The road bends to the right. In 0.2 mile find the Little Si parking lot on the left (north). *Delorme: Washington Atlas and Gazetteer:* Pages 64 A-2 and 80 D-2.

## THE HIKE

From the parking lot the trail takes off steeply on switchbacks on a rocky slope. The view opens up to the south, exposing a fine panorama from Rattlesnake Mountain to Cedar Butte along with the Cedar River watershed. In springtime notice the urn-shaped white flowers of salal along with their glandular, red floral receptacles. The plants are subject to a smut that causes splotches on the leaves, reducing salal's importance as an significant subsidiary forest product. Salal belongs to the same family as madrone and bearberry—plainly evident when comparing the blossoms.

Leaving the rocky slope behind, the trail tops out in 0.3 mile and enters a stand of lovely second-growth. The trail here seems perpetually damp from the deep shade of the forest; this is prime banana slug habitat. Wetter areas have been raised abovegrade with occasional log causeways. Other sections are not so lucky and are becoming wider and wider as hikers step around the mud and puddles. Pass several unmarked waytrails leading off into the trees. Continue straight ahead on the doublewide Little Si Trail.

In 0.6 mile reach an unmarked trail junction on the right (northwest) for the old Mount Si Trail. Continue on the wider Little Si Trail, crossing an ephemeral stream. After 1.0 mile reach a split cedar fence and a DNR sign requesting that you stay on your side in order to allow plant regeneration to proceed on the other. This is an inviting spot for lunch, especially on hot hiking days: cool and moist and with many convenient logs and rocks to sit on.

The trail continues to climb, first gently and then steeply, in its never-ending quest to reach the summit. Pass several marked signposts for the rock-climbing area located below the summit. Come here at the right time of year and you'll hear the clink, clang, and tinkling of climbing hardware and the sounds of climbers' voices wafting dreamlike high above you through the trees.

In 1.2 miles reach a bench embedded with a brass plaque. The bench memorializes Doug Hansen, who disappeared after reaching the summit of Mount Everest on May 10, 1996—a story covered in Jon Krakauer's best seller *Into Thin Air.*

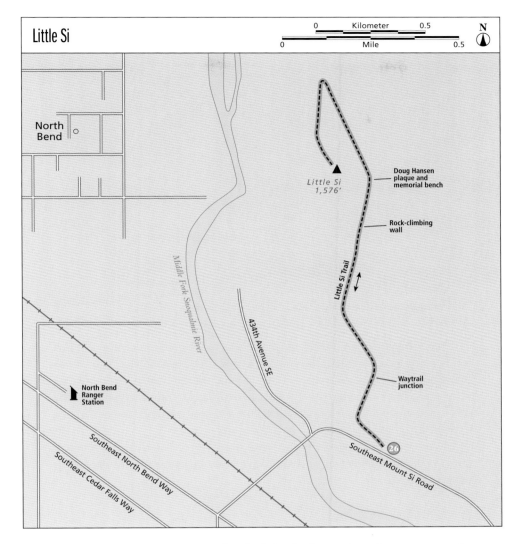

## Little Si

| 0 | Kilometer | 0.5 |
| 0 | Mile | 0.5 |

**N**

North Bend

Middle Fork Snoqualmie River

Little Si
1,576'

Doug Hansen
plaque and
memorial bench

Rock-climbing
wall

Little Si Trail

434th Avenue SE

North Bend
Ranger
Station

Waytrail
junction

Southeast North Bend Way

Southeast Cedar Falls Way

Southeast Mount Si Road

26

A few steps later cross a cedar-plank footbridge and another causeway; the trail begins to climb in earnest. This signals the final uphill stretch of the trail and is steeper and longer than any previous section. The trail swings around the north nose of Little Si. Highway and other sounds rise up from North Bend, making hikers realize that it has been quiet for quite some time—due to the trail passing between the Little Si and Mount Si.

Near the summit are a few openings in the trees, affording dramatic views of the south shoulder and summit of Mount Si. If you choose to step out onto the rock ledges to enjoy the views, watch your step! It's a long way straight down to the bottom. A few feet below the top of Little Si are several waytrails made by impatient hikers attempting shortcuts. At 1.5 miles reach the top.

This bench memorializes Doug Hansen, a local climber who died climbing Mt. Everest

The summit views up the Snoqualmie River Valley are impressive. If it isn't windy and cold, have a seat. Stop and stay a while. If you're eating lunch, be aware that many others have eaten here in the past and will eat here in the future. Pick up any crumbs; refrain from the temptation to toss apple cores, orange peels, and other food waste into the trees. It's unsightly and rude and encourages begging from the local rodents and birds.

To return to the trailhead, retrace your steps. The trail always looks different from the opposing direction, so don't be in a hurry. Enjoy the reverse as much as the forward direction.

## MILES AND DIRECTIONS

**0.0**    Trailhead along Southeast Mount Si Road: N47° 29.215' / W121° 45.217'

**1.0**    Rock climbing wall: N47° 29.751' / W121° 45.292'

**1.2**    Memorial bench: N47° 29.862' / W121° 45.248'

**1.5**    Summit: N47° 29.917' / W121° 45.358'

**3.0**    Return to trailhead: N47° 29.215' / W121° 45.217'

## HIKE INFORMATION

There are two benches and two wheelchair-accessible parking spaces at the trailhead. Pay attention to the No Parking signs along SE Mount Si Road—they mean business. The old trailhead, which began at 434th Avenue SE, is decommissioned and abandoned. Lots of No Parking signs there as well. Pay attention, or pay the man!

After your hike, stop at George's Bakery at 127 North Bend Way, where hot caffeinated or caffeine-free drinks, luscious Danish pastries, or a light lunch can be had for reasonable prices.

## Foxglove

Foxglove (*Digitalis purpurea*) is a ubiquitous herbaceous plant found along trails and other disturbed areas. The soft, hairy leaves are toothed, ovate, and lance-shaped in a basal rosette.

Its tall spikes of colorful purple, pink, rose, yellow, or white flowers entice picking fingers to return home with a blossom or two. But beware! All parts of the plant are toxic.

Because it's such a common plant, foxglove is usually assumed to be native to the Pacific Northwest. Sadly, no. It might have first been introduced to the Pacific Northwest by Dr. William Fraser Tolmie (1812–1886). Tolmie was a surgeon, trader and, later, Chief Factor of the Fort Nisqually Hudson Bay Company fur post between 1833 and 1859. After leaving Washington, Tolmie settled in Victoria, British Columbia, and apparently never practiced medicine again.

A source of the heart medicine digitoxin, foxglove was a common medicinal herb in European gardens during the nineteenth century. It makes sense that it would have been in Dr. Tolmie's pharmacopoeia. Today it's a popular cultivar for vertical accents in flower gardens and is a frequent garden escape.

Other common names for foxglove include the more colorful, and perhaps descriptive, witches glove, dead man's bells, and bloody fingers.

Foxglove

*Looming over the town of North Bend like a giant stegosaurus, Mount Si is all that remains of an oceanic plate volcano. There are many classic hikes in the Seattle area, and the summit of Mount Si is the classic of classics. Without a doubt, it's one of the most popular hikes in our area. Given its popularity, it's interesting to note that within 4.0 miles the trail rises 3,600 feet. Hiking to the top of Mount Si is like climbing the Space Needle six times. This is not a hike for the faint of heart—or the out of shape!*

**Start:** Mount Si Natural Resources Conservation Area trailhead
**Distance:** 8.3-mile circuit
**Approximate hiking time:** 6 to 8 hours
**Difficulty:** Moderate due to steepness
**Trail surface:** Forested path; rocky
**Seasons:** Year-round
**Other trail users:** Runners
**Canine compatibility:** Leashed dogs permitted
**Land status:** Washington Department of Natural Resources
**Nearest town:** North Bend
**Services:** Gas, restaurants, grocer-ies, lodging; vault toilet at trail-head
**Northwest Forest Pass:** No
**Maps:** Green Trails No. 206S, side A: Mount Si NRCA; USGS North Bend; USDAFS Mount Baker–Snoqualmie National Forest
**Trail contacts:** Middle Fork Sno-qualmie: www.midforc.org. Mount Si: www.mountsi.com. Depart-ment of Natural Resources, South Puget Sound District, 950 Farman Street N, P.O. Box 68, Enumclaw, WA 98022-6381; (360) 825-1631
**Special hazards:** Loose rock; exposure

**Finding the trailhead:**
From Seattle drive east on Interstate 90 to exit 32, 432nd Avenue SE. Road signs before the exit proclaim IRON HORSE STATE PARK‡JOHN WAYNE PIONEER TRAIL. At the stop sign at the end of the off-ramp, turn left (north) and proceed north for 0.6 mile. Turn left (west) onto Southeast North Bend Way. In 0.3 mile turn right (north) onto Southeast Mount Si Road. After crossing the Middle Fork Sno-qualmie River, the road curves right (northeast) and in 0.5 mile passes the trail-head to Little Si, arriving at the Mount Si trailhead in an additional 1.8 miles.

 The gated parking lot opens at dawn and closes at dusk. It is subject to video surveillance by the King County Sheriff's Department due to the high

incidence of car prowls. Lock your car and take all valuables with you. The parking lot is often full even during the week and can be overflowing on weekends or holidays. No parking is permitted along Southeast Mount Si Road. Pay attention to the signs if you don't want your car hauled away. *Delorme: Washington Atlas and Gazetteer:* Pages 64 A-2 and 80 D-2.

## THE HIKE

Fans of the early 1990s television show *Twin Peaks* will recognize Mount Si from a distance as the backdrop for many of the show's exterior scenes. The program was filmed primarily on soundstages in Los Angeles, although Twede's Restaurant in North Bend was used as the diner where FBI Special Agent Cooper enjoyed some of the Northwest's famous coffee.

The trail begins north of the vault toilet, picnic tables, and water spigot and quickly passes the wheelchair-accessible 0.2-mile Creek Side Loop Trail, which is dedicated to North Bend resident Frances North. As a state legislator during the 1970s, North was instrumental in setting aside 1,100 acres of Mount Si for public use. The Mount Si Natural Resources Conservation Area now consists of 9,000 acres—once again because of North's vision.

Cross the creek, enter deep second-growth forest, and climb steeply on a wide, rocky trail. The rocks protruding from the ground are worn shiny and smooth by the boots of the 80,000 people who yearly make use of this trail. The way to the top of Mount Si is continually a work in progress as stout bridges replace rotten logs over ephemeral stream courses, and trail rerouting eliminates the steeper sections that in some places once went straight up hill. Where the trail is too steep for switchbacks, there are tall stone steps. Signs are posted every 0.5 mile to assist hikers in charting their progress.

On any given day the route up Mount Si sees a number of extremes. There are Lycra-clad trail runners hauling dual bottles of water on their hips, hikers who look like they just stepped out of an REI catalog, other hikers bedecked in all sorts of glacier climbing gear as they train to summit Mount Rainier, moms and dads with tiny tots riding in backpacks, young and old out for a forest stroll, high school students with manly attitudes, people walking their dogs—even the occasional walker in flip-flops sans hat, pack, water or food. Well, that's what popularity is all about. The important point is that they are all outside, enjoying their public lands.

Whatever your reason for climbing Mount Si, it's a sweat inducer. Be sure to carry plenty of liquids to replace those precious bodily fluids lost to us by evaporative cooling during the ascent.

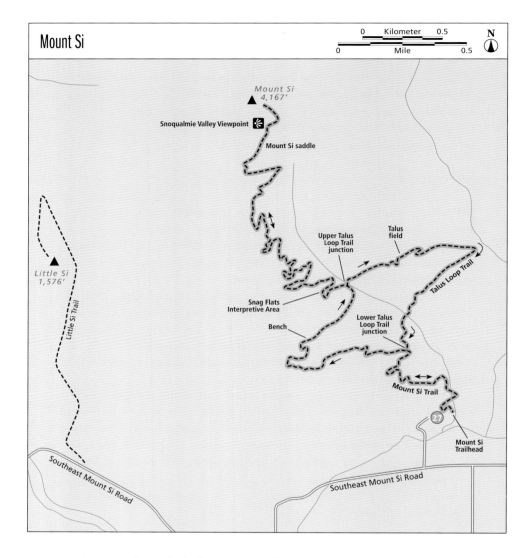

Mount Si

Mount Si
▲ 4,167'

Snoqualmie Valley Viewpoint

Mount Si saddle

Upper Talus
Loop Trail
junction

Talus
field

Talus Loop Trail

Little Si
1,576'

Snag Flats
Interpretive Area

Bench

Lower Talus
Loop Trail
junction

Little Si Trail

Mount Si Trail

27

Mount Si
Trailhead

Southeast Mount Si Road

Southeast Mount Si Road

In 0.75 mile reach the bottom end of the Talus Loop Trail on the right (east). This junction is unmarked, although people have occasionally marked it with rock cairns or flagging tied to trees.

After 1.5 miles the trail levels out briefly. Three benches here give weary hikers an opportunity to rest. This is also a popular place for people to leave their toilet paper beneath softball-size rocks. Don't be one of them—even the most casual observer will notice the TP does not go away in any appreciably short period of time. Pack it in, pack it out.

In 1.7 miles the trail forks at a signpost. Turn left (northwest) to continue on to the summit. Turn right (east) for the Talus Loop Trail (see below), marked The Creek. For the next few hundred feet the trail mellows out, crossing seasonally wet areas on stout wooden bridges and reaching the Snag Flats Interpretive Area, where the role of fire in forest health is explained.

Once again the trail takes off uphill with a vengeance—this time on a series of long switchbacks. There are several older sections of trail through here, and some maps still show them. However, it is best to leave these to the old-timers who know them well from past decades and stay to the newly constructed trail sections. This will prevent erosion and allow the forest to reclaim these older sections for itself.

At 3.7 miles pop out of the trees at a saddle in a large rocky area. There are usually many exhausted hikers lying about on the rocks and admiring the first views to the south of Mount Rainier. Keep on going, though—the top is nearby along with better views and great lunch spots. In winter this is usually as far as snow and ice will permit hikers to proceed.

The trail picks its way through the rocks. Follow signs to the Snoqualmie Valley Viewpoint and Haystack Scramble. The Scramble is a Class 3, 150-foot climb to the actual summit of Mount Si. It requires hands and feet along with caution and care,

Mount Si and Little Si from North Bend

and it is not advised for inexperienced climbers. Views of the Snoqualmie Valley are just as good from any of the vantage points below the summit. There are cliffs here with loose rock. Watch your step!

Some maps show the Mount Si Trail continuing eastward to Mount Teneriffe. This rough route is consigned only to the truly adventurous, since logging activity has obliterated the middle section between Mount Si and Mount Teneriffe. Map and compass can be used to bridge the gap and reach the wide gravel road that serves as a trail to Teneriffe's summit. Otherwise, retrace your steps down the Mount Si Trail to Snag Flats Interpretive Area and the Talus Loop Trail.

Turn left (east) on the lightly used but well-established Talus Loop Trail. Soon cross an ephemeral creek and then a short talus field. Continue through thick forest for 1.3 miles until meeting up again with the Mount Si trail at the unmarked junction mentioned earlier. Turn left (south) and reach the parking lot in 0.7 mile.

## MILES AND DIRECTIONS

**0.0**   Trailhead at Mount Si Natural Resources Conservation Area: N47° 29.305' / W121° 43.385'

**0.7**   Lower Talus Loop Trail junction: N47° 29.588' / W121° 43.692'

**1.7**   Upper Talus Loop Trail junction and Snag Flats Interpretive Area: N47° 29.845' / W121° 43.891'

**3.7**   Mount Si saddle and Snoqualmie Valley view: N47° 30.283' / W121° 44.367'

**4.0**   Mount Si summit: N47° 30.462' / W121° 44.385'

**6.3**   Upper Talus Loop Trail junction and Snag Flats Interpretive Area: N47° 29.845' / W121° 43.891'

**8.3**   Return to trailhead: N47° 29.305' / W121° 43.385'

## HIKE INFORMATION

Mount Si was named for local homesteader Josiah "Uncle Si" Merritt. After the hike, if you're thirsty for the best root beer float within 100 miles, stop along the main drag in downtown North Bend at Scott's Dairy Freeze, 234 North Bend Way. You won't be sorry.

Twede's Restaurant in North Bend, at 137 North Bend Way on the corner of North Bend Way and Bendigo Boulevard, touts its fame as the diner from the early 1990s television show *Twin Peaks* with a sign proclaiming, FAMOUS TWIN PEAKS PIES. For those not seeking fame, two doors east, at 127 North Bend Way, is George's Bakery, where luscious Danish pastries or a light lunch can be had for reasonable prices.

# Cairns and Ducks

Cairns are piles of rocks used to mark a trail or locate a geographic or historic place. They can be as simple as three stones placed one atop the other or as complex as some elaborate summit cairns standing several feet high and comprising hundreds of rocks.

Cairns used for marking trails are found all over the world, predominantly in mountainous areas, but are also used in deserts. In the hardwood forests of the United States, tree blazes were historically used to mark trails. This practice is also used in our Northwest forests. An ax-cut into a tree truck is placed over a long vertical cut—almost like dotting a lowercase i.

The predominant builders of cairns are hikers who, skilled in the trials and tribulations of Hansel and Gretel, don't wish to leave a trail of breadcrumbs behind to mark their way. Permanence, even something as transitory as a pile of rocks, is more comforting than returning from a journey only to find your trail devoured by ravenous ravens or field mice.

"Duck" is another common term for cairn. The term supposedly comes from a time when the topmost rock was used as a pointer, like a bird's beak, showing the proper direction to follow.

Following duck trails is problematic. Subsequent hikers can't be assured whether the builders knew where they were going. It's been found that ducks tend to occur where they are least needed, given that trailblazers are too occupied with finding their own way to mark it for others. It's best to rely upon yourself and your ability to read a map, use a compass, and interpret landscapes based on your own abilities and experience.

Cairns, or ducks, marking trails

# Snoqualmie Valley Highlands

Alders arching over Taylor River

Nearly every popular trail on the north side of Interstate 90 leads into the 362,789-acre Alpine Lakes Wilderness. The Middle Fork Snoqualmie River Road (Forest Road 56) deeply penetrates the wilderness area, which spans the Cascade Mountain crest from Snoqualmie Pass to Stevens Pass.

Congress established the Alpine Lakes Wilderness in 1976 after previous efforts to create a national park failed. Since 1998 the Forest Service has conducted studies to recommend expanding the wilderness boundaries. It looks like the Pratt River Valley, a tributary of the Middle Fork Snoqualmie, could be added, as well as land closer to trailheads.

In 2007 FR 56 was permanently closed to automobile traffic at Dingford Creek. A new campground near the Taylor River Road was opened, and extensive work was done to repair and extend the Middle Fork Trail. Meanwhile, road and restoration work on FR 56 continues. It's all for a good cause, and we can hardly wait for all the labor to be done.

Since 1998 the Forest Service has conducted studies to recommend expanding the boundaries of the spectacular Alpine Lakes Wilderness.

Upper Melakwa Lake

*Barely within the boundaries of the Alpine Lakes Wilderness, Myrtle Lake is a popular place. Snow and high-water creek crossings make reaching Myrtle Lake a challenging prospect in spring. Best to wait until July or August, when the snow is gone and creek levels have dropped or dried up.*

**Start:** Dingford Creek trailhead at gate on Middle Fork Snoqualmie Road (Forest Road 56)

**Distance:** 9.0 miles out and back

**Approximate hiking time:** 4 to 5 hours

**Trail Numbers:** USDA Forest Service Trail 1005

**Difficulty:** Moderate due to a steep trail, several stream crossings; high water and snow in early season

**Trail surface:** Forested path; rocky

**Seasons:** Summer and fall

**Other trail users:** Closed to bikes and horses

**Canine compatibility:** Leashed dogs permitted

**Land status:** Mount Baker–Snoqualmie National Forest, Alpine Lakes Wilderness Area; USDAFS Snoqualmie Ranger District

**Nearest town:** North Bend

**Services:** Gas, restaurants, groceries, lodging; no toilet at trailhead

**Northwest Forest Pass:** Yes

**Maps:** Green Trails No. 175: Skykomish; USGS Snoqualmie Lake; USDAFS Mount Baker–Snoqualmie National Forest, Alpine Lakes Wilderness

**Trail contacts:** Alpine Lakes Protection Society (ALPS): www.alpinelakes.org. Middle Fork Snoqualmie: www.midforc.org. Mount Baker–Snoqualmie National Forest, Snoqualmie Ranger District, North Bend Office, 42404 Southeast North Bend Way, North Bend, WA 98045; (425) 888-1421; www.fs.fed.us/r6/mbs/recreation

**Special hazards:** Stinging nettle; loose rock; creek crossings

**Finding the trailhead:**
Drive east from Seattle on Interstate 90 to exit 34, North Bend. Turn left (north) onto 468th Avenue. After 0.6 mile turn right (east) onto Southeast Middle Fork Road (FR 56). After 12.2 miles pass the Middle Fork Campground; cross the Taylor River Bridge, and turn right (east) to continue on FR 56. Plans are afoot to improve the road, but for now FR 56 is rough and rocky and subject to washouts where it crosses ephemeral streams (no culverts). Early in the season this part of FR 56 may be muddy and impassable for two-wheel-drive or low-clearance vehicles. It is not recommenced to people who care deeply about their tires, suspension, or all-around automobile cleanliness.

Continue for 6.7 miles to the trailhead at Dingford Creek. As of June 27, 2007, the Middle Fork Road is closed permanently at this point.

Park on the right (south) side of the road in a wide but rocky area overlooking the Snoqualmie River. Find the trailhead, marked by a small reader board, on the north side of the road and sign in at the register for entering the Alpine Lake Wilderness. *Delorme: Washington Atlas and Gazetteer:* Page 81 D-5.

## THE HIKE

From the parking area the trail climbs steadily for 0.5 mile on steep switchbacks before entering the Alpine Lakes Wilderness on a heavily eroded and rocky tread. This area is so deep in the woods that heavy logging didn't reach here until after World War II—at the same time, opening the region to recreation. Note the giant stumps, already mostly rotted away—testament to our moist environment and the action of decomposition.

Dingford Creek roars far below the trail in early season. The rare glimpse of it through the trees, foaming over rocks and under fallen forest giants, is exhilarating.

An early spring excursion to Myrtle Lake

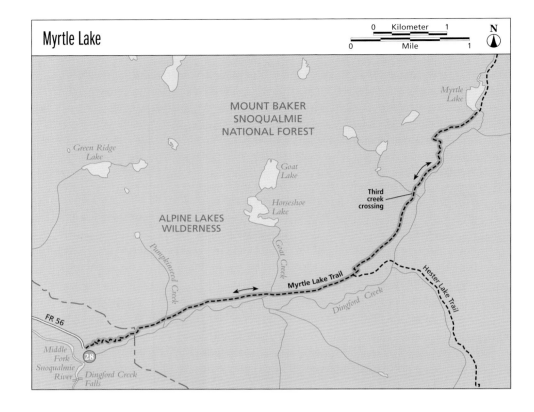

# Myrtle Lake

MOUNT BAKER
SNOQUALMIE
NATIONAL FOREST

Green Ridge
Lake

Goat
Lake

Myrtle
Lake

Third
creek
crossing

Horseshoe
Lake

ALPINE LAKES
WILDERNESS

Pumpkinseed Creek

Goat Creek

Myrtle Lake Trail

Hester Lake Trail

Dingford Creek

FR 56

Middle
Fork
Snoqualmie
River    Dingford Creek
Falls

28

Passing the wilderness boundary, the trail climbs at a reasonable grade, staying above Dingford Creek. Cross the outflow of Pumpkinseed Lake in 0.8 mile, stopping to appreciate the waterfall sliding down a wonderful slab of rock. The braided Goat Creek is crossed in 1.7 miles (high in early season) across rocks, and the trail (what else?) keeps on climbing.

After 2.5 miles reach a trail junction. A small sign nailed to a convenient snag announces that to the right (south) is Hester Lake (Trail 1005.1). Instead, turn left (northeast).

Continue climbing toward Myrtle Lake, crossing many side channels—many of which dry up later in the season. At 3.3 miles cross another braided creek (high and difficult in spring) on rocks, and begin the push toward the lake.

Trees around the shore and rocky cliffs create a pleasant setting for Myrtle Lake. Fishing is said to be fair here. A campsite is located on the other side of the outlet. The trail continues up the drainage toward Little Myrtle Lake and disappears in the upper part of the basin.

28

**0.0**   Dingford Creek trailhead: N47° 31.056' / W121° 27.275'

**0.5**   Alpine Lakes Wilderness boundary: N47° 31.171' / W121° 26.675'

**0.8**   Pumpkinseed Creek crossing: N47° 31.300' / W121° 26.371'

**1.7**   Goat Creek crossing: N47° 31.436' / W121° 25.267'

**2.5**   Junction with Hester Lake Trail: N47° 31.635' / W121° 24.216'

**3.3**   Third creek crossing: N47° 32.184' / W121° 23.661'

**4.5**   Myrtle Lake: N47° 32.834' / W121° 23.027'

**9.0**   Return to trailhead:  N47° 31.056' / W121° 27.275'

**Options:** From the trail junction for Myrtle and Hester Lakes, turn right and walk up to Hester Lake. In early season this alternative to Myrtle Lake involves a dangerous ford of Dingford Creek—wide, deep, and cold with snowmelt. The remainder of the trail, faint in many places and difficult to follow, eventually reaches Hester Lake after 3.0 miles. There are a few campsites near the lake, and no campfires are allowed.

*Note:* Closure of FR 56 (Middle Fork Snoqualmie Road) at Dingford Creek and the Myrtle Lake-Hester Lake trails completes implementation of the 2005 Middle Fork Snoqualmie Access Travel Management Plan. According to the Mount Baker—Snoqualmie National Forest, "This road-to-trail conversion is in conjunction with the recently completed Middle Fork Trail, which will provide multiple trail loop opportunities of up to 28 miles in length." Also part of this project is a new footbridge across the Middle Fork Snoqualmie River at the Goldmyer Hot Springs.

The effort to close FR 56 beyond Dingford Creek and convert the last 7.6 miles of road into a multiuse trail is an outgrowth of cooperative citizen planning efforts begun in the early 1990s and is supported by user groups, environmental groups, landowners, and the Forest Service.

Though road closure equates to loss of vehicle access to the upper reaches of the Middle Fork Snoqualmie, it means scarce maintenance funds during an era of tight budgets can be dedicated to more critical areas of the forest. Some of these resources include enhancements for recreational users on the more heavily used sections of the Snoqualmie River: improved river access, sanitation facilities, vegetation restoration, and increased law enforcement presence to prevent dumping and other illegal activities.

# Taylor River

A walk along Taylor River is perfect during the two- or three-week period in summer when Seattle is suffocating in our yearly 80-degree temperatures. Tree-tunnels provide ample shade, and periodic use-trails down to the river make for splashing opportunities. Water at Marten Creek and Big Creek is also available to wash off the sweat of the hike. The canyon is cool here from downcanyon drift.

The Taylor is a tributary of the Middle Fork Snoqualmie, and its trail (a long-abandoned road) follows above the river for 5 miles to the bridge over Big Creek. Along the way are side trails to Marten Lake and Otter Falls. Spring brings water to many side streams that cross the trail and feed two impressive waterfalls.

**Start:** Snoqualmie Lake trailhead on Middle Fork Road (Forest Road 56)

**Distance:** 10.0 miles out and back

**Approximate hiking time:** 5 hours

**Trail Number:** USDA Forest Service Trail 1002

**Difficulty:** Easy; wide and gentle trail

**Trail surface:** Forested path, gravel road; rocky

**Seasons:** Spring, summer, and fall

**Other trail users:** Bikes, horses, runners

**Canine compatibility:** Leashed dogs permitted

**Land status:** USDAFS Snoqualmie Ranger District

**Nearest town:** North Bend

**Services:** Gas, restaurants, groceries, lodging; no toilet at trailhead

**Northwest Forest Pass:** Yes

**Maps:** Green Trails No. 174: Mount Si and No. 175: Skykomish; USGS Quad Lake Philippa and Snoqualmie Lake; USDAFS Mount Baker–Snoqualmie National Forest

**Trail contacts:** Alpine Lakes Protection Society (ALPS): www. alpinelakes.org. Middle Fork Snoqualmie: www.midforc.org. Mount Baker–Snoqualmie National Forest, Snoqualmie Ranger District, North Bend Office, 42404 Southeast North Bend Way, North Bend, WA 98045; (425) 888-1421; www.fs.fed.us/r6/mbs/recreation

**Special hazards:** Loose rock; no potable water at trailhead or on trail

**Finding the trailhead:**

Drive east from Seattle to North Bend on Interstate 90 to exit 34 (468th Avenue SE/Edgewick Road). During winter closures of Snoqualmie Pass, this is as far east as you can drive. Turn left (north) at the stop sign and proceed past a truck stop, gas stations, and a restaurant. In less than 1 mile arrive at Southeast Middle Fork Road (Forest Road 56) and turn right (east). In 1 mile bear right at a wye onto Lake Dorothy Road. Pavement ends in 1.6 miles at a pull-out and small parking lot for the Mailbox Peak Trail, and the road becomes FR 56 (Forest Road 5600 on some maps).

After 2.6 miles on this good hardpack road with patches of gravel and occasional heavy zones of potholes, pass the popular Granite Creek put-in for kayakers. Cross a well-built concrete bridge and, in 2.1 miles, pass the Bessemer Mountain trailhead. Pass the Middle Fork Snoqualmie River trailhead in another 4.5 miles. Pass a Forest Service campground on your left (northeast), cross the Taylor River on a smaller concrete bridge, and turn left at a junction to reach Snoqualmie Lake trailhead in 1 mile.

The road ends here at a gate and a small parking area. If the lot is full, drive back for 0.2 mile to the bridge and park along the wide spots along the road. *Delorme: Washington Atlas and Gazetteer:* Page 64 A-2, 3.

## THE HIKE

The 1921 USGS Sultan quad shows a ranger station just downstream of the confluence with the Taylor and Snoqualmie Rivers and a trail poking up the Middle Fork. Leave your car at the Snoqualmie Lake trailhead, and pass around the stout metal gate. Immediately on the right is a short trail down to a side channel of the Taylor. It has plenty of sitting spots for lunch and bountiful views up- and downstream. Some have even used it as an informal camping area. The tall trunks of a mature streamside red alder forest provide shade on hot days. To continue, return to the wide pathway.

A newly constructed heavy-duty wooden bridge crosses Marten Creek in 3.0 miles. Look left (north) for a small cairn beside the trail marking a use trail up to Marten Lake. The Taylor River Trail begins to narrow now from its earlier, wider character and crosses several streams. The trail is rough in parts but is never difficult to follow.

After 4.5 miles of hiking, another use trail left (north) beside the trail leads to Otter Falls and a nice swimming hole. In another 0.5 mile arrive at the Big Creek Bridge—incongruously large and overbuilt given the setting. Expect to see an amazing waterfall skittering down long slabs of rock throughout the year.

Turn around and return to your car. It's possible to continue on to Dorothy Lake with a car shuttle at U.S. Highway 2 to lengthen your trip.

Enjoying a waterfall at Big Creek Bridge

## MILES AND DIRECTIONS

**0.0**    Snoqualmie Lake trailhead (Taylor River Trail): N 47° 33.634' / W 121° 31.937'

**1.0**    Quartz Creek Road: N47° 33.965' / W121° 31.810'

**3.0**    Marten Creek: N47° 35.170' / W121° 29.593'

**4.5**    Otter Falls Trail junction: N47° 35.132' / W121° 28.076'

**5.0**    Big Creek Bridge: N47° 35.217' / W121° 28.929'

**10.0**    Return to trailhead: N 47° 33.634' / W121° 31.937'

🍃 **Green Tip:**
*Never let your dog chase wildlife.*

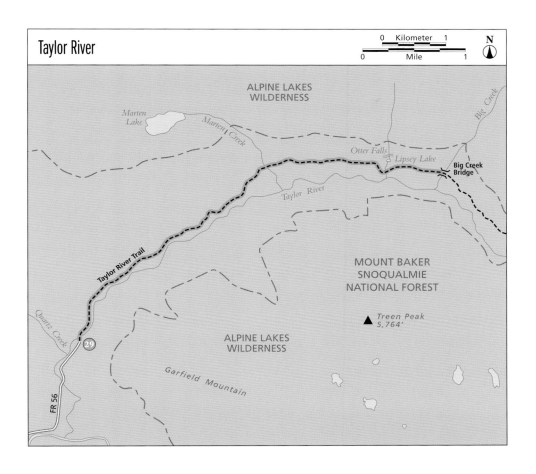

Taylor River

0 Kilometer 1
0 Mile 1
N

ALPINE LAKES
WILDERNESS

Marten
Lake

Marten Creek

Big Creek

Otter Falls

Lipsey Lake

Big Creek
Bridge

Taylor River

Taylor River Trail

MOUNT BAKER
SNOQUALMIE
NATIONAL FOREST

▲ Treen Peak
5,764'

Quartz Creek

29

ALPINE LAKES
WILDERNESS

Garfield Mountain

FR 56

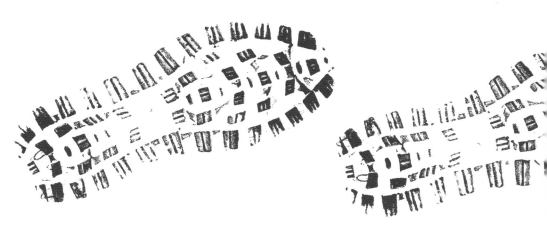

# Snoqualmie Lake–Lake Dorothy

*This hike provides an opportunity to backpack from the Snoqualmie River to the Skykomish River, with a car shuttle to bring you back home again. This backpacking traverse across the divide combines two popular day hikes with a lightly traveled middle section. Done in reverse, the Lake Dorothy Trail is a family-worthy jaunt as far as Camp Robber Creek. Thereafter it becomes a plodding uphill trudge. A day hike to Lake Dorothy is challenging without walking a considerable distance.*

**Start:** Snoqualmie Lake trailhead 1002 on Forest Road 56
**Distance:** 17.0-mile point-to-point shuttle
**Approximate hiking time:** 2 to 3 days
**Trail Numbers:** USDA Forest Service Trails 1002 and 1072
**Difficulty:** Moderate, with occasional steep terrain
**Trail surface:** Forested path, puncheon, gravel road; rocky
**Seasons:** Summer and fall
**Other trail users:** Runners; bikes (for the first 6.5 miles from the trailhead to Nordrum Lake trail junction), horses (not recommended by Forest Service)
**Canine compatibility:** Leashed dogs permitted
**Land status:** Mount Baker–Snoqualmie National Forest, Alpine Lakes Wilderness Area; USDAFS Snoqualmie Ranger District
**Nearest town:** North Bend, Baring, Sultan

**Services:** Gas, restaurants, groceries, lodging; pit toilet at Lake Dorothy trailhead; no toilet at Snoqualmie Lake trailhead
**Northwest Forest Pass:** Yes
**Maps:** Green Trails No. 174: Mount Si and No. 175: Skykomish; USGS Lake Philippa and Snoqualmie Lake; USDAFS Mount Baker–Snoqualmie National Forest
**Trail contacts:** Alpine Lakes Protection Society (ALPS): www .alpinelakes.org. Middle Fork Snoqualmie: www.midforc.org. Mount Baker–Snoqualmie National Forest, Snoqualmie Ranger District, North Bend Office, 42404 Southeast North Bend Way, North Bend, WA 98045; (425) 888-1421; www.fs.fed.us/r6/mbs/recreation. Skykomish Ranger District, 74920 Northeast Stevens Pass Highway, P.O. Box 305, Skykomish, WA 98288; (360) 677-2414; www.fs.fed .us/r6/mbs/about/srd.shtml
**Special hazards:** Loose rock; no potable water at trailhead or on trail; water purification required

**Finding the trailhead:**

***Snoqualmie Lake trailhead:*** From Seattle drive east to North Bend on Interstate 90 to exit 34 (468th Avenue SE/Edgewick Road). During winter closures of Snoqualmie Pass, this is as far east as you can drive. Turn left (north) at the stop sign and proceed past a truck stop, gas stations, and a restaurant. In less than 1 mile arrive at Southeast Middle Fork Road and turn right (east). In 1 mile bear right at a wye onto Lake Dorothy Road. Pavement ends in 1.6 miles at a pullout and small parking lot for the Mailbox Peak Trail, and the road becomes FR 56 (Forest Road 5600 on some maps).

After 2.6 miles on this good hardpack road with patches of gravel and occasional heavy zones of potholes, pass the popular Granite Creek put-in for kayakers running the Middle Fork Snoqualmie. Cross a well-built concrete bridge and, in 2.1 miles, pass the Bessemer Mountain trailhead. The Middle Fork Snoqualmie River trailhead is passed in another 4.5 miles. Pass a Forest Service campground on your left (northeast), cross the Taylor River on a smaller concrete bridge, and turn left at a junction to reach Snoqualmie Lake trailhead in 1 mile.

The road ends here at a gate and a small parking area. If the lot is full, drive back for 0.2 mile to the bridge and park along the wide spots along the road.

***Lake Dorothy trailhead:*** Drive 4.4 miles east of Baring on U.S. Highway 2 and Der Bering Store to Money Creek Road. Turn right (south) onto a paved two-lane road, immediately bridging the South Fork Skykomish River. Drive for 1 mile, crossing railroad tracks and passing USDAFS Money Creek Campground (on both sides of the road).

Turn right (south) onto Miller River Road (Forest Road 6410), a good dirt road. In about 2 miles pass the USDAFS Miller Creek group campground. After 3.7 miles reach a locked gate and bear left (east), continuing on the main road (Forest Road 6412). After 9 miles reach the trailhead.

Park in the large lot. On busy days, don't be surprised to see cars lining the road for 0.5 mile before the parking area. *Delorme: Washington Atlas and Gazetteer:* Page 80 D-4, 81 D-5.

## THE HIKE

The 1921 USGS Sultan quad shows a ranger station just downstream of the confluence with the Taylor and Snoqualmie Rivers and a trail poking up the Middle Fork. Leave your car at the Snoqualmie Lake trailhead, and pass around the stout metal gate. Immediately on the right is a short trail down to a side channel of the Taylor. It has plenty of sitting spots for lunch and bountiful views up- and downstream. Some have even used it as an informal camping area. The

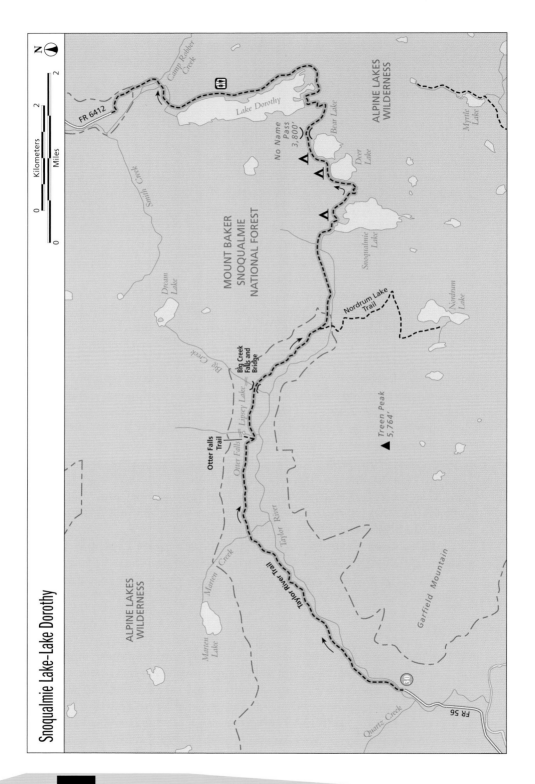

Snoqualmie Lake–Lake Dorothy

tall trunks of a mature streamside red alder forest provide shade on hot days. To continue, return to the wide pathway.

A newly constructed heavy-duty wooden bridge crosses Marten Creek in 3.0 miles. Look left (north) for a small cairn beside the trail marking a use trail up to Marten Lake. The Taylor River Trail begins to narrow now from its earlier, wider character and crosses several streams. The trail is rough in parts but is never difficult to follow.

After 4.5 miles of hiking, another use trail left (north) beside the trail leads to Otter Falls and a nice swimming hole. In another 0.5 mile arrive at the Big Creek Bridge—incongruously large and overbuilt given the setting. Expect to see an amazing waterfall skittering down long slabs of rock throughout the year.

From the highway bridge across Big Creek, continue east on Trail 1002 toward Snoqualmie Lake. There is plenty of water in Big Creek Falls throughout the summer.

The route becomes less like a road as it pushes into the forest. The roadbed continues to narrow and deteriorate and eventually ends altogether at a trail junction 1.2 miles from Big Creek. Bear left (east) to stay on route to Snoqualmie Lake. Right (south) goes to the Nordrum Lake Trail. This is the limit of permissible travel for bicycles.

The sometimes rocky and heavily eroded trail begins to climb through a young forest and enters the Alpine Lakes Wilderness, where the first thing you notice is the increased tree size. Taylor River thunders far below. Many small side streams are captured and diverted by the trail. Don't be surprised at having to walk through mud or standing and flowing water.

The trail reaches Taylor River—no longer a horizontally raging torrent but a tremendous series of cataracts. Walk off the trail a few feet to admire the river in all its vertical glory as it drops 100 feet over a staircase of rocks.

The trail climbs and finally calms down a bit 0.5 mile before reaching Snoqualmie Lake. Enter a talus field, and either plot a course through it or rely on the kindness of strangers who have ducked and/or flagged the route. Within shouting distance of the river, the trail makes one final push and reaches the heavily forested shores of Snoqualmie Lake. Two log booms have been laid across the outlet and filled in with rocks to raise the level of this already large lake. Camping is limited, of unremarkable quality, and dispersed between the outlet and a marshy area 0.2 mile farther up the trail.

Backpackers unable to locate a campsite will have to trudge up switchbacks for another mile to Deer Lake. At the end of the day, this crisscrossing uphill might seem extra steep and especially hard, so it's important to trust in the map and have faith that there is indeed a lake at the top. As recompense for having to hike farther, there are nice views of Snoqualmie Lake and its basin.

An extremely poor camping area lies within a stone's throw of tree-lined Deer Lake and right in the middle of the trail. Less marginal camping exists on the northeast shore. If those sites are occupied, walk another 0.8 mile to Bear Lake, where waytrails lead to three small campsites located along the north shore adjacent to a babbling brook. Where they are accessible from the trail, both Deer and Bear Lakes have shallow shorelines.

If you've come this far in a day, you must be tired. Set up your tent (mosquitoes and flies love it here), eat some dinner, and rest up for tomorrow.

From Bear Lake the trail ascends 0.5 mile eastward to an unnamed pass at 3,800 feet where all views are obscured by thick forest. Long switchbacks begin to drop down to Lake Dorothy. Peekaboo views through the trees transition to full-on vistas of Lake Dorothy when the trail finally reaches the water. Cool off in the lake and give your knees a well-deserved respite before the trail plunges back into the woods.

Skirt several campsites (no fires allowed), cross a wide creek coming down from Marlene and Moira Lakes, and begin a course that contours Lake Dorothy's shore. There are many fine views of the lake, with sporadic access to the water and a few campsites. The two largest camping areas have pit toilets; watch for signs.

There are many wet areas to cross on causeways. Puncheons are helpful in keeping boots and feet dry. At a junction below the lake outlet, turn left (south) to get closer to the lake; or turn right (east) and start plunging downhill on rock steps and inclined causeways.

Until reaching Camp Robber Creek, the trail hardly touches earth. Lake Dorothy has always been a popular hike, and the amount of money and effort directed

Taking a break next to a waterfall on the way to Snoqualmie Lake

toward minimizing human impacts is evident in the puncheons and inclined causeways throughout the next mile.

At Camp Robber Creek, cross on a strong metal bridge and admire views upstream and down. Even in late summer the amount of water coming down Camp Robber Creek is impressive as it slides and falls over rock smoothed by eons of runoff. This is a fine place for hikers in the opposite direction to stop for lunch and contemplate the upcoming steep trail! Careful people will find plenty of scenic resting areas below the bridge, along with a nice swimming hole for times when the water level is low.

Rejoining the trail, it's a simple matter to walk the remaining 0.5 mile to the Lake Dorothy trailhead.

## MILES AND DIRECTIONS

**0.0**  Snoqualmie Lake trailhead (Taylor River Trail): N47° 33.634' / W121° 31.937'

**1.0**  Quartz Creek Road: N47° 33.965' / W121° 31.810'

**3.0**  Marten Creek: N47° 35.170' / W121° 29.593'

**4.5**  Otter Falls Trail junction: N47° 35.132' / W121° 28.076'

**5.3**  Big Creek: N47° 35.217' / W121° 28.929'

**6.5**  Nordrum Lake junction: N47° 34.471' / W121° 26.673'

**10.9**  Snoqualmie Lake: N47° 34.359' / W121° 24.958'

**11.9**  Deer Lake: N47° 34.263' / W121° 24.205'

**12.7**  Bear Lake: N47° 34.480' / W121° 23.876'

**13.4**  Unnamed Pass: N47° 34.599' / W121° 23.385'

**14.9**  Upper Lake Dorothy: N47° 34.625' / W121° 22.937'

**16.5**  Camp Robber Creek: N47° 36.108' / W121° 22.707'

**17.0**  Lake Dorothy trailhead: N47° 36.541' / W121° 23.147'

**Options:** A rough, hard-to-find and hard-to-follow 2.5-mile trail leads to Nordrum Lake (Trail 1004) from the Snoqualmie Lake Trail about 1.2 miles southeast (N47° 34.471' / W121° 26.673') of Big Creek. Continuing on to Nordrum Lakes requires fording Taylor River. At the north end (outlet) of Nordrum Lake, the trail forks, with the main trail leading directly to the lake and the other trail continuing around the lake. Campsites can be found at the end of either route. This trail is not recommended for inexperienced hikers.

Regulations in the Alpine Lakes Wilderness limit campfires to below 4,000 feet in elevation west of the crest of the Cascade Mountain Range and below 5,000 feet in elevation east of the crest. Campfires may be restricted below these elevations due to high use and/or lack of fuel.

## Trail Hazards 3

The biggest trail hazards are caused by the smallest creatures: insects. They bite, they sting, and they suck. And there is precious little we can do except grin and bear it.

Biting flies, like the deerfly, are practiced at landing unobserved on exposed skin and causing painful bites that weep and itch for days. They are active during the day, especially around ponds, streams, and marshes. No-see-ums are small biting flies, or midges. They're extremely brutal and persistent biters active at dawn and dusk. The first aid for fly bites is to wash the bite area with soap and water and apply a bactericide and an anti-itching ointment.

Yellow jacket wasps, the bane of picnickers everywhere, can bite or sting. Yellow jackets that nest in the ground cause the biggest concern for hikers, and a misplaced foot can cause an angry nest of insects to attack. Their bite is bad; their sting is worse. Either can cause life-threatening anaphylaxis in people who are allergic. Bears, on the other hand, see yellow jackets as a huge protein source and will tear apart nests, oblivious to hordes of angry insects.

Since the introduction of West Nile virus to the United States, mosquitoes have screamed to the top of every list of concern. Only the female bites, inserting her proboscis under the skin and injecting an anticoagulant before slurping up a meal of blood. Their larvae ("wigglers") are easily found in still water. The best defense against mosquitoes is to avoid their habitat or to sparingly use repellent. Getting bitten by a mosquito is communing with nature in the most fundamental way—entering at the bottom of the food chain!

Yellow jacket wasp

# Dirty Harry's Peak

*This trail does nothing but go up until there is no more up to go—gaining 3,000 feet in less than 4 miles. The elevation gain and constantly walking over loose cobbles on the barest excuse for a trail make this route more challenging than Mount Si or McClellan Butte. But the views in all directions from the summit of Dirty Harry's Peak are stunning, and you're unlikely to run into other people up there. Ignore any flagging you see, and stick to the defined trail.*

**Start:** Southeast Grouse Ridge Road on the way to the Washington State Patrol Fire Training Center
**Distance:** 7.5 miles out and back (additional 2.5 miles out and back if parking outside the Fire Academy gate)
**Approximate hiking time:** 4 to 6 hours
**Difficulty:** Difficult; steep, rocky trail
**Trail surface:** Old rocky road
**Seasons:** Spring, summer, and fall
**Other trail users:** None
**Canine compatibility:** Leashed dogs permitted
**Land status:** Washington Department of Natural Resources; Mount Baker–Snoqualmie National Forest
**Nearest town:** North Bend
**Services:** Gas, restaurants, groceries; lodging; no toilet at trailhead
**Northwest Forest Pass:** No
**Maps:** Green Trails No. 206S: Mount Si NRCA–Snoqualmie Pass Gateway Peaks; USGS Bandera; USDAFS Mount Baker–Snoqualmie National Forest

**Trail contacts:** Alpine Lakes Protection Society (ALPS): www.alpinelakes.org. Middle Fork Snoqualmie: www.midforc.org. Mount Baker–Snoqualmie National Forest, Snoqualmie Ranger District, North Bend Office, 42404 Southeast North Bend Way, North Bend, WA 98045; (425) 888-1421; www.fs.fed.us/r6/mbs/recreation. Department of Natural Resources, South Puget Sound District, 950 Farman Street N, P.O. Box 68, Enumclaw, WA 98022-6381; (360) 825-1631. Washington State Patrol Fire Academy, 50810 Southeast Grouse Ridge Road, P.O. Box 1273, North Bend, WA 98045; (425) 453-3000; www.wa.gov/wsp/fire/fireacad.htm
**Special hazards:** Loose rock, exposure; no potable water (at trailhead or on trail)

**Finding the trailhead:**
Take Interstate 90 east from Seattle to exit 38, following signs to the Washington State Fire Training Academy. Turn right at the stop sign onto Old U.S.

Highway 10, and pass over the South Fork Snoqualmie River. Drive past Olallie State Park, and in 1.8 miles pass under the freeway and curve right onto Southeast Grouse Ridge Road. Pass through a yellow pole gate, which is posted as closing daily by 4:00 p.m. Cross over the river again, and reach the trailhead in 1.4 miles from passing under the freeway. Opposite the trailhead is AT&T post 798, with various signs indicating it as a cable route.

Parking is limited at the unmarked and unsigned trailhead to a very few wide spots along the road. Park off the pavement, and beware of soft shoulders. There is more, and better, parking available a mile back down the road at the Fire Academy gate. *Delorme: Washington Atlas and Gazetteer:* Page 64 A-3.

## THE HIKE

The trailhead is subtle—and it isn't marked. Look for it directly across from a wooden cable route post placed by AT&T with 798 on it. There is a concrete block, mostly overgrown with ferns and moss, on one side of the trailhead.

The trail is an old logging road built by a tree cutter known by the cognomen "Dirty Harry." The name predates the Clint Eastwood movie, but enough pretend history has been written about Harry Gault to confuse the issue of who he really was. Additional anonymity has been gained over the past thirty years since Harry's departure as the ort from his operations has been swallowed by a forest grown thick and tall. Since that time his road has devolved into a creekbed, and slippery cobbles add a touch of ankle danger to inattentive hikers.

A rotting bridge appears after 0.5 mile. Cross the creek and continue trudging uphill. In about another mile reach a waytrail junction leading to Dirty Harry's Balcony. Turn right (east) for a 0.5-mile detour to a lunch spot with amazing views up and down Snoqualmie Valley.

Too soon for lunch? Then continue left (northwest). Cross the creek again at a place known as Dirty Harry's Museum. Somewhere hidden in the overgrowth are rusted remnants of Harry's logging operation, including a truck: proof positive in the twenty-first century that somebody actually did drive a vehicle on this terrible road. Finding Harry's Museum entails bushwhacking up the creek through increasingly impenetrable brush.

The trail soon jogs right (east) and climbs around a rockslide. Where the trail levels out at another jog, a faint waytrail leads right (east) 0.9 mile across a humongous talus slope to tiny Lake 4353, above Granite Lakes. In another mile reach the summit of Dirty Harry's Peak after a brief, very steep climb. There are stunning peekaboo views in every direction, and trees on the summit conceal an equally stunning drop into Granite Lake below.

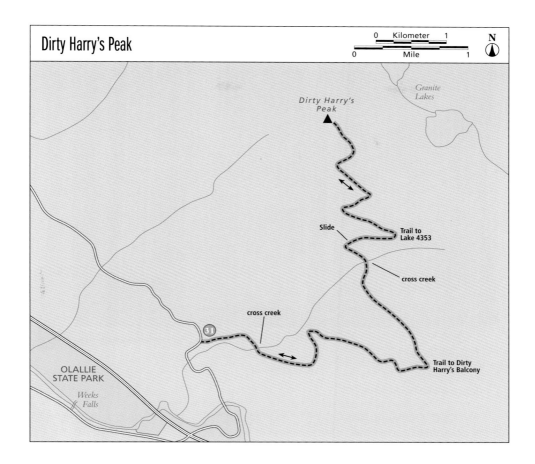

The return trip is nothing remarkable, except for the affect the steep trail and lower section cobbles have on hikers' knees.

## MILES AND DIRECTIONS

**0.0**   Trailhead on Southeast Grouse Ridge Road: N47° 26.194' / W121° 38.028'

**0.5**   Cross creek on rotting bridge: N47° 26.148' / W121° 37.656'

**1.4**   Trail junction to Dirty Harry's Balcony: N47° 26.108' / W121° 36.743'

**2.0**   Cross creek: N47° 26.520' / W121° 37.106'

**2.3**   Rockslide: N47° 26.592' / W121° 37.229'

**2.5**   Trail junction to Lake 4353: N47° 26.623' / W121° 36.932'

**3.75**  Summit of Dirty Harry's Peak: N47° 27.077' / W121° 37.298'

**7.5**   Return to trailhead: N47° 26.194' / W121° 38.028'

View from the summit

## HIKE INFORMATION

The lower end of the trail, between the road and turnoff to Dirty Harry's Balcony, is occasionally attempted on snowshoes.

Defiance Ridge runs from Mailbox Peak on its northwest end to Dirty Harry's Peak on its southeast. Below its base is flat-topped Grouse Ridge—part of the Puget Glacier's terminal moraine. The glacier descended from Canada and moved up Snoqualmie Valley.

The Fire Training Academy, located on the edge of Grouse Ridge, serves local communities, state agencies, and industry by providing live fire training to public and private fire and emergency response personnel.

> *"I had better admit right away that walking can in the end become an addiction . . . even in this final stage it remains a delectable madness, very good for sanity, and I recommend it with passion."*
> —Colin Fletcher,
> The New Complete Walker

# Bandera Mountain

*Fantastic springtime wildflower displays and distant views are the order of the day on Bandera Mountain, but hikers have to work hard for it. The steep trail gains nearly 3,000 feet in 3.0 miles and hopscotches over talus, never actually reaching the true summit. But views to the south of Mount Rainier and Mount Adams, west to the Olympics, and north to Mount Baker (even Vancouver Island on especially clear mornings) are stunning nonetheless and negate the noise of cars whooshing by on Interstate 90 far below. If those drivers only they knew how much they were missing! At the height of spring, vast fields of blooming bear grass overrun Bandera Mountain's unforested slopes.*

**Start:** Trailhead parking for Ira Spring Trail (1038)
**Distance:** 6.0 miles out and back
**Approximate hiking time:** 4 hours
**Hike Number:** USDA Forest Service Trail 1038
**Difficulty:** Strenuous; short, steep trail with talus
**Trail surface:** Forested path, old road; rocky
**Seasons:** Late spring, summer, and fall
**Other trail users:** None
**Canine compatibility:** Leashed dogs permitted
**Land status:** USDAFS Snoqualmie Ranger District; Alpine Lakes Wilderness Area
**Nearest town:** North Bend
**Services:** Gas, restaurants, groceries, lodging; unisex vault toilet at trailhead

**Northwest Forest Pass:** Yes
**Maps:** Green Trails No. 206: Bandera; USGS Bandera; USDAFS Mount Baker–Snoqualmie National Forest, Alpine Lakes Wilderness
**Trail contacts:** Alpine Lakes Protection Society (ALPS): www.alpinelakes.org. Middle Fork Snoqualmie: www.midforc.org. Mount Baker–Snoqualmie National Forest, Snoqualmie Ranger District, North Bend Office, 42404 Southeast North Bend Way, North Bend, WA 98045; (425) 888-1421; www.fs.fed.us/r6/mbs/recreation
**Special hazards:** Talus, exposure; no potable water at trailhead or on trail; no shade on second half of hike

**Finding the trailhead**
From Seattle drive east on I-90 to exit 45 (Lookout Point Road, Forest Road 9030, and Forest Road 9031). Turn left (north) at the stop sign and pass under I-90. In 0.5 mile reach a pay station on the left (south) to purchase a day-use

32

Mount Defiance from the Ira Spring Trail

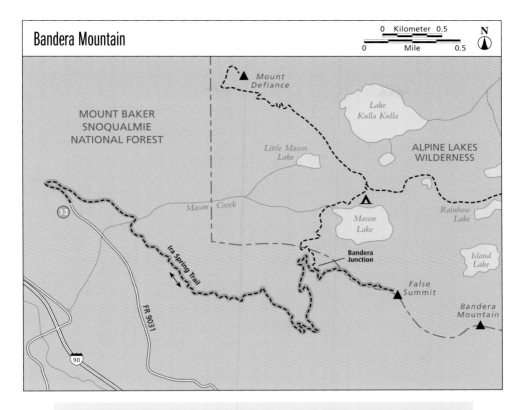

# Bandera Mountain

Northwest Forest Pass. The pavement ends and the road becomes narrow hardpack dirt with many potholes. In 0.3 mile pass the road to Talapus Lake and Trail 1039. Continue on FR 9031. After 1.6 miles pass an old logging road on the right (north). In 3.3 miles reach the large trailhead parking lot. *Delorme: Washington Atlas and Gazetteer:* Page 64 A-4.

## THE HIKE

At the trailhead, next to a vault toilet at the west end of the parking lot, is a picnic bench and a view southwest to I-90. Start on the trail, really an old road, and begin climbing at a good rate to reach Mason Creek after a short walk. Just beyond, signs of the former Mason Lake Trail that once climbed straight up along Mason Creek, are in evidence on the left (north).

The road/trail reaches a talus slope and momentarily dives out of the trees. Take this opportunity to look across the Snoqualmie Valley. The two swaths cutting east to west in the opposite slope are the John Wayne Pioneer Trail and a power line. A second talus slope means more views across the valley before the trail ducks back into the trees. The road portion soon ends in a tangle of brush, and the trail constructed in 2003 takes off up the hill.

Ascend steeply, and contemplate how much steeper the old trail must have been and how fortunate we are that the Forest Service saw fit to change things around. A third break in the forest offers more-limited views than those previous but more than makes up for it by a sidehill meadow, chock-full of wildflowers and a view up toward Bandera Mountain. Don't get your hopes up—it's still a long way to the top.

A fourth, viewless break in the forest quickly follows. Young trees are reclaiming this opening. A fifth break in the trees arrives at a switchback and affords the first good eastward view. That switchback is soon matched by another, as thinning forest segues into straggling trees. There are occasional opportunities to walk through maturing forest, but the trend is fewer trees the higher you go. This makes it possible to appreciate the scree and talus slope that marks the old route up Mason Creek. In no time, the new trail reaches those rocks, missing the worst of it by swinging east.

By this point, if it's a hot, sunny day, you're probably regretting not taking an extra liter of water, a hat, and sunscreen. If you're not prepared for more sun, it's best to consider turning back. There will be no more shade until you reach the ridge running to the summit of Bandera Mountain. A small consolation exists in fine views to the south toward Mount Rainier.

Now completely out of the trees and into talus, views keep getting better and better in all directions. Mount Defiance is the forested peak to the northwest. At 2.0 miles a sign directs hikers to Bandera Peak. Leaving the main trail, turn right (northeast) and begin climbing a trail that could use stairs and ladders.

It's all wildflowers and rocks as the trail, such as it is, climbs straight up toward a copse of trees on the Bandera ridgeline. This is a route that underlines the importance of stairclimbing as a training aid! When you're not looking at your feet, the feet of the person in front of you, or the many species of wildflowers, there are plenty of views to occupy the eye and amaze the geographer.

Once trees are reached again, the trail curves to the right (east) and, rather than going up, up and away, traverses below the ridge and hip-hops from one small stand of trees to another. The false summit of Bandera is now revealed.

If you've had it, stop here, appreciate the view, and think about going home— the views don't really get any better except for a glimpse of Mason Lake over the edge to the north.

On the other hand, if a hike isn't a hike to you without a tangible achievement (like a named peak), continue climbing along the ridge through scattered trees and talus. The trail is steep here but feels mellow compared to the first stage.

There are a few more ladderlike aspects of the trail as well as a large boulder field. If you lose your way, don't be foolish by continuing on. Be wise and backtrack

View from the summit of Bandera Mountain

to your last known location. Peekaboo views open northward with plenty of the same prodigious east, south, and west views.

Finally, dynamic views burst open to the north where many jagged mountains push their sharp peaks and ridges into the sky. There they brush up against the bottom of the powderpuff clouds that give such beauty and dramatic backdrop to azure Cascade Mountain skies.

All of a sudden the trail ends on a tiny, lightly treed promontory. Consulting their maps upon reaching the summit, many hikers are disappointed to discover they're not on the summit at all—that Bandera Mountain lies another 0.25 mile farther east. The truly disappointed continue on with arduous and heinous bushwhacking to place a tick mark beside a list of peaks they've conquered. The merely happy go no farther, enjoying the same view before returning back down the trail to their cars.

## MILES AND DIRECTIONS

**0.0**  Parking area for Ira Spring trailhead: N47° 25.485' / W121° 35.010'

**2.0**  Bandera junction: N47° 25.163' / W121° 33.375'

**3.0**  Bandera false summit: N47° 25.074' / W121° 32.858'

**6.0**  Return to trailhead: N47° 25.485' / W121° 35.010'

## HIKE INFORMATION

Bandera Mountain was named by the Mountaineers Club, evidently for the Milwaukee Railroad station of Bandera 1.5 miles to the south.

Tim's Tastee Freeze in North Bend has the best french fries and root beer floats in the world!

*"Never ride when you can walk."*
*—Bill Gale,*
**The Wonderful World of Walking**

Columbine

# Wildflowers

A famous paleobotanist by the name of Daniel Axelrod was dismayed at the amount of attention his field trip students paid to all the annual wildflowers encountered along a trail. He was accustomed to working with fossil plants preserved in stone and in terms of tens or hundreds of millions of years. Herbaceous plants are fairly recent arrivals—at least in terms of geologic time. Full of disdain, he addressed the class with, "I don't know why you're looking at that ground trash. It's going to be gone in a million years!"

It's safe to say that the only plants many people see during their perambulations around the countryside are "ground trash." In an ocean of green, the bright yellows, reds, and blues of herbaceous wildflowers are sure manifestations of spring. Bear grass (*Xerophyllum tenax*), with its basal rosette of pointy leaves and tall cluster of tiny white flowers, is found in sidehill meadows along with bistort (*Polygonum bistortoides*)—a flower that looks like somebody ran a miniature sheep up a flagpole! Some other common species seen include the bright orange of Indian paintbrush (*Castilleja* sp.), red columbine (*Aquilegia formosa*), and spotted leopard lily (*Lilium* sp.). Wet meadows are home to marsh marigold. A shrubby white wildflower is ground dogwood (*Cornus canadensis*)—a plant best known by its bark. Another shrubby plant, salal (*Gaultheria shallon*), produces urn-shaped flowers with glandular hairs. But the true harbinger of spring is the pretty, three-petaled trillium (*Trillium ovatum*).

All wildflowers bring joy and delight to our eyes. Avoid any impulse to pluck these beauties from the ground. Leave them, not only for the enjoyment of others, but also for the insects, birds, and mammals that require them for food and shelter.

Ground dogwood

# 33

## McClellan Butte

*Carved by glaciers, McClellan Butte is a prominent landmark along Interstate 90 between North Bend and Snoqualmie Pass. Heading east to the pass, look south of the highway for a sharp peak that resembles an eagle about to take flight. Though the trail has seen oodles of work in recent years, it is still brutally steep in most places, and there are precious few views to reward hikers until they almost reach the top. That said, it's an excellent alternative to Mount Si, covering a nearly equal amount of miles and eleva-tion gain, with the extra delight of significantly fewer crowds. The only real disappoint-ment with hiking to McClellan Butte is never really getting away from the interstate noise except for a very short section on the mountain's southern flank.*

**Start:** Parking area for McClellan Butte trailhead
**Distance:** 9.0 miles out and back
**Approximate hiking time:** 6 to 7 hours
**Trail Numbers:** USDA Forest Ser-vice Trail 1015
**Difficulty:** Difficult; an extremely long, steep trail
**Trail surface:** Forested path; rocky
**Seasons:** Summer and fall
**Other trail users:** None
**Canine compatibility:** Leashed dogs permitted
**Land status:** USDAFS Snoqualmie Ranger District
**Nearest town:** North Bend
**Services:** Gas, restaurants, grocer-ies, lodging; unisex vault toilet at trailhead

**Northwest Forest Pass:** Yes
**Maps:** Green Trails No. 206: Bandera and No. 206S, side B: Mount Si NRCA; USGS Bandera; USDAFS Mount Baker–Snoqualmie National Forest, Alpine Lakes Wil-derness
**Trail contacts:** Alpine Lakes Protection Society (ALPS): www. alpinelakes.org. Middle Fork Sno-qualmie: www.midforc.org. Mount Baker–Snoqualmie National For-est, Snoqualmie Ranger District, North Bend Office, 42404 South-east North Bend Way, North Bend, WA 98045; (425) 888-1421; www .fs.fed.us/r6/mbs/recreation
**Special hazards:** Exposure (at summit); no potable water at trailhead or on trail

**Finding the trailhead:**
From Seattle drive east on I-90 to exit 42 (Tinkham Road). Turn right (south) at the stop sign, cross South Fork Snoqualmie River, and travel 0.3 mile on Forest Road 55, a good gravel road. It is 0.2 mile to the parking lot. *Delorme: Washington Atlas and Gazetteer:* Page 64 A-3.

The summit

## THE HIKE

Find the trailhead at the southwestern end of the parking lot next to the toilet. Walk 100 feet and self-register at the kiosk. In 0.1 mile pass under power lines; 0.2 mile later cross an old road. In another 0.2 mile reach the Iron Horse Trail (John Wayne Pioneer Trail) and pass under another set of power lines. Turn right (north) and in 200 feet reach picnic tables, a vault toilet, and several camping pads used by bicyclists peddling the entire Iron Horse Trail—a 100-mile rail-to-trail following the bed of the Chicago, Milwaukee, St. Paul, and Pacific Railroad. It's also known as the "Milwaukee Road." In 0.4 mile cross Alice Creek, bypassing a waytrail down to the creek, and reach the McClellan Butte Trail. Turn left (southwest).

Start climbing through thick forest. The trail angles toward but never meets Alice Creek. Cross Forest Road 9020 in 0.5 mile and continue straight (northwest) up the hill. Don't be surprised to see lots of big trees, particularly as the trail climbs

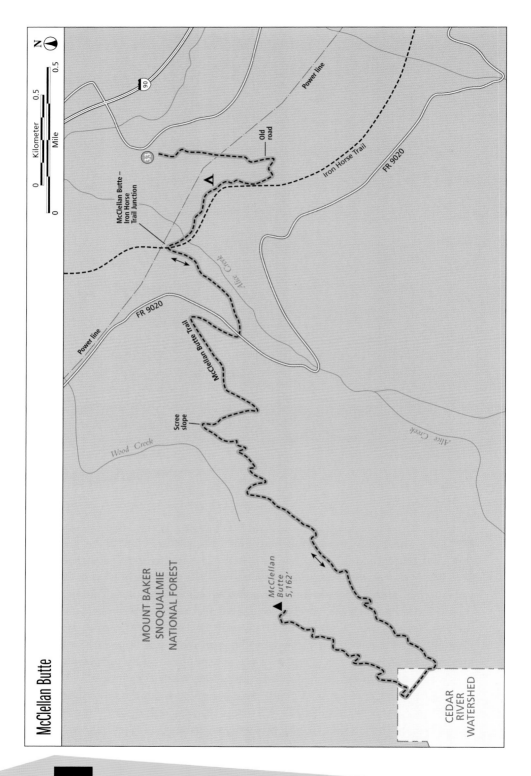

# McClellan Butte

N

| Kilometer | 0.5 |
| Mile | 0.5 |

90

33

Power line

McClellan Butte – Iron Horse Trail Junction

Old road

Iron Horse Trail

FR 9020

Alice Creek

FR 9020

Power line

McClellan Butte Trail

Scree slope

Wood Creek

Alice Creek

MOUNT BAKER SNOQUALMIE NATIONAL FOREST

McClellan Butte 5,162'

CEDAR RIVER WATERSHED

higher and higher. The way is wide and the switchbacks well graded, but this does nothing to alter how steep the trail is.

The switchbacks do, eventually, end. But the trail continues to climb by traversing upward while approaching the south side of McClellan Butte. The advantage of switchbacks becomes obvious after a minute of travel. They aren't as steep as the traverse, but by this point, everything looks vertical.

About 4.0 miles from the trailhead, views southward to Mount Rainier are possible along with a good glimpse below of Howard Hanson Reservoir in the Seattle Municipal Watershed Reserve. Don't be discouraged by the roads fairly close below the trail—no one but watershed employees is allowed to drive on them. The watershed is closed to all public use in order to safeguard Seattle's municipal water supply.

The trail actually loses some elevation before leaving its forest chrysalis and popping out onto the summit ridge. The trail ends not long afterward. From trail's end there is a short, extremely exposed Class 3 scramble to the actual summit of McClellan Butte.

Whitewater kayakers look at three elements when assessing a run. How exciting and fun will it be? How difficult? And what will the penalty phase be if anything goes awry? The route from the end of the trail to the top of McClellan Butte is not hard, and the reward in terms of viewscape is pretty good. But the penalty phase is very high. One mistake, one slip, and a person would fall and tumble all the way down to the Iron Horse Trail. For that reason, many people are more than content to go no farther. The scenery at trail's end is already good enough.

To return to the parking lot, turn around and retrace your route.

## MILES AND DIRECTIONS

**0.0**   Trailhead on Forest Road 55: N47° 24.729' / W121° 35.358'

**0.6**   Iron Horse Trail (John Wayne Pioneer Trail): N47° 24.470' / W121° 35.486'

**1.5**   Cross FR 9020: N47° 24.542' / W121° 36.160'

**4.5**   McClellan Butte: N47° 24.377' / W121° 37.363'

**9.0**   Return to trailhead: N47° 24.729' / W121° 35.358'

## HIKE INFORMATION

McClellan Butte is named for General George B. McClellan, famous for inventing the McClellan cavalry saddle and for never quite getting his act together to successfully attack the Confederate Army of Virginia during the Civil War. Insubordinate to his commander in chief, McClellan was finally relieved of command by President Abraham Lincoln.

McClellan was also the unsuccessful 1864 Democratic presidential candidate. He was forced to repudiate his party's platform of seeking an early end to the war with a negotiated settlement with the Confederacy. He served as governor of New Jersey and spent his later years writing articles and books that defended his actions during the War between the States. McClellan was an engineer by training and in 1853 helped survey rail routes across the Cascade Mountains. He preferred Yakima Pass, having failed to consider Stevens or Snoqualmie.

## Tree Stories 2

Western hemlock (*Tsuga heterophylla,* or "differently-leaved hemlock") is a common associate of Douglas fir. Viewing the branches on-end, western hemlock needles appear like little starbursts. The needles are of different lengths, and each one stands on a peglike base. From a distance, western hemlock gives the impression of being tired and fatigued (probably from trying to keep up with the distribution of its best friend and associate); the tree crown always lies limp and lazy. The dense canopy of mature western hemlock forests retards a well-developed shrub layer. The tree grows faster than any other forest tree in the Northwest. Trees reach heights of 200 feet with diameters of 3 feet. *Tsuga* is the native name for Japanese hemlocks.

Western red cedar (*Thuja plicata,* or the cedar with "leaves folded into plaits") is found growing near the coast from Alaska to Humboldt County, California, and inland to Montana. It was a popular provider of shelter, clothing, tools, and transportation to the Native Americans.

The leaves of western red cedar consist of flat, overlapping scales. Trees reach heights of 200 feet with diameters of 16 feet. Older trees are well known for possessing a tremendous buttress. A walk through a mature western red cedar forest is an olfactory enchantment verging on the divine. And yes, there is an eastern red cedar (*Juniperus virginiana*).

Western hemlock

# Mason Lake and Mount Defiance

*Mount Defiance is prominently displayed to motorists heading west on Interstate 90. They never suspect the peak harbors vast fields of wildflowers or views that stretch south to north from Oregon to Canada and west to east from the Olympic Mountains to eastern Washington. Strong hikers frequently make the round-trip journey to Mount Defiance in one day, but it's much more pleasant as an overnight excursion, with a stay at Mason Lake. There are many options to continue on as a multiday backpack trip.*

**Start:** Trailhead parking for Ira Spring Trail 1038
**Distance:** 6.4 miles out and back to Mason Lake; another 4.0 miles out and back to Mount Defiance from Mason Lake
**Approximate hiking time:** 4 to 8 hours or overnight (depending on options)
**Trail number:** USDA Forest Service Trail 1038
**Difficulty:** Strenuous; short, steep trail with talus; no water; no shade on second half of hike to Mason Lake
**Trail surface:** Forested path, old road; rocky
**Seasons:** Summer and fall
**Other trail users:** None
**Canine compatibility:** Leashed dogs permitted
**Land status:** USDAFS Snoqualmie Ranger District; Alpine Lakes Wilderness Area

**Nearest town:** North Bend
**Services:** Gas, restaurants, groceries, lodging; unisex vault toilet at trailhead
**Northwest Forest Pass:** Yes
**Maps:** Green Trails No. 206: Bandera (2002 revision shows the new trail); USGS Bandera; USDAFS Mount Baker–Snoqualmie National Forest, Alpine Lakes Wilderness
**Trail contacts:** Alpine Lakes Protection Society (ALPS): www.alpinelakes.org. Middle Fork Snoqualmie: www.midforc.org. Mount Baker–Snoqualmie National Forest, Snoqualmie Ranger District, North Bend Office, 42404 Southeast North Bend Way, North Bend, WA 98045; (425) 888-1421; www.fs.fed.us/r6/mbs/recreation
**Special hazards:** Talus; exposure; no potable water at trailhead or on trail

**Finding the trailhead:**
From Seattle drive east on I-90 to exit 45 (Lookout Point Road/Forest Roads 9030 and 9031). Turn left (north) at the stop sign and pass under I-90. In 0.5 mile stop at a pay station on the left (south) to purchase a day-use Northwest

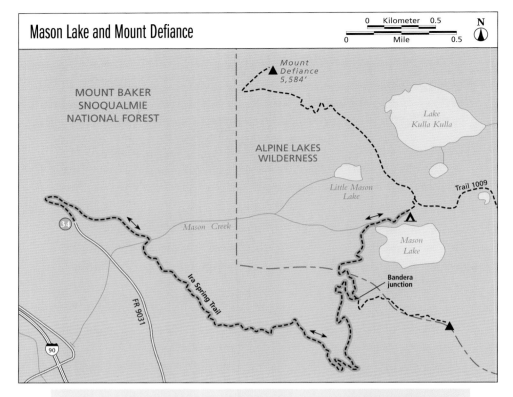

## Mason Lake and Mount Defiance

Mount Defiance 5,584'

MOUNT BAKER SNOQUALMIE NATIONAL FOREST

ALPINE LAKES WILDERNESS

Lake Kulla Kulla

Little Mason Lake

Trail 1009

Mason Creek

Mason Lake

Ira Spring Trail

FR 9031

Bandera junction

Forest Pass. The pavement now ends and the road becomes narrow, hard-pack dirt with many potholes. In 0.3 mile pass the road to Talapus Lake and Trail 1039. Continue on FR 9031. After 1.6 miles pass an old logging road on the right (north). In 3.3 miles reach the large trailhead parking lot. *Delorme: Washington Atlas and Gazetteer:* Page 64 A-4.

## THE HIKE

The trailhead for the Ira Spring Trail is located at the western end of the parking area. Self-register for travel in the Alpine Lakes Wilderness and begin walking on an old road that ascends gently through a thick forest to Mason Creek, accompanied by traffic noise from I-90. This is a lovely and cool spot to stop and rest or eat a late lunch before proceeding up the trail.

At 2.0 miles is a sign for Bandera Junction. Turn left (northwest) and traverse a slope, bare of trees, overflowing with shrubs and herbaceous growth. The wildflowers are quite stupendous through here during spring and summer. The trail doesn't exactly cease its climb, but it does mellow a bit. Cross into Alpine Lakes Wilderness and follow the trail down to Mason Lake, bidding adieu to whooshing cars and I-90. The lake was named by James Tilton, territorial surveyor during the 1850s, for Charles H. Mason, first secretary of Washington Territory.

If Mason Lake is your final destination, explore the shore or make a short hike to Little Mason Lake. If camping is your objective, there are four marginal campsites on the north shore of the lake. Wooden signs bolted to trees mark each site. No campfires are allowed. There is no toilet at the lake. Though staying at Mason Lake may not be as popular as other places in Alpine Lakes Wilderness, it can be crowded, and late campers can expect to find the sites already occupied.

If Mason Lake is not your final destination and you're looking for more adventure, the trail to Mount Defiance continues northward. Climb over a short divide and descend to a junction with Trail 1009. Right (west) leads to Rainbow Lake, Island Lake, and another junction with Trail 1007 to Pratt and Olallie Lakes. Left (west) leads to Mount Defiance.

Mason Lake

Mount Rainier from the trail

Proceeding along Trail 1009, look right (east) to occasional views through thick forest to Lake Kulla Kulla. The name is Chinook jargon and is related to the word for bird. Word repetition suggests the bird was a big one.

Soon enough the trail resumes its upward cant, and once again hikers will be huffing and puffing. Switchbacking for about a mile through heavy forest, the trail emerges onto the south slope of Mount Defiance and another wildflower and scree garden. Views southward to Mount Rainier and Mount Adams are fantastic. East is a great view of Bandera Mountain, with Mason Lake below.

Traverse west across the open slope for around 0.5 mile. Just before the trail goes around a corner to plunge back into the forest, find an unmarked and narrow waytrail leading straight up the west flank of Mount Defiance. Hike to the broad, sparsely forested summit in about 0.25 mile. Views northward into the heart of the Cascades, all the way to Glacier Peak and Mount Baker, will knock your socks off. All of Puget Sound is also visible, leading right up to the Olympic Mountains.

Retrace your steps, returning to Mason Lake or Ira Spring trailhead.

## MILES AND DIRECTIONS

**0.0**   Ira Spring trailhead: N47° 25.485' / W121° 35.010'

**2.0**   Bandera Junction: N47° 25.163' / W121° 33.375'

**3.2**   Mason Lake: N47° 25.506' / W121° 33.168'

**5.2**   Mount Defiance: N47° 26.118' / W121° 33.860'

**10.4**   Return to trailhead: N47° 25.485' / W121° 35.010'

**Options:** From Mason Lake it is possible to continue on to Thompson Lake (northwest on Trail 1009) or Rainbow, Island, Pratt, Olallie, and Talapus Lakes (east on Trail 1009, Trail 1007, and Trail 1039) with car shuttles.

## HIKE INFORMATION

This trail is named to memorialize photographer, author, and activist Ira Spring, who, with help from Volunteers for Outdoor Washington, urged the Forest Service to close the original trail to Mason Lake. Originally built in 1958 to enable fire crews access to the lake, the old route was badly eroded and went straight up Mason Creek, gaining 1,700 feet within a mile. The new trail was built in 2003.

> *"An early morning walk is a blessing for the whole day."*
> —*Henry David Thoreau*

*This popular and well-known trail has everything: a rushing and thundering creek, waterfalls, old-growth forest, wildflowers, views, camping, and a lake.*

**Start:** Trailhead parking for Annette Lake Trail 1019 and Asahel Curtis Nature Trail
**Distance:** 7.2 miles out and back, including side trip to campsites
**Approximate hiking time:** 4 to 5 hours
**Trail number:** USDA Forest Service Trail 1019
**Difficulty:** Moderate, with several steep sections
**Trail surface:** Forested path; rocky
**Seasons:** Spring, summer, and fall
**Other trail users:** Runners
**Canine compatibility:** Leashed dogs permitted
**Land status:** USDAFS Snoqualmie Ranger District
**Nearest town:** North Bend

**Services:** Gas, restaurants, groceries, lodging. USDAFS Tinkham, Commonwealth, and Denny Creek Campgrounds nearby along I-90; unisex vault toilet at trailhead
**Northwest Forest Pass:** Yes
**Maps:** Green Trails No. 207: Snoqualmie; USGS Lost Lake and Snoqualmie Pass; USDAFS Mount Baker–Snoqualmie National Forest
**Trail contacts:** Mount Baker–Snoqualmie National Forest, Snoqualmie Ranger District, North Bend Office, 42404 Southeast North Bend Way, North Bend, WA 98045; (425) 888-1421; www.fs.fed .us/r6/mbs/recreation
**Special hazards:** No potable water at trailhead or on trail

**Finding the trailhead:**
From Seattle take Interstate 90 east to exit 47 (Tinkham Road/Denny Creek–Asahel Curtis). At the stop sign turn right (south) onto Tinkham Road and cross the Snoqualmie River on a narrow two-lane bridge. At the T intersection turn left (east) onto Forest Road 55. Drive for 0.4 mile and park in a huge paved lot. *Delorme: Washington Atlas and Gazetteer: Page 65 A-5.*

Annette Lake

## THE HIKE

Find the Annette Lake Trail at the southeast end of the parking lot between the Asahel Curtis Nature Trail and a gated, wide gravel road. Begin your 1,200-foot climb to Annette Lake by ascending to the sound of I-90 on a narrow, well-trod forest path. In a hundred feet is a self-serve trail register. Cross Humpback Creek on a stout new log bridge funded in part in 2003 by the Spring Trust for Trails. The creek is an impressive cataract and would be impassible without the bridge.

Cross the old road observed at the trailhead, and continue going up the trail. Cross the road again in a few hundred feet. In 0.6 mile pass under a power line and then plunge back into the forest. In 0.7 mile cross the John Wayne Pioneer Trail (Old Milwaukee Railroad grade) and find the Annette Lake Trail continuing on the other side.

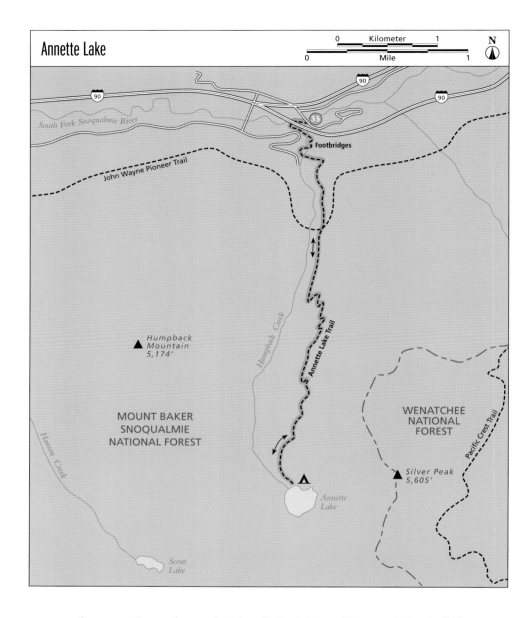

Cross a pretty creek on a double split-log bridge with a sturdy handrail. The higher you go, the bigger the trees. Soon enter an old-growth forest and reach a wet meadow, a short boardwalk, and an interesting bridge. In a burst of creativity, trail builders incorporated a fallen cedar log in their span, cutting steps into the trunk and adding a handrail. This sort of artistic sense is a sure sign that the trail crew saw more than just ground to be traversed. Applaud their work!

The trail steepens, and switchbacks begin. Let your gaze rise away from the ground periodically, past and through the trees—as you go higher, views across Snoqualmie Valley and down Humpback Creek begin to open up. In about 3.2 miles the trail finally flattens out as it climbs over the lip of a hanging valley and begins its last push to the lake.

Reach Annette Lake in 3.5 miles. Cross the creek to a small day-use area in and among the trees. Or find a seat with the crowds beside the outflow. A better idea is to turn left (east) and walk 0.1 mile on waytrails to the camping area. There is lake access here, as well as fine picnicking with nice views across the lake to a waterfall, Silver Peak, and Humpback Mountain. Please respect those people who have chosen to camp here by remaining outside their campsites and away from their tents. Thank you.

Retrace your route to reach the parking lot.

## MILES AND DIRECTIONS

**0.0**   Trailhead parking for Annette Lake Trail 1019: N47° 23.565' / W121° 28.427'

**0.2**   Bridge over Humpback Creek: N47° 23.445' / W121° 28.439'

**0.7**   John Wayne Pioneer Trail: (Old Milwaukee Railroad grade): N47° 23.091' / W121° 28.231'

**3.5**   Annette Lake: N47° 21.617' / W121° 28.520'

**3.6**   Campsites: N47° 21.603' / W121° 28.406'

**7.2**   Return to trailhead: N47° 23.565' / W121° 28.427'

**Options:** The Asahel Curtis Nature Trail begins right next door to the Annette Lake Trail. The nature trail is a perfect introduction to the forest for children and newcomers to Seattle. Use caution walking on the cedar boardwalk—the planks become slippery when wet. A pamphlet for a self-guided walk on the nature trail is often available at the trailhead.

Silver Peak was a popular climb for The Mountaineers during the 1930s. A route exists from the Pacific Crest Trail on the east side of the peak to the summit. People very experienced in off-trail hiking and scrambling over boulders and scree have been known to make their way up Silver Peak from Annette Lake. Hikers have also made the difficult traverse from Silver Peak to Humpback Mountain via Abiel Peak across steep slopes with loose rock, exposure, and lots of bushwhacking.

Asahel Curtis, a photographer (and brother of photographer Edward Curtis) who documented the natural history and historical events of Washington, wrote: "One comes more intimately in touch with the mountains when he travels the trails. In the valleys the forests seem lower, the giant trees rise from one's side to tremendous heights, and the lower growth reaches out a friendly hand to bid you welcome; but it is on the untrodden mountain heights that the traveler receives a true reward for his toil. Here where vegetation makes its last stand amid a world of ice and snow, with the lower world stretching away to the distant horizon, nature unfolds in all her beauty."

**Green Tip:**
*Reuse zip-top bags.*

# Melakwa Lake

*Most hikers know the Denny Creek Trail for its waterslide—admittedly a worthy goal, especially on a hot day or with small children in tow. Ah! But there is so much more to amaze and delight farther up the trail, including old-growth forest, two long waterfalls, wildflower gardens, and a subalpine lake with limited camping possibilities. This is a popular trail; don't be surprised to see large groups of people, especially on weekends.*

**Start:** Denny Creek trailhead
**Distance:** 8.0 miles out and back to Melakwa Lake; 9.0 miles out and back to Upper Melakwa Lake
**Approximate hiking time:** 6 hours
**Trail number:** USDA Forest Service Trail 1014
**Difficulty:** Moderate, with steep sections and exposure at waterfall viewpoints
**Trail surface:** Forested path; rocky
**Seasons:** Summer and fall
**Other trail users:** Llamas
**Canine compatibility:** Leashed dogs permitted. The Forest Service frequently patrols this trail and issues expensive tickets to owners of unleashed dogs
**Land status:** USDAFS Snoqualmie Ranger District, Alpine Lakes Wilderness

**Nearest town:** North Bend
**Services:** Gas, restaurants, groceries, lodging; limited services at Snoqualmie Pass; camping at USDAFS Denny Creek Campground; unisex vault toilet at trailhead
**Northwest Forest Pass:** Yes
**Maps:** Green Trails No. 207: Snoqualmie Pass; USGS Snoqualmie Pass; USDAFS Mount Baker–Snoqualmie National Forest
**Trail contacts:** Mount Baker–Snoqualmie National Forest, Snoqualmie Ranger District, North Bend Office, 42404 Southeast North Bend Way, North Bend, WA 98045; (425) 888-1421; www.fs.fed.us/r6/mbs/recreation
**Special hazards:** Devil's club; loose rock; exposure; no potable water at trailhead or on trail

**Finding the trailhead:**
 From Seattle take Interstate 90 east to exit 47 (Tinkham Road/Denny Creek–Asahel Curtis). Turn left (north) at the stop sign, cross over I-90, and turn right (east) at the T intersection. Pass under I-90, and after 0.2 mile reach Denny Creek Road (Forest Road 58); turn left (north). Cross Denny Creek on a metal bridge in 1.8 miles, continuing on the paved road. After 2.1 miles reach the USDAFS Denny Creek Campground and continue on FR 58 past the campground. In 0.2

mile turn left (west) onto Forest Road 5830, a paved road. Cross Denny Creek on a narrow concrete bridge, pass parking for Franklin Falls Trail 1036, and continue to the end of a gradually worsening road in 0.3 mile. Pay attention to No Parking signs along the road in the vicinity of the private cabins, and do not block driveways in the parking permitted areas. Parking at the trailhead lot is limited. Be kind: Use only one space and leave room for others. *Delorme: Washington Atlas and Gazetteer:* Page 65 A-5.

## THE HIKE

The trail begins on the northwest side of the parking lot, adjacent to the unisex vault toilet. Begin on a level stretch with noisy Denny Creek nearby. The trail soon climbs on a series of stairs and after about 0.1 mile reaches a bridge over Denny Creek. Rocky and log choked, the creek loudly flows below. Look upstream and see the I-90 viaduct high above; after 0.5 mile pass under it.

The trail now begins to climb in earnest on a well-constructed and well-graded trail. Cross the Alpine Lakes Wilderness boundary in about 1.0 mile. Sounds from Denny Creek are still evident in places, but highway noise is completely gone. There are plenty of opportunities to step off the trail and admire Denny Creek and its cataracts.

Cross Denny Creek again after 1.1 miles to reach the famous Denny Creek waterslide. Most families stop here, and it's easy to see why. This popular place is a playground for children of all ages. Sit on the big slab of granite and soak up the rays or dip your body in the cold, refreshing creek. Maintain a watchful eye on young children, and keep dogs on their leash. Explore upstream a few hundred feet to a small cascade. Look downstream and observe the old bridge—a sawn log.

Find the Main Trail sign, and resume the route to Melakwa Lake with significantly fewer people. The trail punches out of the forest and into the open after 1.6 miles with views upcanyon. Climbing through this open slope on switchbacks, the trail reaches a viewpoint of Keekwulee Falls in another 0.2 mile.

Cross a talus field and reenter the forest. Sharp eyes will spot several waytrails through the trees and underbrush to Denny Creek and the lip of the falls. Switchbacks play hide-and-seek with talus and forest, zigzagging in and out of each. There are plenty of viewpoints down sheer cliffs to Denny Creek.

In 0.4 mile the switchbacks top out. There is no access to Snowshoe Falls. Cross Denny Creek on a sawn log, and traverse another, longer talus slope. Up the canyon is forested Hemlock Pass. Downstream are views to Snoqualmie Valley. At your feet are gardens of wildflowers, including columbine (*Aquilegia furmosa*), bluebells (*Mertensia* sp.), various sedges (*Carex* sp.), marsh marigold (*Caltha* sp.), shooting stars (*Dodecatheon* sp.), saxifrage (*Saxifraga* sp.), bracken fern (*Pteridium aquilinum*), yellow violets (*Viola sempervirens*), and red alder (*Alnus rubra*).

Melakwa Lake

Tighter and tighter switchbacks lead to Hemlock Pass (no view), where the trail descends through thick forest to a trail junction. Turn left (west) to drop steeply in 2.9 miles and visit Tuscohatchie Lake on Trail 1011. Continue straight (north) and quickly reach Melakwa Lake after a short uphill push. Cross the outlet stream on a logjam. A small sign bolted to a tree directs hikers and campers to an outhouse.

Camping around the outlet is limited and of poor quality. The best sites are located on the opposite shore. No fires are permitted.

An optional 0.5-mile hike continues along the west shore of Melakwa Lake and leads to Upper Melakwa Lake, which affords more solitude. This tiny basin is surrounded by huge talus fields, one of which leads upward to Melakwa Pass, with Kaleetan Peak on the west and Chair Peak to the east.

Return to the trailhead by retracing your route over Hemlock Pass and down Denny Creek.

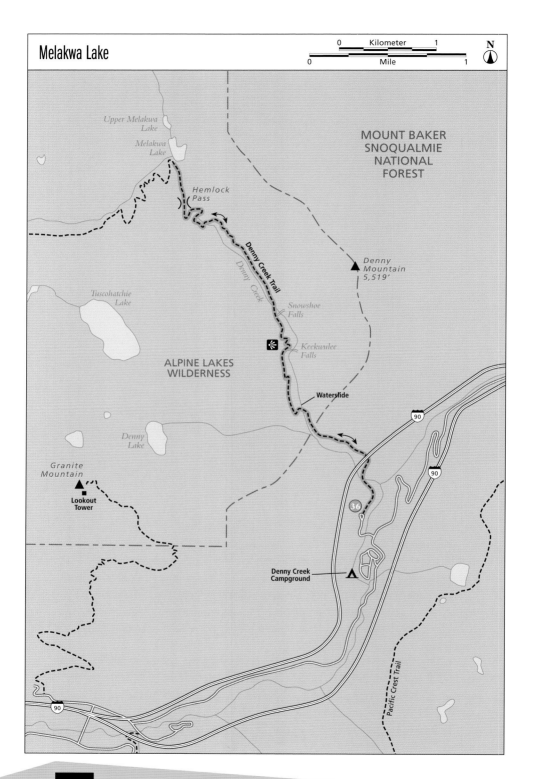

# Melakwa Lake

Kilometer

Mile

**N**

Upper Melakwa Lake

Melakwa Lake

Hemlock Pass

Denny Creek Trail

Denny Creek

Denny Mountain 5,519'

**MOUNT BAKER SNOQUALMIE NATIONAL FOREST**

Tuscohatchie Lake

Snowshoe Falls

Keekwulee Falls

**ALPINE LAKES WILDERNESS**

Waterslide

Denny Lake

Granite Mountain

Lookout Tower

90

90

36

Denny Creek Campground

Pacific Crest Trail

90

**0.0**   Denny Creek trailhead: N47° 24.914' / W121° 26.589'

**0.9**   Alpine Lakes Wilderness boundary: N47° 25.346' / W121° 26.960'

**1.1**   Waterslide: N47° 25.508' / W121° 27.096'

**1.8**   Keekwulee Falls viewpoint: N47° 25.791' / W121° 27.248'

**3.5**   Hemlock Pass: N47° 26.673' / W121° 28.083'

**4.0**   Melakwa Lake: N47° 26.958' / W121° 28.180'

**4.5**   Upper Melakwa Lake: N47° 27.118' / W121° 28.189'

**9.0**   Return to trailhead: N47° 24.914' / W121° 26.589'

**Options:** Franklin Falls (2.0 miles out and back). Access to Melakwa Lake on Trail 1011 (3.2 miles) via Pratt Lake Trail 1007 (5.5 miles).

## HIKE INFORMATION

*Melakwa,* or *malakwa,* means "mosquito" in Chinook jargon, the pidgin language forced upon natives of the Pacific Northwest as a *lingua franca* by French, English, and American traders too lazy to learn the actual languages of the region. During spring and summer, expect several different kinds of annoying flies at the lake, too.

Arthur A. Denny was leader of the party that founded the city of Seattle in 1852. Being first on the scene, Denny was well situated to profit from those who came later and, as one of the city fathers, encourage and finance Seattle's expansion. During the late 1860s Denny poked around the Snoqualmie Pass area, prospecting for ore and scouting a hoped-for wagon road, or even railroad, over the Cascades. Denny Creek and Denny Mountain honor his pioneering efforts. There are many other places in King County with the Denny moniker, including a major street in Seattle. The Denny family plot in Lake View Cemetery on Capitol Hill is not to be missed. It uses impressive amounts of granite, features a Teutonic eagle–topped pillar, and occupies a large swath of property.

> *"I may not have gone where I intended to go, but I think I have ended up where I intended to be."*
> —*Douglas Adams, English humorist and science fiction novelist*

*There is a cost to popularity. Along with Talapus Lake, Olallie Lake has long been heavily overused and will probably continue to be so. The two lakes, beautifully situated in forested basins, are fairly close to the trailhead, relatively easy to reach, and provide both fishing and swimming opportunities.*

**Start:** Pratt Lake trailhead

**Distance:** 6.0 miles out and back

**Approximate hiking time:** 4 hours

**Hike number:** USDA Forest Service Trail 1007

**Difficulty:** Moderate

**Trail surface:** Forested path; rocky

**Seasons:** Summer and fall

**Other trail users:** None

**Canine compatibility:** Leashed dogs permitted

**Land status:** USDAFS Snoqualmie Ranger District, Alpine Lakes Wilderness Area

**Nearest town:** North Bend

**Services:** Gas, restaurants, groceries, lodging; vault toilet at trailhead

**Northwest Forest Pass:** Yes

**Maps:** Green Trails No. 207: Snoqualmie Pass and No. 206: Bandera; USGS Snoqualmie Pass; USDAFS Mount Baker–Snoqualmie National Forest, Alpine Lakes Wilderness

**Trail contacts:** Alpine Lakes Protection Society (ALPS): www .alpinelakes.org. Middle Fork Snoqualmie: www.midforc.org. Mount Baker–Snoqualmie National Forest, Snoqualmie Ranger District, North Bend Office, 42404 Southeast North Bend Way, North Bend, WA 98045; (425) 888-1421; www .fs.fed.us/r6/mbs/recreation

**Special hazards:** Devil's club; no potable water at trailhead or on trail

**Finding the trailhead:**
From Seattle drive east on Interstate 90 to exit 47 (Tinkham Road/Denny Creek–Asahel Curtis). At the stop sign turn left (north); cross over I-90, and in 0.1 mile turn left (west) at the intersection onto a good gravel road. Follow signs to Granite Mountain Lookout, and in 0.3 mile reach the trailhead parking. *Delorme: Washington Atlas and Gazetteer:* Page 65 A-5.

Olallie Lake

## THE HIKE

The large sign announcing Pratt Lake Trail 1007 lists ten lakes and one fire lookout as destinations for this popular route. The wide and rocky trail begins past the information kiosk. Self-register for the Alpine Lakes Wilderness, and begin walking up the trail on a decent grade over long, loosely structured, meandering switchbacks. The sounds of I-90 filter through the thick forest of old trees. Cross numerous seasonal creeks in the first 0.5 mile. At 1.0 mile from the parking area, continue straight (west) past a trail leading east and north to Granite Mountain Lookout. Soon afterward cross two channels of an ephemeral stream that can run high early and late during the year.

At 1.5 miles pass through a narrow, rocky dell below an attractive cataract. The water crosses over slabs of rock with many small waterfalls. Following a brief steep section, the trail starts a traverse of Granite Mountain, reaching a long boardwalk that keeps hikers' feet dry and an equally long sidehill meadow from being trampled to death. At the end of the boardwalk, enter Alpine Lakes Wilderness.

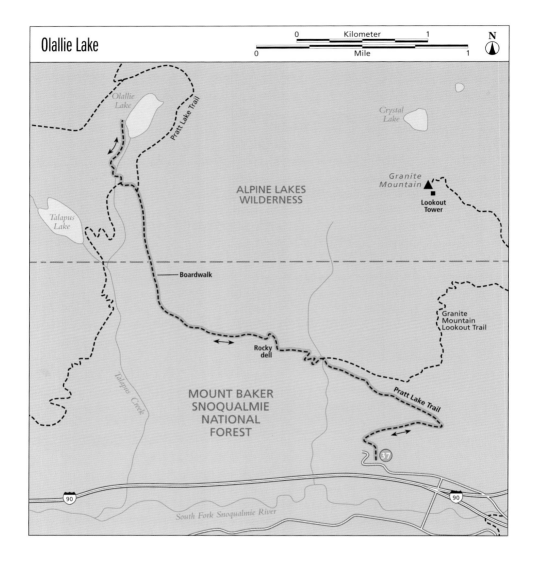

Kilometer

Mile

N

Olallie
Lake

Pratt Lake Trail

Crystal
Lake

Granite
Mountain

Lookout
Tower

ALPINE LAKES
WILDERNESS

Talapus
Lake

Boardwalk

Granite
Mountain
Lookout Trail

Rocky
dell

Pratt Lake Trail

MOUNT BAKER
SNOQUALMIE
NATIONAL
FOREST

Talapus Creek

37

90

90

South Fork Snoqualmie River

At the junction of Pratt Lake and Olallie Lake Trails, turn left (west). Hikers who continue straight (north) pass 100 feet or so above Olallie Lake, reaching a viewpoint of the lake before crossing a divide and plunging down to Pratt Lake.

In 0.15 miles cross Talapus Creek on rocks and reach a junction, turning right (north) toward Olallie Lake. A few switchbacks and 0.2 mile later, Olallie Lake comes into view.

Campsites are small and scattered. No fires are allowed at Olallie Lake. Swimming is good; fishing is fair. There is a pretty view to the north and the head of the lake to gentle slopes, forest and, talus fields. To return home, retrace your route back down the trail.

**0.0** Pratt Lake trailhead: N47° 23.872' / W121° 29.189'

**1.0** Pratt Lake Trail and Granite Mountain Lookout Trail junction: N47° 24.192' / W121° 29.247'

**1.5** Rocky dell: N47° 24.332' / W121° 29.791'

**2.0** Alpine Lakes Wilderness boundary: N47° 24.822' / W121° 30.591'

**2.7** Pratt Lake Trail and Olallie Lake Trail junction: N47° 25.029' / W121° 30.624'

**2.8** Olallie Lake Trail and Talapus Lake Trail junction: N47° 25.094' / W121° 30.814'

**3.0** Olallie Lake: N47° 25.315' / W121° 30.735'

**6.0** Return to trailhead: N47° 23.872' / W121° 29.189'

> *"Part of the pleasure of any kind of walking for me is the very idea of going somewhere—by foot."*
> —*Ruth Rudner,* **Forgotten Pleasures: A Guide for the Seasonal Adventurer**

## There's a Fungus Among Us

Mushrooms are the most commonly seen fungus, but there are many other kinds, including athlete's foot and ringworm fungi, bread molds, and the penicillin-producing mold that grows on oranges. What we see as a mushroom is actually the fruiting body of an organism that grows below the soil surface, living off the detritus produced by plants and animals. Loosely interpreted, this makes mushrooms the equivalent of an apple or tomato with the fungal spores being equivalent to seeds.

At one time mushrooms were considered plants because they were non-motile. But biologists now agree that plants must photosynthesize, and since fungi don't ... Also, plant cell walls consist of cellulose and lignin. Fungal cells are made of chitin, a substance also found in the hard outer shells of insects and other arthropods.

The body of mushroom fungi consists of whitish or grayish strands called hyphae. The hyphae absorb moisture and nutrients, growing over, under, around, and through the soil and often by growing into an object. Some fungi are involved in a mycorrhizal association with the roots of conifers. In this complex relationship, the fungus derives photosynthate from the tree. In return, the fungus provides the tree with a greater surface area to absorb water and mineral nutrition from the soil.

Fly agaric

# Snow Lake

*The popular (25,000 annual visitors) route up to Snow Lake swarms with people during summer, and finding a place to hang out along the lake's rocky beach is close to impossible on sunny weekends. Still, the lake sits within a gorgeous setting and should not be missed. An excursion in the fall to pick huckleberries is bound to find fewer people. Such is the popularity of the lake that even a rainy day sees plenty of visitors but at least no crowds. In spring, fields of wildflowers bloom at regular intervals along the trail—another reason for the lake's popularity.*

**Start:** Trailhead parking at Alpental Ski Area
**Distance:** 7.0 miles out and back
**Approximate hiking time:** 6 hours
**Trail number:** USDA Forest Service Trail 1013
**Difficulty:** Moderate, with steep areas
**Trail surface:** Forested path; rocky
**Seasons:** Summer and fall
**Other trail users:** Llamas and goats
**Canine compatibility:** Leashed dogs permitted
**Land status:** USDAFS Snoqualmie Ranger District, Alpine Lakes Wilderness Area
**Nearest town:** Snoqualmie Pass
**Services:** Gas, restaurants, lodging; unisex vault toilet at trailhead

**Northwest Forest Pass:** Yes
**Maps:** Green Trails No. 207: Snoqualmie Pass; USGS Snoqualmie Pass; USDAFS Mount Baker–Snoqualmie National Forest, Alpine Lakes Wilderness
**Trail contacts:** Alpine Lakes Protection Society (ALPS): www.alpinelakes.org. Middle Fork Snoqualmie: www.midforc.org. Mount Baker–Snoqualmie National Forest, Snoqualmie Ranger District, North Bend Office, 42404 Southeast North Bend Way, North Bend, WA 98045; (425) 888-1421; www.fs.fed.us/r6/mbs/recreation
**Special hazards:** Loose rock; no potable water at trailhead or on trail

**Finding the trailhead:**
From Seattle drive east on Interstate 90 and take exit 52 (west summit to Snoqualmie Pass). Turn left (north) onto Forest Road 9040 (unmarked) and then turn right (north) at Alpental Road, the second street. After 1.5 miles enter a large gravel parking lot used by Alpental Ski Area. Park in the northernmost section of the lot. There is a vault toilet hidden behind some trees. *Delorme: Washington Atlas and Gazetteer:* Page 65 A-5.

Snow Lake

## THE HIKE

Cross Alpental Road from the parking area (no public access is allowed past the car park) and find the marked trailhead. There is a self-registration station for Alpine Lakes Wilderness and an information kiosk. Climb a series of stairs constructed of logs, which finally ends at a rocky trail that traverses the hillside across several avalanche chutes. The area around Snoqualmie Pass is part of the Naches Formation, volcanic rocks interlaid with sandstone that were deposited around forty-five million years ago. There are good exposures of Eocene andesite in the cliffs and rocks around these chutes.

The trees around here are big. If hiking the Puget Sound lowlands has taken the edge off experiencing western hemlock (*Tsuga heterophylla*), enjoy these big boys—they are mountain hemlock (*Tsuga mertensiana*). The cones are much smaller than their lowland relatives, and the tree needles lack the distinctive starburst appearance of western hemlock. Both species share the characteristic tree crown, which bends over like a limp wrist.

Ascend through the forest and avalanche chutes, cross talus fields, and in 2.0 miles reach the Source Lake Overlook Trail junction. This 1.0-mile round-trip spur trail takes hikers across rock slopes to look down upon the source of South Fork Snoqualmie River.

Continuing east and north to Snow Lake, the trail begins to switchback uphill. The sometimes-rocky trail rises upslope, at times crossing the same avalanche chute visited below. The upper part of the trail is replaced in steeper areas by log steps. Cross the Alpine Lakes Wilderness boundary at 2.5 miles; cross over the lip into Snow Lake basin, and begin to descend.

The lake is visible through the trees as the trail crosses a talus field and keeps on dropping. Above the lakeshore is a sign, perhaps left by Paul Bunyan, directing hikers to campsites, the main trail, and ruins of a stone-walled cabin and cautioning everyone that no fires are allowed.

Walk past the toilet, a cute waterfall and pool, lots of blocked-off waytrails, and the vaguely delimited main trail that continues on up the valley. Reach the cabin

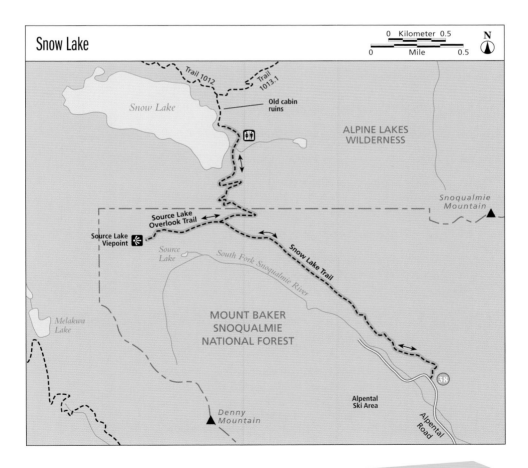

Snow Lake

ruins—a house really, and a large one at that. Many of the rock walls are still standing, as is what must have been a very nice fireplace. Campsites and lake access lie below.

It's impossible to hike in the Pacific Northwest without spending some time walking in the rain. There are advantages to this! In popular places like Snow Lake, expect fewer people on the trails. Rain walking is a great opportunity to leave your stuffy house, and it beats being cooped up all day. In autumn there are huckleberries to pick and fall colors to enjoy. And at the end of the day, no matter how wet you are, you can always go home and take a hot shower. Just make sure you come prepared for wet weather by bringing along the best rain gear you can afford, plenty of warm (and dry) clothes, food, and energy snacks.

Campsites at Snow Lake are poor, and many of the best are now prohibited from use so that the ground can recover from generations of heavy abuse. No fires are allowed, and group size is limited to twelve. Good luck, though, finding ample camping close to one another if you have a group that big.

On the return, retrace your steps down the Snow Lake Trail. At the junction with Source Lake Overlook, detour 0.5 mile to admire the cliffs and numerous creeks where South Fork Snoqualmie River begins. Come back to the main trail and keep heading downhill to the parking lot at Alpental.

## MILES AND DIRECTIONS

**0.0**  Trailhead at Alpental parking lot: N47° 26.719' / W121° 25.411'

**2.0**  Source Lake Overlook Trail junction: N47° 27.484' / W121° 26.877'

**2.5**  Alpine Lakes Wilderness boundary: N47° 27.606' / W121° 26.817'

**3.0**  Old cabin (ruins): N47° 27.835' / W121° 26.783'

**3.0**  Snow Lake: N47° 27.854' / W121° 26.801'

**4.5**  Source Lake view: N47° 27.437' / W121° 27.307'

**9.0**  Return to trailhead: N47° 26.719' / W121° 25.411'

**Options:** From Snow Lake, Trail 1012 goes on, faintly in parts, to Gem and Upper Wildcat Lakes. Or follow Trail 1013.1 to the Middle Fork Snoqualmie (car shuttle required).

*"Before you criticize someone, you should walk a mile in their shoes. That way when you criticize them, you're a mile away and have their shoes."*
—*Frieda Norris*

# Lake Lillian

*Because it begins by climbing a clear-cut hillside, this isn't as popular a route as found elsewhere around Snoqualmie Pass. But that prejudice aside, the trail soon enters an old-growth forest and leads to a beautiful lake surrounded by awesome cliffs and craggy mountains. Along the way are dynamite views across the spine of the Cascades plus a shot at Mount Rainier. Wildflowers are abundant during summer in wet meadows surrounding Twin Lakes and the talus field below Lillian Lake.*

**Start:** Margaret Lake trailhead parking
**Distance:** 9.0 miles out and back
**Approximate hiking time:** 6 to 7 hours
**Trail number:** USDA Forest Service Trail 1332
**Difficulty:** Difficult, with sections of narrow trail that are straight up and down
**Trail surface:** Forested path; rocky
**Seasons:** Summer and fall
**Other trail users:** Illegal use by mountain bikers is a problem on this hikers-only trail
**Canine compatibility:** Dogs prohibited
**Land status:** Wenatchee National Forest, Cle Elum District; Alpine Lakes Wilderness Area
**Nearest town:** Snoqualmie Pass
**Services:** Gas, restaurants, lodging; no toilet at trailhead

**Northwest Forest Pass:** Yes
**Maps:** Green Trails No. 207: Snoqualmie Pass; USGS Chikamin Peak; USDAFS Mount Baker–Snoqualmie National Forest, Alpine Lakes Wilderness
**Trail contacts:** Alpine Lakes Protection Society (ALPS): www.alpinelakes.org. Middle Fork Snoqualmie: www.midforc.org. Wenatchee National Forest, Cle Elum Ranger District, 803 West Second Street, Cle Elum, WA 98922; (509) 852-1100; www.fs.fed.us/r6/wenatchee. Mount Baker–Snoqualmie National Forest, Snoqualmie Ranger District, North Bend Office, 42404 Southeast North Bend Way, North Bend, WA 98045; (425) 888-1421; www.fs.fed.us/r6/mbs/recreation
**Special hazards:** Loose rock; no potable water at trailhead or on trail

**Finding the trailhead:**
From Seattle take Interstate 90 east to exit 54 (Gold Creek). Turn left (north) at the end of the off-ramp. Proceed 0.2 mile, go under the interstate, and pass the on-ramp to I-90 westbound. Turn right (east) on Gold Creek Road (Forest Road 4832), and begin paralleling I-90. After 2.0 miles the road narrows to one lane, becoming gravel at 2.4 miles. At 2.7 miles the road makes a switchback, leaving I-90 behind.

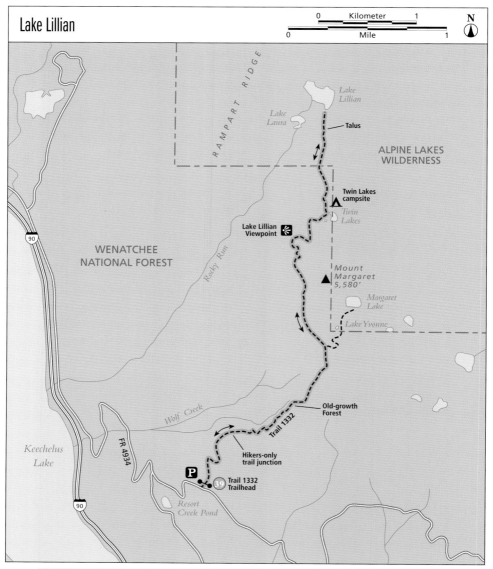

0      Kilometer      1

0      Mile      1

N

RAMPART RIDGE

Lake Lillian

Lake Laura

Talus

ALPINE LAKES WILDERNESS

Twin Lakes campsite

Twin Lakes

Lake Lillian Viewpoint

WENATCHEE NATIONAL FOREST

Rocky Run

Mount Margaret 5,580'

Margaret Lake

Lake Yvonne

Old-growth Forest

Wolf Creek

Trail 1332

Keechelus Lake

FR 4934

Hikers-only trail junction

P

39   Trail 1332 Trailhead

Resort Creek Pond

Though the road is in good shape, consider bringing some laundry—it's heavily washboarded. The road climbs steadily to another switchback at 3.7 miles and then another switchback at 3.9 miles and a fork in the road. Bear left onto Forest Road 4934, following the road sign to Trail 1332 1/2. The road narrows, switchbacks at 4.3 miles, and switchbacks again at 4.4 miles. Continue straight ahead (northwest) into the Mount Margaret parking area. The sounds of I-90 can be heard faintly below. *Delorme: Washington Atlas and Gazetteer:* Page 65 A-6.

## THE HIKE

To find the trailhead, leave the parking lot and turn left (north), returning to FR 4934. Walk 0.2 mile up the road and take the gated spur road to the left (east). Begin walking along this old road through a forest of vine maple (*Acer circinatum*), willow (*Salix* sp.), red alder (*Alnus rubra*), and maturing Douglas fir and mountain hemlock. Stay on the main road despite opportunities to turn off until reaching a junction marked by a fiberglass Forest Service stick-sign announcing a hikers-only trail. An older metal sign bolted onto a 4-by-4–inch, 8-foot-tall post declares this trail is closed to motor vehicles, saddle horses, and pack stock. Turn north, then east onto a narrow trail and climb through a regenerating clear-cut. As the trail climbs there are plenty of vistas east, west, and south to such familiar sights as I-90, Mount Rainier, Keechelus Lake, and the ski slopes of Snoqualmie Pass.

Small meadow along the trail to Lake Lillian

Keechelus Lake is also known by the sobriquet "Stump Lake" for its prevalence of tree stumps exposed in wintertime when the reservoir is low. A 128-foot-tall earth-fill structure, built in 1917 and operated by the U.S. Bureau of Reclamation, controls the lake capacity and discharge for agriculture. Keechelus, which is supposed to mean "few fish" in the local Indian dialect, is the source of the Yakima River. Downstream is Kachess Lake, which supposedly means "more fish."

Cross an old dirt road and continue up the trail. After nearly 2.0 miles from the parking area, enter an old-growth forest and begin a series of nicely graded switchbacks. In 2.5 miles reach the top of a ridge and the junction to Margaret Lake on the right (east). Continue straight ahead (north). Pass several waytrails (northeast) that lead to views of Rampart Ridge.

The trail skirts below the summits of two peaks, including Mount Margaret, and reaches a viewpoint. More of Rampart Ridge can be seen, along with a piece of Lake Lillian, a couple of ribbon waterfalls, and Rocky Run, the stream that drains the lake. Begin descending toward Twin Lakes on a trail that sometimes could use a ladder. In 1.0 mile reach the lakes and cross into the Alpine Lakes Wilderness.

Twin Lakes are small and shallow and seasonally provide beautiful habitat for large hordes of mosquitoes. The first lake is the larger of the two and has a poor campsite about midway up the lake—though the scenery is nice to look at. Some people choose to camp on a small island close to shore. This is a bad idea and is discouraged, since it's impossible to get 100 feet away from water in any direction—a requirement for good campers everywhere.

Leaving the larger lake, the trail follows a creek to the smaller lake and traverses even better mosquito habitat. Climb steeply and in earnest for a short while, and then proceed to lose elevation as the trail avoids having to deal with some heinous cliffs. Cross through a wide talus field and regain all the elevation lost since passing the Margaret Lake Trail junction. A brief flat spot is reached before you ascend the remaining part of the hillside—straight up! Where's that ladder?

It's not a long climb, fortunately, before the trail reaches a lip; in 100 feet Lake Lillian pops into view, surrounded by an amphitheater of rock and jagged peaks. There is no place to go from here except for mountain goats and rock climbers.

Camping sites, located back at the lip, are paltry and far from level. Impressive views down the cliffs to Lake Laura, Rocky Run, clear-cuts, and Forest Road 136 are nearby. Return to the trailhead by the same route.

## MILES AND DIRECTIONS

**0.0**   Trailhead off FR 4934: N47° 21.799' / W121° 21.369'

**0.5**   Junction with hikers-only trail: N47° 22.111' / W121° 21.112'

**1.0**   Cross dirt road: N47° 22.141' / W121° 20.780'

**2.0**    Enter old-growth forest: N47° 22.326' / W121° 20.503'

**2.5**    Lake Lillian/Margaret Lake Trail junction: N47° 22.581' / W121° 20.347'

**3.5**    Alpine Lakes Wilderness boundary and Twin Lakes: N47° 23.356' / W121° 20.332'

**4.0**    Talus: N47° 23.759' / W121° 20.474'

**4.5**    Lake Lillian: N47° 23.943' / W121° 20.372'

**9.0**    Return to trailhead: N47° 21.799' / W121° 21.369'

# Margaret Lake

*Reaching Margaret Lake occupies much of the same trail as getting to Lake Lillian, with the added pleasure of being a shorter hike. Another major difference between the destinations is that past the junction with Margaret Lake, the trail to Lake Lillian is steep, rough, and in many places almost straight up and down. In comparison, the entire way to Margaret Lake is along a nice and easy-to-follow route. In autumn an immense slope of huckleberries at Margaret Lake makes for good grazing. The lake is also a suitable swimming hole in summer.*

**Start:** Margaret Lake trailhead parking

**Distance:** 7.0 miles out and back

**Approximate hiking time:** 4 to 6 hours

**Trail number:** USDA Forest Service Trail 1332

**Difficulty:** Moderate, with steep sections

**Trail surface:** Forested path; rocky

**Seasons:** Summer and fall

**Other trail users:** Illegal use by mountain bikers is a problem on this hikers-only trail.

**Canine compatibility:** Dogs prohibited

**Land status:** Wenatchee National Forest, Cle Elum District; Alpine Lakes Wilderness Area

**Nearest town:** Snoqualmie Pass

**Services:** Gas, restaurants, lodging; no toilet at trailhead

**Northwest Forest Pass:** Yes

**Maps:** Green Trails No. 207: Snoqualmie Pass; USGS Chikamin Peak; USDAFS Mount Baker–Snoqualmie National Forest, Alpine Lakes Wilderness

**Trail contacts:** Alpine Lakes Protection Society (ALPS): www.alpinelakes.org. Middle Fork Snoqualmie: www.midforc.org. Wenatchee National Forest, Cle Elum Ranger District, 803 West Second Street, Cle Elum, WA 98922; (509) 852-1100; www.fs.fed.us/r6/wenatchee. Mount Baker–Snoqualmie National Forest, Snoqualmie Ranger District, North Bend Office, 42404 Southeast North Bend Way, North Bend, WA 98045; (425) 888-1421; www.fs.fed.us/r6/mbs/recreation

**Special hazards:** Loose rock; no potable water at trailhead or on trail

**Finding the trailhead:**

From Seattle take Interstate 90 east to exit 54 (Gold Creek). Turn left (north) at the end of the off-ramp. Proceed 0.2 mile, go under the interstate, and pass the on-ramp to I-90 westbound. Turn right (east) onto Gold Creek Road (Forest Road 4832) and parallel I-90. In 2.0 miles the road narrows to one lane. After 2.4 miles the road turns to gravel and at 2.7 makes a switchback, leaving I-90 behind.

This good road climbs steadily to a switchback at 3.7 miles, another switchback at 3.9 miles, and then a fork in the road. Bear left onto Forest Road 4934, following the sign to Trail 1332 1/2. The road narrows, switchbacks at 4.3 miles, and at 4.4 miles switchbacks again. Continue straight ahead (northwest) into the Mount Margaret parking area at what looks like an old log-loading platform. The sounds of I-90 can be heard faintly below. *Delorme: Washington Atlas and Gazetteer:* Page 65 A-6.

Stump Lake from Margaret Lake Trail

## THE HIKE

To find the trailhead, leave the parking lot and turn left (north), onto FR 4934. After 0.2 mile take the gated spur road to the left (east). Begin walking along this old road through a forest of vine maple (*Acer circinatum*), willow (*Salix* sp), red alder (*Alnus rubra*), and maturing Douglas fir and mountain hemlock. Despite opportunities to turn off, stay on the main road until you reach a junction marked by a fiberglass Forest Service stick-sign announcing a hikers-only trail. An

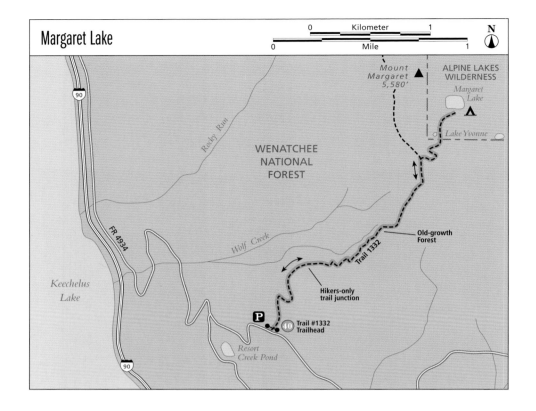

# Margaret Lake

| 0 | Kilometer | 1 |
| 0 | Mile | 1 |

**N**

Mount Margaret 5,580'

ALPINE LAKES WILDERNESS

Margaret Lake

Lake Yvonne

WENATCHEE NATIONAL FOREST

Rocky Run

FR 4934

Wolf Creek

Old-growth Forest

Trail 1332

Keechelus Lake

Hikers-only trail junction

**P**

10 Trail #1332 Trailhead

Resort Creek Pond

older metal sign bolted onto a 4-by-4–inch, 8-foot-tall post proclaims this trail is closed to motor vehicles, saddle horses, and pack stock. Turn north, then east onto a narrow trail and climb above Wolfe Creek through a regenerating clear-cut. There are copious vistas to such familiar sights as I-90, Mount Rainier, Keechelus Lake, and the ski slopes of Snoqualmie Pass as the trail climbs.

Cross an old dirt road and continue up the trail. Nearly 2.0 miles from the parking area, enter an old-growth forest and begin a series of nicely graded switchbacks. The preceding clear-cut walk is hot, dry, and sunny during summer and a real sweat inducer. Of course there is the added value of seeing more wildflowers in logged areas, but the old-growth forest shade is always welcome. During spring and late autumn the ground is a veritable cornucopia of fleshy fungi.

In 2.5 miles reach the top of a ridge and the junction to Margaret Lake on the right (east). Turn here and drop precipitously on regular and nicely constructed switchbacks for 0.5 mile.

Pass into the Alpine Lakes Wilderness and notice no change except for the end of the switchbacks. After walking 0.1 mile farther, pass by the pond marked on maps as Yvonne Lake. Another 0.2 mile of flat walking reaches a lip overlooking Margaret Lake. Drop down to the lake and turn right (east) at the shore. Quickly reach a poor but heavily impacted campsite on a knoll above the lake and the end of the trail.

Margaret isn't a large lake, but it's certainly bigger than Yvonne. On the west side of Margaret Lake is a huge talus field leading up to tree-covered Mount Margaret. Much of the talus is choked with huckleberries, which in autumn provide riotous fall colors.

## MILES AND DIRECTIONS

**0.0**   Trailhead off FR 4934: N47° 21.799' / W121° 21.369'

**0.5**   Junction with hikers-only trail: N47° 22.111' / W121° 21.112'

**1.0**   Cross dirt road: N47° 22.141' / W121° 20.780'

**2.0**   Enter old-growth forest: N47° 22.326' / W121° 20.503'

**2.5**   Lake Lillian/Margaret Lake Trail junction: N47° 22.581' / W121° 20.347'

**2.9**   Alpine Lakes Wilderness boundary: N47° 22.679' / W121° 20.276'

**3.0**   Lake Yvonne: N47° 22.720' / W121° 20.241'

**3.5**   Margaret Lake: N47° 22.826' / W121° 20.133'

**7.0**   Return to trailhead: N47° 21.799' / W121° 21.369'

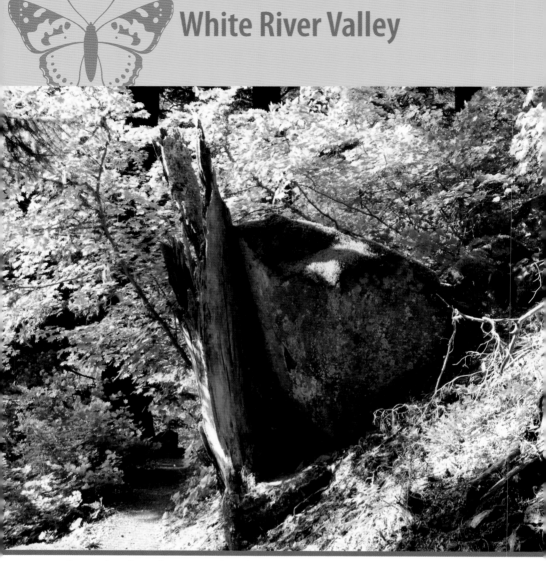

Large rocks outlasting large trees on the trail to Snoquera Falls

The White River begins in Mount Rainier National Park at the Emmons Glacier. The river has a history of flooding, and Mud Mountain Dam was built in 1948 to keep it under control. During a flood in 1906, the White River changed its course when a debris jam blocked the river channel. The White River was diverted from flowing into the Green River and ultimately into Elliot Bay. Instead the river entered the Stuck River, which flows into the Puyallup River and then Commencement Bay in Tacoma. Highway 410 follows the river closely between Greenwater and Mount Rainier, and there are plenty of hiking and picnicking spots to choose from.

> Highway 410 follows the White River closely between Greenwater and Mount Rainier, and there are plenty of hiking and picnicking spots to choose from.

Skookum Falls

# Skookum Falls

*The lack of appreciable vertical relief makes the first part of this trail suitable as an out-and-back walk for young children. Views of the river, a plethora of picnic sites both in the forest and along the bluff, and spring wildflowers all contribute to making this a pleasant experience. For through-hikers, trail washouts and destruction of the suspension bridge over White River—all from the November 2006 storms and flood—make this route best done with a car shuttle.*

**Start:** Skookum Flats trailhead on Forest Road 73
**Distance:** 5.4 miles point-to-point shuttle, with optional 1.0-mile round-trip excursion to site of washed-out suspension bridge and Buck Creek crossing; 10.8 miles out and back without shuttle
**Approximate hiking time:** 4 to 5 hours
**Trail number:** USDA Forest Service Trail 1194
**Difficulty:** Moderate, with trail washouts
**Trail surface:** Forested path, boardwalks
**Nearest town:** Greenwater
**Services:** Gas, restaurants, groceries; USDAFS campground at The Dalles, approximately 2 miles south of Forest Road 73 along Highway 410; hotels and shopping malls in Enumclaw; no toilet at starting point along FR 73; vault toilet at Buck Creek Recreation Area end point

**Seasons:** Summer and fall
**Other trail users:** Bikes
**Canine compatibility:** Leashed dogs permitted
**Land status:** Mount Baker–Snoqualmie National Forest, White River Ranger District
**Northwest Forest Pass:** Yes
**Maps:** Green Trails No. 238: Greenwater; USGS Suntop and White River; USDAFS Mount Baker–Snoqualmie National Forest
**Trail contacts:** Mount Baker–Snoqualmie National Forest, White River Ranger District, 450 Roosevelt Avenue E, Enumclaw, WA 98022; (360) 825-6585. Camp Berachah Ministries, 19830 Southeast 328th Place, Auburn, WA 98092-2212; (253) 939-0488 or (800) 859-CAMP; www.campberachah.org
**Special hazards:** Trail washouts; bridge washout; no potable water at trailhead or on trail; swift and cold White River unsafe for swimming

**Finding the trailhead:**
From the intersection of Highways 410 and 169 in Enumclaw, drive east 24.7 miles on Highway 410 to Huckleberry Creek Road (FR 73). The highway is also known through here as the Mather Memorial Parkway. Turn right (west, and then head south), bearing left in 0.1 mile. After another 0.3 mile cross the White River on a narrow bridge; park either on the side of the road or in the trailhead parking lot. There is a lone picnic table here overlooking the river. *Delorme: Washington Atlas and Gazetteer:* Page 64 D-4.

## THE HIKE

**B**egin by crossing FR 73 to the trailhead. Many parts of this trail were washed out by the November 2006 storm and flood. Smaller washouts were repaired with logs from deadfall and sediment hauled up from the river. Larger washouts, including a suspension bridge over White River (Trail 1169) had not been repaired as of summer 2007.

The path instantly enters an old-growth forest, with White River on your left. There is a dense ground cover of mahonia, or Oregon grape (*Berberis repens*), trillium (*Trillium ovatum*), ground dogwood (*Cornus canadensis*), salal (*Gaultheria shallon*), ferns, and western hemlock seedlings, all within the sun breaks of the tall forest, along with an abundance of fallen trees. Such familiar species as devil's club (*Oplopanex horridus*) and stinging nettle (*Urtica dioica*), common to highly disturbed areas, are absent.

The trail winds its mostly flat way through the forest with occasional hills to climb. They are neither steep nor long—all of which makes this first section of trail a great walk for young children. You can choose to turn back at any time the kiddies are ready. The trail plays peekaboo with the river, crossing many wet spots on various-length bridges in various stages of disrepair and rot. If your foot falls through it won't fall far, though it may stick between the slats or in deep muck.

In 2.1 miles cross a new bridge, reaching a side trail and sign marked Falls directing hikers right (west) up a very steep and rocky slope with plenty of deadfall to Skookum Falls. The top end of the trail splits into several braids where past hikers have sought their own level to observe the falling water. When ready to proceed, backtrack 0.2 mile to the main trail, turn right (east), and continue upstream.

The trail drops to a small grove of Sitka spruce (*Picea sitchensis*) at river level after 3.0 miles. From here look across the river to broken views of a rock formation called the Palisades. Water in Snoquera Falls can also be seen prior to summer (look for a long white splotch in the darker rock of the Palisades).

In 3.7 miles reach the unmarked Buck Creek Trail junction (Trail 1169). A suspension bridge once crossed the river here and Trail 1194 continued upstream, but

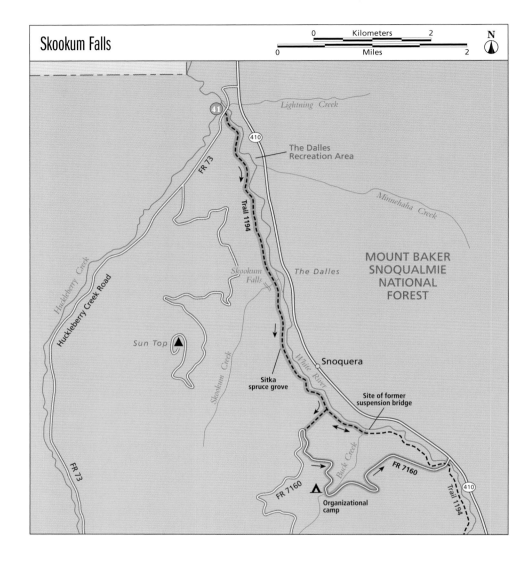

Kilometers

0                2

0            Miles           2

N

Lightning Creek

The Dalles
Recreation Area

Minnehaha Creek

Trail 1194

FR 73

Skookum
Falls

The Dalles

MOUNT BAKER
SNOQUALMIE
NATIONAL
FOREST

Huckleberry Creek

Huckleberry Creek Road

Sun Top

Skookum Creek

White River

Snoquera

Sitka
spruce grove

Site of former
suspension bridge

FR 73

Buck Creek

FR 7160

FR 7160

Trail 1194

410

FR 7160

Organizational
camp

no longer. Both bridge and trail were washed away by floods. It's still an interesting trip down to the water, where you can spot the remains of the suspension bridge on the opposite bank.

Returning from the river, either turn around for a long day hike or head uphill on a switchback with bright light streaming in from a clear-cut. This section of trail is not marked on the Green Trails map. In 0.6 mile the increasingly faint trail crosses the upper reaches of Buck Creek on a rickety bridge and emerges at an organizational camp, operated by Camp Berachah Ministries under a Forest Service special-use lease. Walk downhill (east) through the camp to Buck Creek Road (Forest Road

41

Skookum Falls

7160), and emerge at Highway 410 in the Buck Creek Recreation Area after 1.1 miles. Retrieve your car from the parking lot (vault toilet).

## MILES AND DIRECTIONS

**0.0**    Trailhead on FR 73: N47° 04.659' / W121° 35.140'

**2.1**    Skookum Falls: N47° 03.023' / W121° 34.450'

**3.0**    Sitka spruce grove: N47° 02.250' / W121° 34.175'

**3.7**    Trail 1169 down to White River: N47° 01.773' / W121° 33.609'

**4.3**    Buck Creek Church Camp: N47° 01.287' / W121° 33.425'

**5.4**    Trail ends at junction with FR 7160 and Highway 410: N47° 01.354' / W121° 32.164'

**Options:** It's possible to continue hiking up Trail 1194 for about 2.0 miles to the boundary with Mount Rainier National Park.

## HIKE INFORMATION

Ash and lava are not the only things produced by volcanoes. About 5,800 years ago the Osceola Mudflow from Mount Rainier flew down the White River and spread out over 100 square miles, burying what is now the townsite of Enumclaw under 70 feet of debris and reaching the current site of Kent. White River, beginning at the snout of Mount Rainier's Emmonds Glacier, gets its plaster color from "glacial flour," finely ground debris created by the action of ice crunching away the bedrock of the mountain. All this sediment, held in suspension, doesn't seem to bother the fish, though. There are five runs of anadromous fish on the White River, including coho, sockeye, and chinook salmon.

# Tree Stories 3

Bigleaf maple (*Acer macrophylla,* or "maple with large leaves") has the largest leaves of any maple—up to 10 inches in width and sometimes more! It's found near the Pacific coast, from southern Alaska to southern California and inland in the foothills of the Sierra Nevada. The fruit is a paired, winged samara resembling a helicopter rotor. The edible flowers are sweet and have been used in salads.

Maples are widespread, with about 120 species worldwide. Bigleaf maple can grow to heights of 120 feet with a diameter of 3 feet. When grown by itself, bigleaf maple produces a generous, rounded crown.

Red alder (*Alnus rubra,* or "red Alnus"—the old Latin name for the species) is the most common tree species to grow in west Cascade forests immediately after logging, fire, or other disturbance. A member of the birch family, it can grow as tall as 130 feet with diameters up to 30 inches in prime habitat. Normally, though, red alder is found in subprime habitat: poorly drained, oxygen- and nutrient-depleted soils. Fortunately a bacterium (*Frankia* sp.) growing in alder roots takes atmospheric nitrogen, which is inert, and coverts it to a usable form, giving the tree a competitive advantage over other associated plants.

Red alder is deciduous and can live to a ripe old age of fifty years. The male and female flowers are separate; the latter developing into hard woody structures that resemble teeny-tiny toy pinecones. This trait makes them favorite test objects in plant identification classes. The tree is distributed from Alaska to northern California and eastward through the Rocky Mountains.

Seeds from bigleaf maple

*If you can find your way around the confusing array of Forest Service trails and trails generated by the Boy Scout camp, Snoquera Falls is a great destination—especially during spring when the water is gushing. Though it's a short way up to the bottom of Snoquera, the steep trail will preclude all but the hardiest of children. An option to continue on Trail 1167 after reaching the falls is possible, but the way is not maintained. It's a rough row to hoe, requiring talus hopping, screeing, and route-finding. There are at least two trailheads to choose from to start your hike.*

**Start:** Trailhead for White River Trail (1199) at Camp Sheppard or Buck Creek (1169) along Highway 410

**Distance:** 2.4 miles, more or less; options for out-and-back, lollipop, or circuit hike

**Approximate hiking time:** 2 to 3 hours

**Trail numbers:** USDA Forest Service Trails Buck Creek Trail 1169, White River Trail 1199, and Snoquera Falls Trail 1167

**Difficulty:** Strenuous; steep trail and misleading signage

**Trail surface:** Forested path; gravel road (through Camp Sheppard); rocky

**Seasons:** Year-round

**Other trail users:** Bikes and horses lower down; runners

**Canine compatibility:** Leashed dogs permitted

**Land status:** Mount Baker–Snoqualmie National Forest, Snoqualmie Ranger District; Boy Scouts of America, Chief Seattle Council

**Nearest town:** Greenwater

**Services:** Gas, restaurants, groceries; USDAFS campground at The Dalles, approximately 2 miles south of Forest Road 73 along Highway 410; hotels and shopping malls in Enumclaw; vault toilet at the Camp Sheppard trailhead

**Northwest Forest Pass:** Yes

**Maps:** Green Trails No. 238: Greenwater; USGS Suntop and White River; USDAFS Mount Baker–Snoqualmie National Forest

**Trail contacts:** Mount Baker–Snoqualmie National Forest, White River Ranger District, 450 Roosevelt Avenue E, Enumclaw, WA 98022; (360) 825-6585. Seattle Council, BSA, Seattle Service Center, 3120 Rainier Avenue South, P.O. Box 440408, Seattle, WA 98114; (206) 725-5200. Camp Sheppard Camping Department (open Monday through Friday 8:30 a.m. to 5:00 p.m.); (206) 725-0361; www.seattlebsa.org/; e-mail: council@seattlebsa.org

**Special hazards:** Loose rock, exposure; water crossing (to continue on past Snoquera Falls); no potable water at trailhead or on trail

**Finding the trailhead:**
From the intersection of Highways 410 and 169 in Enumclaw, drive east on Highway 410, passing the Skookum Falls viewpoint at 26.8 miles and reaching the Camp Sheppard trailhead at 28.2 miles. Turn left (east) onto Forest Road 7155, and in 0.1 mile park in the large lot. To access Trail 1169, alternative parking for about ten cars is available 0.2 mile farther east on Highway 410 on the north side of Mather Memorial Parkway. A quarter mile past this is the actual trailhead for Trail 1169, with parking at a wide spot on the south side of the parkway. *Delorme: Washington Atlas and Gazetteer:* Page 64 D-4.

## THE HIKE

Starting from the Buck Creek Trail (1169) alongside Highway 410, walk east for 0.3 mile on a gradually ascending trail and reach the junction with the White River Trail (1199). Turn right (southeast) on the Snoquera Falls Trail (1167). A left turn will take you to Camp Sheppard BSA. The signpost says it is 1.0 mile to Snoquera Falls and 3.0 miles to White River Trail.

Begin a nice ascent through a forest of western hemlock, with unending carpets of salal in the understory. For the next 0.3 mile the trail climbs with an even pace; never so steep as to make you want to stop and never so gentle as to make you wish it would flatten out a bit.

Just as the pitch begins to increase, reach another trail junction (Trails 1167 and 1169—signage is unclear) with a very old sign announcing that this trail is not completed for horse or bike use, although work continues. Discouragingly, another sign announces that Snoquera Falls is still 1.0 mile away. No treadmill is obvious, so you have to wonder just what is going on.

If you began the hike at Camp Sheppard on Trail 1199, you have reached this point after 0.7 mile of walking. Hikers can reach this point on the downhill jaunt and either return the way they came or live dangerously and take the alternate route.

Continue ascending through a thick forest with gradually decreasing salal (*Gaultheria shallon*) but thankfully increasing vine maple (*Acer cicinatum*). Late afternoon sun is particularly pretty as it streams through the forest canopy to bathe the maple's palmlike leaves.

Climb, climb, and climb. Whenever in doubt, follow signs to Snoquera Falls, arriving there in 0.5 mile. Once you're at the falls, it's possible to continue on—this is, after all, billed by the Forest Service as a "loop trail." But as the signs warn, it hasn't been maintained for a long time. The next part of the loop requires route-finding skills, talus hopping, and traversing scree. It's recommended that only the experienced adventurer attempt the remainder of the loop.

Cross the outlet to Snoquera Falls, which can be wet and slippery, and find a use trail that heads straight up the hill. Turn right (north) and quickly encounter a 2-inch pipe that siphons water to supply the Boy Scout camp. If you find this upsetting, bear in mind there would be no trail up here without the pipe. A great deal of water also disappears under the talus piled across the trail. Even more is sucked up by the trees growing in the creek.

Climb to the base of the falls through fields of cow parsnip. Once you run out of trail, stop; sit, catch your breath, and admire the view across the valley in the opposite direction. During spring, when the seasonal supply of water is pouring in volume, it might be difficult to get too close. Snoquera Falls is 400 feet tall, with the top end of the drop falling 250 feet.

Return the way you came, or take the alternative way home. The two parking areas are not very far apart. If returning by way of Camp Sheppard, keep an eye on

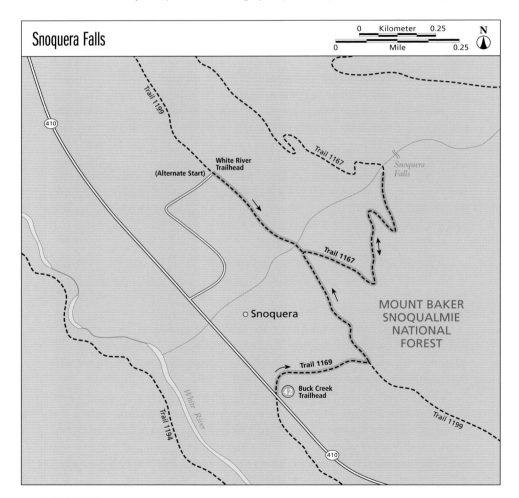

Snoquera Falls

View from the trail

the trail signs; they are confusing. When you see the first buildings for the camp, cut down to the gravel road and follow it out to the Forest Service parking area.

## MILES AND DIRECTIONS

**0.0**   Trailhead for Buck Creek Trail (1169): N47° 01.974' / W121° 33.493'

**1.0**   Snoquera Falls: N47° 02.366' / W121° 33.205'

**2.0**   Return to trailhead: N47° 01.974' / W121° 33.493'

**0.0**   Trailhead for White River Trail (1199): N47° 02.148' / W121° 33.588'

**1.2**   Snoquera Falls: N47° 02.366' / W121° 33.205'

**2.4**   Return to trailhead: N47° 02.148' / W121° 33.588'

> *"The sole criterion is to walk with the senses, with hands that feel, ears that hear, and eyes that see."*
> —*Robert Brown*, **The Appalachian Trail: History, Humanity, and Ecology**

# Appendix A: Resources

Clubs, hiking forums, and access/advocacy groups, including online groups and organizations.

**Alpine Lakes Protection Society**
P.O. Box 27646
Seattle, WA 98125
www.alpinelakes.org
Give thanks to these people for their wilderness advocacy and their excellent 1:100,000 topo map that covers the Alpine Lakes Wilderness and surrounding area.

**American Whitewater**
P.O. Box 1540
Cullowhee, NC 28723
(866) BOAT-4-AW (866-262-8429)
www.Americanwhitewater.org
E-mail: info@amwhitewater.org
American Whitewater restores rivers dewatered by hydropower dams, eliminates water degradation, improves public land management, and protects public access to rivers for responsible recreational use.

**Hiker's Meetup Group (Seattle)**
www.hiking.meetup.com/cities/us/wa/seattle
Sign up and meet people who share your interest in hiking.

**Issaquah Alps Trail Club**
P.O. Box 351
Issaquah, WA 98027
www.issaquahalps.org/index.html
The club serves as a voice for protection of our open spaces, trails, and quality of life. Their mission is to act as custodian of the trails and the lush, open, tree-covered mountaintops known as the Issaquah Alps.

**Local Hikes**
www.localhikes.com/MSA/MSA_7602.asp
A Web site providing information on local hiking opportunities contributed by volunteer reporters.

**Middle Fork Snoqualmie**
www.midforc.org
An educational and information Web site that encourages people to become involved in the protection of the Middle Fork Snoqualmie River Valley.

**The Mountaineers, Seattle Branch**
300 Third Avenue W
Seattle, WA 98119
(206) 284-6310
www.mountaineers.org/seattle/seahike
www.seattlemountaineers.org/
The Pacific Northwest's largest recreation and conservation organization.

## Mountains to Sound Greenway Trust

911 Western Avenue, Suite 523
Seattle, WA 98104
(206) 383-5565
www.mtsgreenway.org
A group trying to reverse the trend along Interstate 90 to become the province of strip malls, billboards, and spreading urban development. They're working to keep an accessible landscape of forests and open spaces as outdoor recreation for people and habitat for wildlife.

## Northwest Hikers

www.nwhikers.net
An online forum to talk about hiking, hiker issues, places to hike, or find a hiking companion.

## Seattle Audubon Society

8050 35th Avenue NE
Seattle, WA 98115
(206) 523-4483
www.seattleaudubon.org
E-mail: info@seattleaudubon.org

## Seattle Hiking Group

www.groups.yahoo.com/group/
seattlehiking
Join people from around the globe exploring the Northwest! Hiking, camping, river rafting, backpacking, stargazing—they want to do it all!

## Sierra Club, Cascade Chapter

180 Nickerson Street, Suite 202
Seattle, WA 98109
(206) 378-0114
www.cascade.sierraclub.org
E-mail: chapter@cascade
.sierraclub.org

## Snoqualmie River Road Project

Federal Highway Administration—
Western Federal Lands
610 East Fifth Street
Vancouver WA 98661
www.mfsnoqualmie.org
E-mail: mfsnoqualmie@fhwa.dot.gov

## Spring Family Trust

5015 88th Avenue SE
Mercer Island, WA 98040
(206) 718-4441
www.springtrailtrust.org/
A charitable trust dedicated to enhancing hiking opportunities in Washington State with grants for trail building and maintenance projects.

## Washington Native Plant Society

Central Puget Sound Chapter
6310 Northeast 74th Street, Suite 215E
Seattle, WA 98115
(206) 527-3210
www.wnps.org/cps
Conservation and preservation of Washington's native flora is combined with education by exposing plant lovers to trails and unique habitats.

**Washington Trails Association**
2019 Third Avenue, Suite 100
Seattle, WA 98121
(206) 625-1367
www.wta.org
WTA protects hiking trails and wild lands, takes thousands of volunteers out to maintain trails, and promotes hiking as a healthy, fun way to explore Washington.

**Wild Wilderness**
248 Northwest Wilmington Avenue
Bend, OR 97701
(541) 385-5261
www.wildwilderness.org
E-mail: ssilver@wildwilderness.org
Wild Wilderness believes that America's public recreation lands are a national treasure that must be financially supported by the American people and held in public ownership as a legacy for future generations.

**Wilderness Society**
Pacific Northwest Office
720 Third Avenue, Suite 1800
Seattle, WA 98104
(206) 624-6430
www.wilderness.org
Their name says it all.

*"Climb the mountains and get their good tidings. Nature's peace will flow into you as sunshine flows into trees. The winds will blow their own freshness into you, and the storms their energy, while cares will drop off like autumn leaves."*
*—John Muir*

# Appendix B: Further Reading

## Field Guides

Mathews, Daniel. 1999. *Cascade-Olympic Natural History*. Raven Editions.

Peterson, Roger Tory. 1998. *A Field Guide to Western Birds*. Houghton Mifflin.

Pojar, Jim. 2004. *Plants of the Pacific Northwest Coast: Washington, Oregon, British Columbia, and Alaska*. Lone Pine Publishing.

Whitney, Stephen, and Rob Sandelin. 2004. *Field Guide to the Cascades and Olympics*. The Mountaineers Books.

## Hiking Guides

Dreisbach, Bob. 2000. *Seattle Outdoors*. Entropy Conservationists.

Smoot, Jeff. 2003. *Hiking Washington's Alpine Lakes Wilderness*. Falcon Press.

Sykes, Karen. 2002. *Hidden Hikes in Western Washington*. The Mountaineers Books.

Zilly, John. 2003. *Beyond Mount Si*. Adventure Press.

## History

Ferguson, Robert L. 1996. *Pioneers of Lake View: A Guide to Seattle's Early Settlers and Their Cemetery*. Thistle Press.

Seidel, William. 2003. *Sons of the Profits*. Nettle Creek Publishing.

## Natural History

Kozloff, Eugene N. 1978. *Plants and Animals of the Pacific Northwest: An Illustrated Guide to the Natural History of Western Oregon, Washington, and British Columbia*. University of Washington Press.

Kruckeberg, Arthur R. 1995. *The Natural History of Puget Sound Country*. University of Washington Press.

Renner, Jeff. 2005. *Mountain Weather: Backcountry Forecasting and Weather Safety for Hikers, Campers, Climbers, Skiers, and Snowboarders*. The Mountaineers.

Renner, Jeff. 1993. *Northwest Marine Weather*. The Mountaineers Books.

> *"The West of which I speak is but another name for the Wild, and what I have been preparing to say is that in Wildness is the preservation of the World. Every tree sends its fibers forth in search of the Wild. The cities import it at any price. Men plow and sail for it. From the forest and wilderness come the tonics and barks which brace mankind. . . ."*
> —Henry David Thoreau

# Hike Index

## About the Author

Peter Stekel is a professional writer and avid backpacker and mountaineer who has hiked throughout the intermountain West as well as along the West Coast, the Pacific Northwest, the Appalachian Trail, eastern Australia, and northern England. He is the author of *The Flower Lover* and 700 feature magazine and newspaper stories about science, adventure travel, sports, history, forestry, natural history, recreation, travel, theatre, and entertainment, including articles on the Sierra Nevada mountains of California, with a focus on Sequoia and Kings Canyon National Parks. His articles have appeared in such publications as *Sierra Heritage, American Forests, High Country News, Canoe & Kayak, Paddler, American Whitewater, Sea Kayaker, Wild West, Appalachia Trailway News, AAA TravelChoices, E The Environmental Journal,* and *EarthFirst!* Stekel and his wife live in Seattle.